Youth in a Changing World

World Anthropology

General Editor

SOL TAX

Patrons

CLAUDE LÉVI-STRAUSS
MARGARET MEAD
LAILA SHUKRY EL HAMAMSY
M. N. SRINIVAS

MOUTON PUBLISHERS · THE HAGUE · PARIS
DISTRIBUTED IN THE USA AND CANADA BY ALDINE, CHICAGO

Youth in a Changing World

Cross-Cultural Perspectives on Adolescence

Editor

ESTELLE FUCHS

MOUTON PUBLISHERS · THE HAGUE · PARIS
DISTRIBUTED IN THE USA AND CANADA BY ALDINE, CHICAGO

General Editor's Preface

Almost no part of the physiological process of change from childhood to adulthood is unaffected by its social and cultural environment; thus, at no level can it be said to have much that is universal about it. And to an even greater degree, one cannot speak, for the species as a whole, about a social class of adolescents or youth. This book therefore describes primarily the significance of differences across cultural, ethnic, and class boundaries. Coming as it does fresh from scholars of the many cultures in a conference before and during a large international Congress, the book is an unusual—if not unique—expression of some very old and some very new concerns.

Like most contemporary sciences, anthropology is a product of the European tradition. Some argue that it is a product of colonialism, with one small and self-interested part of the species dominating the study of the whole. If we are to understand the species, our science needs substantial input from scholars who represent a variety of the world's cultures. It was a deliberate purpose of the IXth International Congress of Anthropological and Ethnological Sciences to provide impetus in this direction. The *World Anthropology* volumes, therefore, offer a first glimpse of a human science in which members from all societies have played an active role. Each of the books is designed to be self-contained; each is an attempt to update its particular sector of scientific knowledge and is written by specialists from all parts of the world. Each volume should be read and reviewed individually as a separate volume on its own given subject. The set as a whole will indicate what changes are in store for anthropology as scholars from the developing countries join in studying the species of which we are all a part.

The IXth Congress was planned from the beginning not only to include as many of the scholars from every part of the world as possible, but also with a view toward the eventual publication of the papers in high-quality volumes. At previous Congresses scholars were invited to bring papers which were then read out loud. They were necessarily limited in length; many were only summarized; there was little time for discussion; and the sparse discussion could only be in one language. The IXth Congress was an experiment aimed at changing this. Papers were written with the intention of exchanging them before the Congress, particularly in extensive pre-Congress sessions; they were not intended to be read aloud at the Congress, that time being devoted to discussions — discussions which were simultaneously and professionally translated into five languages. The method for eliciting the papers was structured to make as representative a sample as was allowable when scholarly creativity — hence self-selection — was critically important. Scholars were asked both to propose papers of their own and to suggest topics for sessions of the Congress which they might edit into volumes. All were then informed of the suggestions and encouraged to re-think their own papers and the topics. The process, therefore, was a continuous one of feedback and exchange and it has continued to be so even after the Congress. The some two thousand papers comprising *World Anthropology* certainly then offer a substantial sample of world anthropology. It has been said that anthropology is at a turning point; if this is so, these volumes will be the historical direction-markers.

As might have been foreseen in the first post-colonial generation, the large majority of the Congress papers (82 percent) are the work of scholars identified with the industrialized world which fathered our traditional discipline and the institution of the Congress itself: Eastern Europe (15 percent); Western Europe (16 percent); North America (47 percent); Japan, South Africa, Australia, and New Zealand (4 percent). Only 18 percent of the papers are from developing areas: Africa (4 percent); Asia-Oceania (9 percent); Latin America (5 percent). Aside from the substantial representation from the U.S.S.R. and the nations of Eastern Europe, a significant difference between this corpus of written material and that of other Congresses is the addition of the large proportion of contributions from Africa, Asia, and Latin America. "Only 18 percent" is two to four times as great a proportion as that of other Congresses; moreover, 18 percent of 2,000 papers is 360 papers, 10 times the number of "Third World" papers presented at previous Congresses. In fact, these 360 papers are more than the total of ALL papers published after the last International Congress of Anthropological and

Ethnological Sciences which was held in the United States (Philadelphia, 1956).

The significance of the increase is not simply quantitative. The input of scholars from areas which have until recently been no more than subject matter for anthropology represents both feedback and also long-awaited theoretical contributions from the perspectives of very different cultural, social, and historical traditions. Many who attended the IXth Congress were convinced that anthropology would not be the same in the future. The fact that the next Congress (India, 1978) will be our first in the "Third World" may be symbolic of the change. Meanwhile, sober consideration of the present set of books will show how much, and just where and how, our discipline is being revolutionized.

The reader will find in this series some of the other books from the Congress which add cross-cultural information and insight to the subjects treated here — books on human biology; species and individual development and adaptation; sex, ethnic, and class differences; urbanization; social and cultural change; medical, linguistic, and psychological anthropology; interrelations of people in primary groups; and education and enculturation.

Chicago, Illinois   SOL TAX
March 28, 1976

Preface

The IXth International Congress of Anthropological and Ethnological Sciences, held in Chicago, Illinois, September 1–8, 1973, offered a unique opportunity to bring together scholars from throughout the world. Therefore, the Congress sought to organize research sessions on important issues to be held immediately preceding the Congress. These research groups were then to present their findings at the Congress deliberations in Chicago.

The International Research Conference on Adolescence, under my direction, was one of these pre-Congress research conferences. Its purpose was to provide an opportunity for scholars to focus attention upon studies of adolescence. Among the topics examined were: the parameters of adolescence (age, distribution, definition); studies of adolescent growth and development contributed by physical anthropologists and other students of human development; changing patterns of socialization (sex role definitions, *rites de passage*, economic functions, etc.); adolescent environments; and identification of questions and priorities for further research.

The papers brought together in this volume originated as contributions to the International Research Conference on Adolescence held in Oshkosh, Wisconsin, August 28–31, 1973. Here, the authors met and discussed their work. Several of the papers, including those by Dr. Malcolm, Dr. Fiawoo, and Benjamin White, had been submitted to the Congress and were included because of their relevance to the topic under discussion; Dr. Rendon's paper was added later. These authors, however, were not present at the Oshkosh Conference.

As an indication of the international nature of the Conference, it should be noted that over seventeen different nationalities and ethnic groups were represented. Equally striking is the fact that scholars from areas which have in the past been the subject of study by Western researchers, were themselves discussing and describing the conditions and issues concerning young people around the globe.

The Conference deliberations were marked by great interest and enthusiasm as anthropologists, social psychologists, physicians, and psychiatrists shared their observations of youth in a changing world. The Conference sessions themselves were attended by many scholars who had not been specifically invited to present papers.

Part of our task was to present the work of the Conference to the IXth International Congress of Anthropological and Ethnological Sciences at an open session. On Wednesday afternoon, September 5, 1973, I chaired a Congress session in Chicago, entitled the International Research Conference on Adolescence. After I presented a summation of the Conference organization and objectives, Drs. Peterson, Kurian, Gokulanathan, and Eckenfels delivered summations of the proceedings. Professor Robert J. Havighurst delivered an overview of the findings. A lively discussion ensued from the floor with participation by scholars from many different nations. It was obvious that the Conference themes had touched on concerns felt around the globe.

A volume such as this is clearly a joint effort, made possible only by the cooperation and efforts of its many contributors. We wish to extend our appreciation to the Ford Foundation, whose financial assistance enabled us to convene the International Research Conference on Adolescence; to Dr. Terry Saario for her encouragement; to Professor Sol Tax, Director of the IXth International Congress of Anthropological and Ethnological Sciences, whose vision made it possible to bring together people from the myriad of cultures around the globe; and to Dr. James Riddill and his hard-working assistants at the University of Wisconsin, Oshkosh, who facilitated Conference arrangements. Our thanks also to Penelope Haile, Madeleine Holzer, Delores Holzer, Julia Brackman, Myra Derkatch, Andrew Fuchs, and William Fuchs for helping in all those many ways necessary to make this volume possible.

Graduate Center   ESTELLE FUCHS
City University of New York
New York, New York

Table of Contents

Introduction

ESTELLE FUCHS

In his foreword to Margaret Mead's classic study of adolescence in Samoa, Franz Boas wrote, "... much of what we ascribe to human nature is no more than a reaction to the restraints put upon us by our civilization ..." (Mead 1928). This comment, and the pioneering work on maturation in the South Pacific, summed up the two basic perceptions which anthropologists use for viewing behavioral phenomena: that the human organism and its responses must be understood within the context of cultural conditioning, and that only by a comparative view of the ways in which different cultures function in time and place can we wholly understand human behavior. While our own particular interests may be directed toward problems of the here and now, or even of the specific individual, the anthropological perspective is essential in order to free us from the myopic distortions of the ethnocentric view.

A cross-cultural view of adolescence enables us to sort out the regularities and differences in the way people approach maturity and offers clues to those phenomena which are universal and those which are imposed by particular cultural systems. This is hardly a simple, uncomplicated task, as a closer look at the issues will reveal.

The very definition of the period to be called adolescence poses problems. It would seem that reference to the physical characteristics of the human species would provide a ready definition, but even here the evidence is blurred, as the articles in Part I of this volume demonstrate. Pubertal growth spurts are well documented for man and may occur in other primates. But at best, given our present knowledge, we are forced to depend upon operational definitions for determining the ages between the onset of puberty and the onset of adulthood. There is evidence for a pubertal growth spurt as early as ages five and a half for girls and eight for boys; menarche does not necessarily tell us that sexual reproduction is actually possible; and different organ systems, tissues, and physiological functions develop at different ages. There is variation in maturation between the sexes, and within either sex. Size alone is no criterion for maturation. We have evidence that while the age of onset of menarche has declined in the more affluent societies of the world, this trend has levelled off. At the same time, there are populations which reach puberty in their late teens (Tanner 1962, 1970; Malcolm 1970), and much remains to be learned about growth in the developing areas of the world.

We cannot, even simplistically, state that physical adulthood starts when growth is completed, for, as Alex Roche asks in this volume, "Growth of what?" Growth in weight does not necessarily cease even in those who are clearly adult. On the other hand, some parts of the body, for example the auditory ossicles, reach adult size during intrauterine life.

Still, while much remains to be investigated by the students of human growth, societies everywhere have created their own systems for dealing with the life cycle. All cultures have recognized the fact that humans are born, mature, and die. That the movement through life is fraught with possible difficulty or danger is also recognized. The *rites de passage* employed by many societies assist individuals as they move from one social status to another. The rites generally consist of three major parts: separation from a previous status, a period of transition, and incorporation into a new status — often involving being claimed by the members of the new status into which one is moving. The timing of these rites varies from culture to culture, but generally they mark important points of transition, such as birth, marriage, and death.

In pre-industrial societies, adolescence as a special period is not well defined. Generally, people moved rather quickly from childhood to adulthood. While puberty was recognized, it signified the beginning of rather early involvement in adult economic production and preparation for marriage and parenthood. The major socializing agency was the extended family group, and the availability of choices as regards life style and economic role was relatively restricted. Although the picture of what to us may seem like idyllic transquillity for adults was occasionally challenged by a rebellious couple, a bold innovator, or carefree adventurer, on the whole, pre-industrial societies managed to control and direct the socialization of their young into a pattern of tradition and stability that insured survival and cultural continuity, even within a framework of moderate change.

The last decades have thrust a radically different perception of youth and adolescence upon the world. Radical though it seems, it reflects the acceleration of change in the world, which, while it has always occurred, has reached monumental proportions since the advent of the industrial revolution. No study of adolescence today can ignore the impact of culture change as it is now occurring.

Indeed, the very definition of adolescence, in the cultural sense, derives its meaning from relatively recent change. Whereas pre-industrial societies moved their young rather quickly from childhood to adulthood, we have not only defined the period in between, but have been constantly expanding the age levels we consider to be within the adolescent framework. As late as 1904, G. Stanley Hall marked the significance of the term itself and legitimized research on twelve- to twenty-year-olds (Hall 1904). Since the emergence of what might be called the youth subculture of the 1960's, the ages have been extended upward. In its recent *Report*, the Panel on Youth of the President's Science Advisory Committee deals with the ages fourteen to twenty-four. The implications of this changed definition of a delineated age grouping, newly isolated and segregated in industrial society, are staggering when one recognizes that throughout much of the world, for example, over half the population is under the age of twenty, and in the United States alone, there are over 40 million young people between the ages of fourteen and twenty-four, an increase in number from 1960 to 1970 of 13.2 million, or 52 percent! We are faced with the extraordinary situation of the industrial, affluent nations having defined an elongated period of life called adolescence. Given the explosion of the post-World War II population, we have defined a whole new age group whose sheer size has presented overwhelming problems to their societies.

The separation of young people into a recognizable period of adolescence in the industrial nations in the nineteenth and early part of the twentieth centuries proceeds from the need for more time for advanced training for the more technologically sophisticated industrial world. It was an uneven development, for the young of the lower classes were not afforded the luxury of this period, moving quickly into the factories, and early adulthood; rural people also retained earlier patterns. Paradoxically, it was the affluence and ever-increasing efficiency of industrial production which made it possible to keep larger and larger segments of young people out of employment, segregated in the ever-expanding schools for longer and longer periods of time. At the same time, young people were exempt from adult economic participation, increasingly segregated in limited environments away from the larger community, their socialization increasingly undertaken by schools and peers. By the 1920's, sociologists in this country were speaking of the adolescent society; by the 1960's, the segregation and isolation of young people had brought about the development of what sociologists have come to call "youth culture" — with adulthood postponed to increasingly later ages.

Industrial societies have come to employ technological and educational criteria for adulthood, giving approval in the form of various degrees of certification. This is closely related to an achievement-oriented value system. While these have been highly functional for the growth and expansion of a technological system, the efforts to universalize these criteria among less achievement-oriented individuals, in their own society as well as among peoples with different cultural ethos, create serious problems.

Non-Western cultures vary in this regard. The Ibo of Nigeria, for example, are highly individualistic and achievement-oriented. Their young people have been extremely successful in adopting the Western educational system and, until the Biafran conflict, moved readily into national and world trade. For some native American youth, on the other hand, there remains the difficulty of resolving a noncompetitive Indian view with the materialistic, competitive demands of the mainstream culture (Fuchs and Havighurst 1972). The school, which requires individualistic, achievement-oriented motivation, may appear to demand more than the young person can give and still retain psychic unity with his group and its value system. To those for whom age or physical maturity are the traditional criteria in defining adult social status, the shift to educational accomplishment, which is the mark of highly motivated individuals seeking their place in a money economy, may generate conflict.

The elongation of the post-pubertal, pre-adult period, associated with requirements for longer and longer periods of educational preparation, has inevitably created problems. The implications of this are evident when we recognize that most societies relate readiness for marriage and parenthood with the capacity to assume adult economic responsibilities. Students of Japanese society have noted how sexual tension in youths increases as a result of middle-class insistence that heterosexual interests must not interfere with occupational preparation, although a double standard has permitted sexual outlets for males during the preparatory period (DeVos 1973). In many industrial societies, including our own, the relaxation of the double standard and the sexual revolution for females has been a response to the changed conditions. Increasingly, an individual who makes a premature permanent marital commitment is considered to have jeopardized his total career pattern, especially if he fathers children before his occupational stability is fully insured; and in our society this is increasingly considered true of girls as well as boys.

While this pattern is fairly obvious for middle-class urban youth in industrial societies around the world, the requirements for prolonged adolescence have profound effects for people who are in the process of change from rural to urban life, for some ethnic groups within the society who still retain other patterns of socialization, as well as for some of the lower classes who cannot afford to maintain their young for long periods.

An example from contemporary Choctaw Indian life in the American Southeast (discussed in this volume) illustrates this dilemma which faces groups in the process of change brought about by contact with impinging industrial society. Formerly a rural, sharecropping people whose children, after puberty, moved quickly into economic production and marriage, their lives have been altered by several changes which have occurred since 1964. These changes take on added significance in view of the fact that 50 percent of the population is under the age of twenty-one.

Since 1964, there has been a decline in farming and a rise in the mechanization of agriculture, resulting in unemployment for older men, out-migration for younger men, and some local factory employment for women. For the first time, a local high school was established with boarding facilities, bringing together Choctaw youth from various localities, taught by predominantly white, middle-class teachers who were accustomed to white, middle-class, adolescent groupings. In addition, there was an increase in consumer items such as television sets, radios, and cars.

As a result of these changes, within the last ten years there has been, in part because of the establishment of the high school, a delay in the timing of marriage; but there has not been adequate opportunity to learn or act out the courtship patterns of the surrounding society. Parental conflict is engendered because some parents do not understand prolonged adolescence for their children. They ask, "Why aren't they married? Why aren't they working?"

At the same time, mating behavior continues, without the ready accessibility of contraceptives or abortion. As a result, many young people find themselves involved in marriage before they are ready. Thus, while professional jobs and other opportunities requiring higher education are opening up for them, many of the brightest young people find themselves married while in high school, or during summer vacation away from college, or while on a visit from a job in the North; and because of the demands of early marriage they are cut off from economic advancement.

The problem of technological employment, even for rural peoples, has forced a universal elongation of the preparatory period. It is perhaps a moot point as to whether the rural dropout, given contact with the larger world via mass media, is in any less difficulty psychologically than his urban counterpart who, because of discrimination, or lack of ability or motivation, etc., also does not move through the established preparatory institutions of the society.

No discussion of adolescence today can ignore the phenomenal impact caused by the diffusion of what might be called the youth culture to every segment of society, both within this country and throughout the world. This youth culture, the sheer size of the youth group, growing affluence, increasing inevitability of modernization, and the rising expectations for the future among peoples of different cultures throughout the world have created formidable problems for societies as they seek to insure survival and continuity by the socialization of their young.

One of the characteristics of this youth culture is its self-conscious recognition of being a separate social grouping. As we have already noted, this has arisen primarily out of the increasing separation and segregation of age groups in industrial societies. The young are in schools much of the time, or in youth groups of one sort or another. They are, as in our society, either not permitted to work or find difficulty in getting work. They are separated from adults who work in institutions away from the young, outside of school, "in the real world." Social life also occurs along age lines. Extended family groupings engaged in economic ventures or social activities which include all age groups come to be an impediment or nuisance, taking time away from school or the company of peers. Our schools encourage this by sorting by age, by assigning tests and papers to be done during holidays, binding students to school rather than family. Our adults encourage this by their recognition (albeit at times reluctant) that the larger institutions of industrial society are better equipped to prepare their children for adult occupations than the parents are. At the same time, this is an uneven process of separation from elders and family and bears the potential of intergenerational conflict and loss of psychic support from the family.

Another characteristic generally assigned to the youth culture is the growth in psychic attachment of young people to others their own age rather than to those within their families. This has resulted in part from the decline of the extended family and the limitations of the nuclear family's ability to provide the time and educative functions during the elongated period of preparation for adulthood. Evidence for this psychic dependence upon other young people in this country can be seen in the evolution of dating, a recent phenomenon growing out of age segregation in the high schools and colleges, which replaced less intimate gatherings such as community parties and dances during this century. Dating was replaced in part by "going steady" in the 1950's, and more recently some have sought closeness through communal living.

The search for psychic attachment is also related to other activities. As Coleman (1973) notes:

This element of psychic need for closeness increasingly unfulfilled by the family is apparent not only in the evolution of the dating system and in communal groups. It probably is an important stimulus to the use of soft drugs and to the religious movement among the young. It is an aspect of youth's current situation which helps spawn activities that are very unlike but tied together by this one need.

Related to the loss of emotional support from the family is the fact that in modern societies the sanctioning of individuals has been removed to impersonal social agencies such as the police and the legal court system. Authority has become impersonalized and sanctioning agencies have become professionalized. For some youth, the professionalized social agencies are regarded as external forms of oppression rather than positive agents of social control. Sometimes this is expressed along class lines. Where ethnic as well as class variables segment society, a greater proportion of alienated youth interact as part of ethnic subcultures. Where the sanctioning agencies are dominated by one or another ethnic group, as opposed to their clients, conflict is exacerbated.

The loss of psychic support from the family, as it moved from extended kin groups with many functions toward the increasingly fragile nuclear unit, has been noted by many observers of industrial society. But this picture may not be accurate for non-Western societies which are moving very rapidly into contact with international economic and cultural systems in the present. There appears to be some evidence that the rapidity of change has become so great that families and their young people are making simultaneous adjustments to a changed world, and that elders and young people are being supportive of one another in the process. There is also evidence that extended kin networks are still operative among some segments of society and act to alleviate the stresses which occur when cultural change moves in the direction of replacing achievement-oriented status for earlier ascribed status among some less mobile, less urban peoples.

An example of this is the illustration of the kinship network displayed among the residents of Holmes County, Mississippi. (See Edward Eckenfels, "Several selves and many homes: black youth's adaptation to geographical and cultural mobility," in this volume.) This Mississippi Delta region is characterized by extreme economic deprivation. In 1970, the median age was between 17 and 18, and around 18 percent, or about 3,500 individuals were adolescents. Two-thirds of all households consisted of husband-wife families. Almost half the families, both husband-wife and woman-headed, were of the extended type. Since 1960 there has been intense out-migration, primarily to Chicago. A good deal of movement to and from the city takes place, and adolescents constitute one of the major groups of returning migrants.

Migration among the young members of minority groups is often considered to have an extremely disruptive effect on individuals' links with family, friends, and historical roots, to the point of behavioral disorganization. In Holmes county it is not unusual to find that before black youths are out of their teens they have lived in both the rural South and urban North. They have been associated with the ghetto street-society in the city, with school-oriented youngsters, and with sharecroppers; they have attended both segregated and desegregated schools. Despite all of this movement, one finds a sense of stability in them maintained through strong family ties, emotional support, and intervention in times of crisis by an extended family network. Maturing youngsters are shielded from the ghetto youth culture by being returned to relatives in the rural South for part of their adolescence; and rural youngsters often spend summers with relatives in the cities. There is growing sophistication, regardless of residence, with respect to the demands of the larger society and the problems faced by black youth in an unisolated urban milieu.

The extended family plays a significant role in cushioning the problems of adjustment faced by these youngsters. Eckenfels reports:

One of the most serious problems that these young people struggle with is how they can become accepted and respected members of the major culture without facing retribution from those blacks who are left behind. Besides having to deal with recriminations of the white majority who believe they should "remain in their place," they are constantly aware of possible criticism from their own cultural group. Those black youths that I have talked with, however, have pointed out to me that throughout their lives their family and friends have helped them prepare for dealing with these conflicts. If anything, their loved ones have shown them that they have a vicarious positive feeling about their personal achievements, and that feeling will grow as they continue to share their accomplishments (this volume, p. 135).

Wilhemina Kalu's study of adolescence among the Ga people of Ghana in West Africa illustrates similar themes. The modern Ga adolescent is brought up in a multicultural milieu with an earlier exposure, through school, to widening horizons for socioeconomic functioning. Thus, he is a child of new cultural patterns created by industrialization and urbanization. Yet he is also socialized through traditional institutions, primarily the extended family which remains operative in the present. The extended families maintain a degree of flexibility and pragmatism, measuring their desire to protect their younger members against what are considered undesirable or frivolous aspects of the developing youth culture, yet at the same time maintaining pride and encouragement for their educated, modern, young people. The result is an adolescent more receptive to a broad range of cultures, curious about other ways of life and uncritical of them until the late adolescent phase, when national consciousness and political idealism gain strength. Recent years have seen the attraction to cultural nationalism, which is likely to ensure the survival of traditional agencies of socialization amidst the adaptations for the new modes of life demanded by modernization and urbanization.

I would suggest that the modern conditions which have accelerated the geographical and cultural mobility of many young people throughout the world have also served to cushion the damaging effects of that mobility. In the past, the crossing of a continent or ocean frequently signified a total break with family, culture, and language. While kinship networks were retained for a while and supported further migration, the distances and time spans were great and therefore the pace of contact was of necessity slow.

In our era these conditions have changed markedly. The jet age has placed the remotest areas within rapid and easy access. The telephone and telegraph, the sharing of exposure to world and even universal events have become available to almost all via satellite communications. The level of shared experience across cultures has reached a point greater than ever before possible in the history of the world. At the same time, pride in one's ethnic roots and native language need not be eroded by isolation. Certainly, for example, the Hispanic migrant to the United States mainland who can visit back and forth KNOWS that Spanish is a splendid language, in contrast to the shame and contempt experienced by migrants of the past in this nation.

At the same time, the modern technology of communication has also been instrumental in diffusing those aspects of the youth culture which intensify youth's view of itself as a distinct group with a sense of deviation from the norms which the adults in their homes, schools and colleges encourage them to hold. Thus new sources of information — not only the ordinary channels of television and radio programs, but also disk jockeys catering to youth, the proliferation of underground newspapers, etc. — legitimized for youth the sense of alienation and estrangement from adult society, feeding into the anti-establishment and anti-adult norms of many young people and providing the possibility of ready diffusion of fads and fashion at a dizzying pace. Belief that this was wholly the creature of the young avoids the recognition that the age delineation grew out of the needs of the larger, increasingly affluent society, as well as the huge size of the post-World War II youth population which provided a ready audience and market.

The dilemma we face today in the industrial societies is that our civilizations have had no previous experience in socializing such vast numbers of peoples whose productive labor is really not essential to an affluent society. With intentions stemming from protective altruism as well as inexperience, we have had no more imaginative schemes for dealing with this issue other than to keep young people in our schools, which are often unprepared for the influx of so many, or in the armed forces. It came as a rude shock that so many young people responded with vigorous protest in the last decade to the growth of impersonalized processing through chaotically expanding educational institutions, or to issues such as the draft.

Modern, industrial nations such as the United States and Japan have tended to produce from their middle classes two subgroups of adolescents. While they represent only a small fraction of youth, perhaps 5 or 10 percent, their groups have attracted considerable attention. Labelled counter-culture, these groups are of two kinds: one moves in the direction of a more emotionally oriented life style, with a rejection of the values of modern, materialistic, Western culture; the other is more committed to thorough political revolution — the group called, in this country, the New Left.

It must be emphasized that the overwhelming majority of young people in industrial, capitalist countries — over 90 percent — are prepared to go along with the achievement values of the larger cultures. They have varying degrees of commitment to social change, but they do not totally reject their parents' values, nor do they expect revolutionary change. They are quite ready to prepare themselves for adult roles in the way the society expects them to. In those societies where there has to be a shift from ascribed status by virtue of kinship to achieved status as the societies enter modern industrial life, there is the possibility, though not the inevitability, of greater conflict between the young and the adult supporters of the status quo.

However, while the vast size of the youth population of the last decade forced the total society into a traumatic confrontation with the young, with reverberations felt throughout the world, we would be foolish indeed to believe that a slowed increase in the numbers of youth in the next decade, and a higher proportion of older persons to younger, will defer the necessity of confronting remaining issues.

Adolescents today are faced with what appears to be a bewildering array of choices to be made in their lives: the choice of lifestyles, possible careers, varying educational preparations, even of mates. Complicating this is the fact that, in some areas, choice is recognized by many as more illusory than real, and dependent on what appear to be the irrational whims of impersonal organizations. Nevertheless, the general opening up of choices for youth, and for others, has occurred and is at once both emancipating and anxiety-provoking.

Over forty years ago, when Margaret Mead (1928) did her classic study which demonstrated that adolescent storm and stress were not inevitable, she made a comment still appropriate today:

... it must be recalled by any student of civilization that we pay heavily for our heterogeneous, rapidly changing civilization: we pay in high proportions of crime and delinquency, we pay in the conflicts of youth, we pay in ever-increasing number of neuroses, we pay in the lack of coherent traditions without which the development of art is sadly handicapped. In such a list of prices, we must count our gains carefully, not to be discouraged. And chief among our gains must be reckoned this possibility of choice, the recognition of many possible ways of life, where other civilizations have recognized only one. Where other civilizations give a satisfactory outlet to only one temperamental type, be he mystic or soldier, business man or artist, a civilization in which there are many standards offers a possibility of satisfactory adjustment to individuals of many different temperamental types, or diverse gifts and varying interests.

Clearly, society is not able to turn back to an era of greater restriction or absence of choice. Adolescents are likely to continue to confront the frequent need for decision-making. However, if choice is to be emancipating and meaningful, society must assume responsibility to see that the opportunity for fulfillment of youthful anticipation or ambition is in reality available.

There is something to be learned from the way in which cultures throughout the history of mankind have dealt with problems of the life cycle. Gokulanathan reminds us of this in "Adolescence in a matriarchal society," as does Mária Kresz in "The community of young people in a Transylvanian village," both in this volume. The *rites de passage* helped to move people across the periods of dangerous transition. One of the difficulties we face is that incorporation into adulthood comes later and is ever more difficult, and the lines of transition are increasingly blurred. We, of course, have our diffuse kinds of secular rites, such as getting a driver's license, or a car, or a license to teach. But what has really emerged as the major difficulty is not so much that we do not have a structured rite understood by all. Neither is it that young people face a world in which there is a multiplicity of things from which to choose. It is rather that there is a dangerous discontinuity between the years of preparation and experimentation for adult occupation and participation, and the absence of any assurance that society can provide the place for one to practice adulthood. If there are no jobs for those who have prepared to teach, no places in graduate school for those who have studied hard at college, no professional posts for those who have gone on to graduate schools, no theatres for those who wish to direct, no families to run — if there is no place to practice what one has been led to believe lies ahead — then we are likely to have enormous numbers of highly educated but deeply disappointed people.

The problems of adolescence are in good measure reflective of the problems of the entire world. Scarcely any society of our time has remained untouched by the vastly accelerating pace of cultural change. Industrialization, high productivity, urbanization, national movements, major social revolutions, thermonuclear power, catastrophic wars, jet transport, satellite communications, and a burgeoning world population have thrust upon all peoples the choices and uncertainties previously held in check by more traditional life styles and have forced new definitions of social roles.

In industrial societies we are faced with the need to design and think through alternative environments in which young people of different temperaments can spend their youth. Most important, the larger society must assume the social responsibility which adults have assumed throughout history — the responsibility to provide, as young people advance in age, the opportunity for participation as productive members of society.

REFERENCES

COLEMAN, JAMES
1973 "Youth culture," in *Youth: transition to adulthood*. Report of the Panel on Youth of the President's Science Advisory Committee, Office of Science and Technology, Executive Office of the President. Washington, D.C.

DE VOS, GEORGE A.
1973 *Socialization for achievement: essays on the cultural psychology of the Japanese*. Berkeley: University of California Press.

FUCHS, ESTELLE, ROBERT J. HAVIGHURST
1972 *To live on this earth: American Indian education*. New York: Doubleday.

HALL, G. STANLEY
1904 *Adolescence: its psychology and its relations to physiology, anthropology, education*. New York: Appleton.

MALCOLM, LAWRENCE
1970 *Growth and development in New Guinea: a study of the Bundi people of the Medang District*. Institute of Human Biology Medang Monograph Series 1.

MEAD, MARGARET
1928 *Coming of age in Samoa*. New York: William Morrow.

TANNER, J. M.
1962 *Growth at adolescence*. Oxford: Blackwell Scientific Publications.
1970 "Physical Growth," in *Carmichael's Manual of Child Psychology*, volume one. Edited by P. H. Mussen. New York: Wiley.

PART ONE

Growth and Health Care in Adolescence

Growth After Puberty

ALEX F. ROCHE

This paper presents some basic concepts relevant to many types of research concerning growth and development, a general survey of growth after puberty, and the findings from some specific analyses.

Because growth is a dynamic process, its study should be dynamic. There are two basic types of growth data, one called "cross-sectional" and the other "longitudinal," or "serial." One of the earliest known serial-growth records was made by Count Gueneau de Montbeillard (Scammon 1927), who recorded the stature of his son at six-month intervals from birth to the age of eighteen years (see Figure 1). His son's growth in stature or recumbent length was more rapid between birth and two years than during any other age interval, with the possible exception of that from thirteen to fifteen years. These changes in growth rate are not obvious when the data are presented as in Figure 1. If the data are used to obtain annual increments, the changes become much more clear (see Figure 2).

Conclusions about growth in individuals must be based on serial data. Cross-sectional data from a population at various ages allows one to determine the differences between means or medians at ages one year apart, for example, between nine years and ten years. This difference is the mean or median increment from nine years to ten years. But cross-sectional data cannot provide the range of increments between successive ages. Such questions, and many others, require serial data.

It is important to stress that serial data can provide information that cross-sectional data cannot provide. It is equally important to stress that

This work was supported by Contract 72–2735 and Grants HD–03472 and HD–04629 from the National Institutes of Health, Bethesda, Maryland.

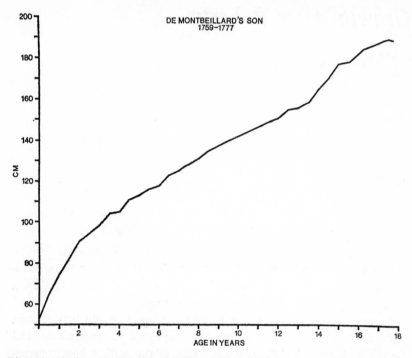

Figure 1. A distance graph of serial-growth data recorded at six-month intervals from birth to eighteen years in one French boy during the eighteenth century (from Scammon 1927)

serial data are not better than cross-sectional data. Which is better depends on which is more suited to the particular purpose. Serial data are essential if the purpose is to study changes in individuals; only cross-sectional data are required to analyze growth attainment in a community or population group. In the latter type of study, sampling is of major importance. Cross-sectional data are likely to be more effective in a population study because it is virtually impossible to obtain the cooperation of a large and fully representative sample in a serial study.

Dictionaries define puberty as the age when sexual reproduction becomes possible, and define adolescence as the period from puberty to adulthood. It is difficult to determine when individuals become capable of sexual reproduction. Certainly, it is not possible to do so in a serial-growth study. Commonly, the age of puberty is accepted as menarche, the development of secondary sex characters, or peak height velocity (the midpoint of the year in which the maximum annual increment in stature occurs, often written as PHV). Peak height velocity is preferable, because it has similar meanings in the two sexes. In addition, it has a natural

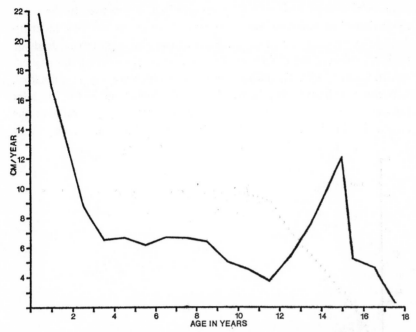

Figure 2.   A graph of annual increments, using the data shown in Figure 1

relationship to another useful criterion of developmental level, that is, the age when growth ceases. This can be regarded as the time when adolescents become adults.

These criteria do not match the dictionary definitions, but they are reasonable working ones. If it is accepted that the transition from adolescence to adulthood is the age when growth ceases, it can be asked: "Growth of what?" Growth in weight has not necessarily ceased, even in those who are clearly adult. On the other hand, some parts of the body, for example, the auditory ossicles, reach adult size during intrauterine life (Scammon 1930; Anson, et al. 1948).

THE CESSATION OF GROWTH IN STATURE

Figure 3 shows what may be the longest serial growth record for an individual. This girl was studied between the ages of one year and forty years. These serial data for recumbent length and stature indicate that she ceased to grow in stature at an age between twelve and twenty-four years. This is not unexpected, but these data should make it possible to determine the age of cessation of growth more precisely. For such an analysis, long-term serial data of high reliability are required. Those used in the study to be described had been recorded by two observers working independently (Roche and Davila 1972). Each of the observers remeasured the subject whenever the differences between pairs of recorded statures exceeded 5 millimeters. The mean interobserver difference was 3 millimeters.

Without such accuracy, the trend of data points would be too irregular for adequate curve fitting. The marked regularity of the trend of the recorded points in Figure 3 should not be overemphasized. This regularity

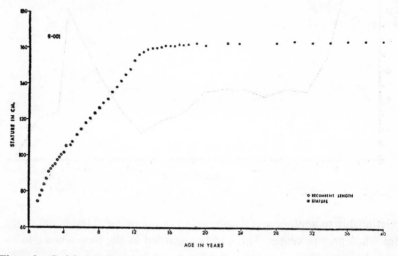

Figure 3. Serial recumbent length and stature data from one to forty years for a girl in the Fels Longitudinal Sample

is less impressive when the data are redrawn, omitting those recorded before twelve years and after thirty years and using a larger ordinate scale (see Figure 4).

It could be assumed, reasonably, that growth in stature ceased after twelve years. Consequently, there was little interest in data recorded during infancy and childhood. These were excluded so that they would not influence the statistical method used. Only data recorded after the age of peak height velocity were used, because it was considered that curves should be fitted to sets of points recorded during corresponding biological intervals for individuals. Similarly, data recorded in middle age were excluded, because they would not have been relevant. Furthermore, they might have led to erroneous conclusions, because of the probable loss of stature in individuals after thirty years (Büchi 1950; Trotter and Gleser 1958).

The analysis was done separately for each individual. The problem was

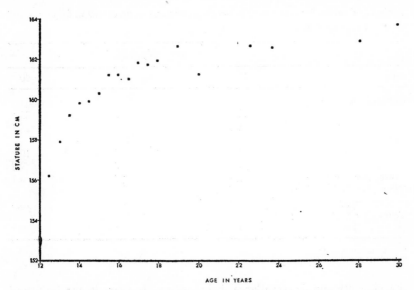

Figure 4. Serial stature data for the same girl as in Figure 3. The age range has been reduced and the vertical scale altered

to determine where growth in stature ceased amongst a set of data points such as those in Figure 4. This was done using piecewise regressions in which two separate polynomial lines were fitted to sets of data points for each individual (Mellits 1965, 1968). One line was fitted to the earlier set and the other to the later set of points. These polynomial lines were fitted using all possible junctions between earlier and later sets. When applying this method, one chooses the degrees of the polynomials that will be used. This choice is based on the known trends of the data and on the results of trials with different-degree polynomials. With the present data, a two-degree polynomial for the left-hand data set and a zero-degree polynomial (horizontal straight line) for the right-hand data set resulted in a good fit. The second-degree polynomial approximates in form the latter part of a sigmoid growth curve. The age at which growth in stature ceased in each individual was taken to be the age of the junction where the goodness of fit was maximized for the two polynomials combined.

The median age at which growth in stature ceased was about four years later in the boys than in the girls; there was a wide spread of these ages in each sex (Table 1). The spread from the tenth to the ninetieth centile was approximately five years in each sex. Growth in stature (median values) ceased 7.8 years after PHV in the boys and 6.0 years after PHV in the girls, indicating that the relationships between these two events differ between the sexes. Again, the ranges of intervals from the tenth to

Table 1.   Centiles for ages (year) at which growth in stature ceased in fifty boys and forty-five girls (Roche and Davila 1972)

Ages	Centiles		
	10	50	90
Chronological age			
(years) Boys	18.4	21.2	23.5
Girls	15.8	17 3	21.1
Years after PHV*			
Boys	4.4	7.8	10.3
Girls	4.6	6.0	9.8
Years after menarche	3.8	4.8	6.7
Years after SA† 13 years			
Boys	4.8	8.1	10.9
Years after SA† 11 years			
Girls	4.7	6.3	9.7

* peak height velocity
† skeletal age

the ninetieth centile were large, being about six years in the boys and about five years in the girls. In the girls, growth in stature ceased 4.8 years after menarche, with a narrower range between the tenth and ninetieth centiles than for the other ages and intervals listed.

The ages of cessation of growth in stature were considered in relation to skeletal age (SA). This measure of bone maturity is determined from a radiograph, and further reference to it will be made later. For the moment, it is sufficient to note that the appearance of the hand-wrist radiograph of a boy with a skeletal age of thirteen years is similar to that of the hand-wrist radiograph of a girl with a skeletal age of eleven years. Nevertheless, after the bones of the hand-wrist had achieved the same maturity appearances in the two sexes, growth in stature continued for about two years longer in the boys than in the girls. There were wide ranges, with a spread from the tenth to the ninetieth centile of about six years in the boys and five years in the girls.

The total increments in stature to twenty-eight years were almost identical with those to the ages when growth in stature ceased (Table 2). This implies that the LEVELS of the junctions between the pairs of polynomials accurately match adult-stature levels. The boys grew considerably more than the girls after both sixteen and eighteen years. When the usual sex differences in rates of maturation were taken into account, by comparing the total increments after eighteen years in boys with those after sixteen years in girls, the difference in growth between boys and girls was small (boys 0.8 centimeters, girls 1.1 centimeters).

In serial-growth studies, it is common to enroll children at a particular

Table 2. Centiles for total increments (in centimeters) in stature after growth and developmental landmarks (Roche and Davila 1972)

	n	10	50	90
16 years — Boys	103	1.2	2.8	7.2
Girls	91	-0.1	1.1	2.7
18 years — Boys	103	-0.3	0.8	2.3
Girls	91	-0.4	0.6	1.4
PHV* — Boys	78	11.6	17.8	23.7
Girls	63	10.8	15.8	22.3
Menarche	90	4.3	7.4	10.6
Femur mature — Boys	31	0.6	1.4	2.7
Girls	35	0.3	1.0	2.0
Tibia mature — Boys	33	0.3	1.2	2.3
Girls	37	0.1	1.1	2.2

*   peak height velocity

high school. Usually, by seventeen years such samples are attenuated, and by eighteen years they are almost nonexistent. The few reported studies concerning the cessation of growth in stature have been based on those students who remained, as a nonrepresentative sample of the educationally slow; or they have been short-term studies of college students over two-to three-year periods (Trotter and Gleser 1958). It is important to note that both the boys and the girls in the present study grew after eighteen years (median values), and that at the ninetieth centile level this growth amounted to 2.3 centimeters in the boys and 1.4 centimeters in the girls.

The total increments after PHV were slightly greater in the boys than in the girls. After menarche, the girls grew 7.4 centimeters (median), with a range of 6.3 centimeters from the tenth to the ninetieth centile.

Girls with an early menarche tend to have more growth after this than do those with a late menarche. There is a negative correlation between age at menarche and growth in stature after menarche ($r = -0.51$, $n = 96$, $p < 0.0005$). This association is illustrated in Figure 5.

Sometimes it is considered that children have ceased to grow in stature when the long bones of the leg are skeletally mature. This is determined from radiographic observations showing that the secondary center of ossification (epiphysis) of each long bone has fused with the corresponding shaft (diaphysis). After this occurs, the long bone cannot elongate. However, growth in stature occurred in both the boys and the girls after the femur and the tibia were mature. At the median level, the total increment was 1.0–1.4 centimeters, being slightly greater in the boys than in the girls. These sex differences in total stature increments after the cessation of elongation in the long bones presumably reflect sex-associated

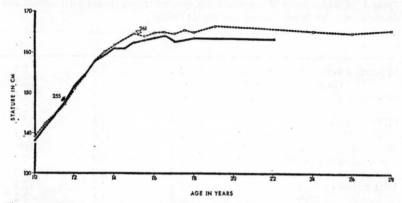

AGE IN YEARS

Figure 5.   Serial stature data for two girls in the Fels Longitudinal Sample who differed markedly in age at menarche. The girl with menarche at 11.6 years (Number 255) grew much more after menarche, and for a longer period, than the girl with menarche at 15.2 years (Number 261)

differences in trunk elongation during adolescence. This involves changes in the vertebral bodies rather than in the intervertebral discs (Anderson, et al. 1965; Roche 1972).

CURVE FITTING

Long-term serial-stature data can be used in other ways. Often this is facilitated by fitting mathematically defined curves to summarize the data in a few parameters. Many possible curves can be fitted, but those curves must be selected that fit the observed data accurately and that can be described by few parameters. It is desirable that these parameters be capable of biological interpretation.

In the method to be described, two separate logistic functions were fitted (Bock, et al. 1973). This parameterization is satisfactory for data from one year to maturity, but it can be fitted only if the serial data extend to at least eighteen years. Recumbent-length data from one year and three months to eighteen years, for a girl who was modal in all parameters, is used as an example (see Figure 6). The first function (A) fitted closely to the early data but then diverged. This prepubertal component of the model rose steeply until about five years and then decelerated, although it was still increasing slightly even at eighteen years. The lower curve (B) began at about five and a half years, increased rapidly from nine to eleven years, and then decelerated. It did not increase after sixteen years. This is the pubertal component of the model. The sum of the two lower curves

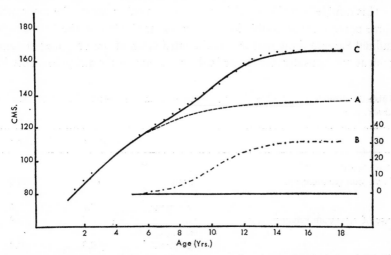

Figure 6. Components of the total fitted curve, using the double logistic model, for recumbent length in a girl who was modal in all parameters (based on Bock, et al. 1973)

$(A + B)$ is shown as the solid line (C) that passes through or near the recorded data points.

The sum of these two logistic curves (C) provided a better fit to the original data points than other models that have been described. Six parameters describe the two curves, but only five are needed, because one can be predicted from the others. This double logistic model has the further advantage that it can be interpreted biologically. The prepubertal component (A) may reflect the ability of chondrocytes to divide in a constant environment — this ability decreases gradually. The pubertal component may reflect the ability of endocrine cells to divide, particularly those that produce somatotropic or steroid hormones. This ability increases gradually and then decreases. This division of endocrine cells produces a change in the environment (levels of circulating hormones). Consequently, chondrocytes divide more rapidly and a growth spurt occurs during pubescence.

This model indicates that the pubertal component of growth begins at about eight years in boys and five and a half years in girls. These ages are earlier than those obtained by analysis of the total curve (Deming 1957; Maresh 1972) because the acceleration of the pubertal component is masked by deceleration of the prepubertal component. Increased levels of circulating steroid hormones occur at about the ages of initiation of the pubertal component, and histological changes associated with puberty occur even earlier in the ovary and testis (Blizzard, et al. 1970).

This double logistic model is interesting in other ways. The means for some parameters of double logistic curves for children in the Fels Longitudinal Sample show that the total contribution of the prepubertal component was considerably larger in the boys than in the girls (see Table 3).

Table 3.   Values for double logistic parameters in the Fels Longitudinal Sample (Bock, et al. 1973)

		Boys	Girls
Prepubertal			
Total gain (centimeters)	mean	149.7	138.0
	standard deviation	7.1	7.1
Age of maximum velocity (years)	mean	0.8	0.4
	standard deviation	0.3	0.4
Pubertal			
Total gain (centimeters)	mean	31.2	29.8
	standard deviation	4.1	6.2
Age of maximum velocity (years)	mean	13.0	11.0
	standard deviation	0.8	0.9

On the other hand, the mean contribution of the pubertal component is only slightly larger in the boys. This differs from corresponding interpretations of total serial-growth curves, which indicate that the gain in stature during the pubertal spurt is considerably greater in boys and that this difference is a major contributor to the systematic stature differences between men and women (Deming 1957; Tanner 1962). The double logistic model implies that adult sex differences in stature reflect the contributions of the prepubertal component.

PUBERTAL GROWTH SPURTS

These are well documented in man, may occur in other primates, almost certainly occur in seals, but have not been substantiated in other animals (Scheffer and Wilke 1953; Tanner 1962). Consequently, this is a field where experimental animals are of little use; studies must be of human beings, and serial data for individuals are necessary. The growth curve for an individual differs markedly from the mean growth curve for a group (see Figure 7). This is most obvious during pubescence, because the timing of pubertal growth spurts varies among individuals. The pubertal spurt

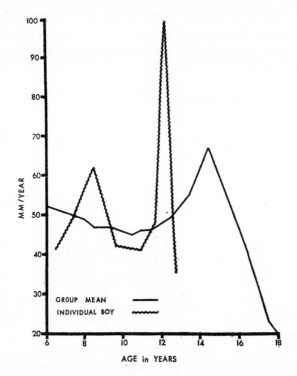

Figure 7. Data from Davenport (1930), showing serial stature data for one boy and the mean for the group

for a child is almost always more dramatic than the changes in the mean growth curve. The serial records that are used must extend from before any possible spurt to after any possible spurt. If the record of this boy (see Figure 7) had extended from six and a half until eleven years only, it might have been concluded, quite wrongly, that his spurt in stature had already occurred and had been completed.

The timing of examinations, also, is important in the study of pubertal spurts. Typically, these are made at birthdays and at half-birthdays — for example, nine, nine and a half, ten, ten and a half, eleven years, etc. Such a schedule implies that biological events occur at birthdays, but the only birthday with biological significance is the day of birth itself, which is significant for the mother and her child. The timing of examinations makes a difference, because the timing of spurts is not necessarily related to birthdays. The four pairs of matching graphs (*A–D*) in Figure 8 illustrate a problem to which van der Linden (1970) directed attention. The data are annual increments in pelvic width (bicristal diameter) in a girl in the Fels Longitudinal Sample. The actual measurements were recorded at birthdays, and the graphs in pair A (matching bar and line graphs) illustrate standard presentations of such data as annual increments. The midpoint of the year with the maximum increment is eleven and a half years.

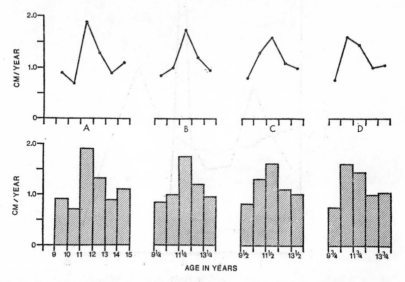

Figure 8.   Annual increments in bicristal diameter (hip width) in a girl in the Fels Longitudinal Sample. The pairs of line and bar graphs (*A-D*) illustrate the theoretical effects on the recorded data of differences in the timing of examinations

If it is assumed that growth was spread equally over each year, and that, instead of being measured on birthdays, this girl had been measured at quarter-birthdays, that is, at nine and a quarter, ten and a quarter years, etc., the form of the graphs would match those in Set B. The midpoint of the year with the maximum increment would be eleven and three-quarter years. If, however, this girl had been measured on half-birthdays, the form of the graphs would be different again (Set C); the midpoint of the annual interval with the maximum increment would be twelve years. Finally, if this girl had been measured on the three-quarter years, that is at nine and three-quarters, ten and three-quarter years, etc., the graphs would match those in Set D and the midpoint of the annual interval with the maximum increment would be eleven and a quarter years.

This methodological problem has general application to any study based on serial data. There is no way to avoid it completely. Ideally, examinations would be made when changes in rates occurred, but these times cannot be known in advance. The only possible solution, and that only a partial one, is to increase the frequency of examinations.

It has been noted that the pubertal growth spurt is more abrupt in an individual than the changes in population means. The spurt in stature results from increased growth rates in various bones — in particular, those of the leg. It can be asked whether all these bones have their spurts at the same time in an individual.

Data made available by the Child Research Council (Denver) were analyzed along with corresponding data from the Fels Longitudinal Sample. The measurements of long bones were made on serial standardized radiographs and are more reliable than standard caliper measurements of the living (Maresh and Deming 1939; Day and Silverman 1952). This analysis failed to achieve its purpose, which was to identify a bone in which the growth spurt occurred very early. It was planned to use the size of this spurt to predict growth in stature during puberty, and thus assist the prediction of adult stature from childhood variables.

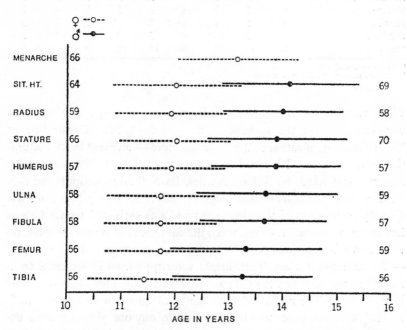

Figure 9. The timing of menarche and of maximum annual increments in six long bones, in stature and in sitting height (SIT HT). The circles indicate means, the lines indicate the range ± 1 standard deviation. The numbers show the sample sizes for girls on the left and boys on the right

As expected, the corresponding mean ages at which the growth spurt occurred were considerably earlier in the girls than in the boys (see Figure 9). While the mean ages differed among the long bones within a sex, these differences were small. The horizontal lines indicate the limits from plus-to minus-one standard deviation. These are large. Thus, it is not surprising that the order of maximum increments varies among individuals.

The order of some maturational events and maximum increments in nine girls from the Fels sample shows marked variability (see Table 4).

Table 4.   Age order for some girls in the Fels Sample of maximum increments and some developmental landmarks (Roche 1974)

	Girls								
	A	B	C	D	E	F	G	H	J
Ossification of US*	1	3	1	3	4	1	1	4	1
Tibia	2	1	3	4	1	1	3	3	3
Ba-S†	2	5	3	10	2	1	6	2	9
Ba-N†	7	5	3	1	5	1	6	8	3
S-N	7	3	1	1	5	5	10	1	10
Metacarpal II	4	5	3	4	5	5	3	10	3
Stature	6	2	7	8	9	5	2	6	2
Radius	4	5	8	4	2	5	3	4	3
Bicristal	7	5	10	4	5	9	8	7	3
Menarche	7	10	9	9	10	10	9	9	8

* ulnar sesamoid
† Ba = basion, S = sella, N = nasion

These girls were chosen randomly from a larger sample of those with complete data for the variables listed (Roche 1974). "Ossification of US" refers to ossification of the ulnar sesamoid — an event in the maturation of the skeleton. Tibia, radius, and metacarpal II are bones of the leg, forearm, and hand. Ba-S (basion-sella), Ba-N (basion-nasion), and S-N (sella-nasion) are cranial base lengths; "bicristal" is a pelvic diameter. Usually ossification of the ulnar sesamoid was early and menarche was late in the sequence. However, when the data are read across the table, no event had a fixed ordinal position in all girls. Some events varied markedly — for example, stature (peak height velocity) varied in sequence from second to ninth. When the data are read vertically, they show the order in individuals. The mean order for the whole group would read 1, 2, 3, … 10. The mean order was not followed by any one girl, and some deviated markedly from it. For example, in Girl E, ossification of the ulnar sesamoid and the spurt in stature were late, but the spurt in the radius was early. Not only is the pubertal spurt in stature more dramatic in an individual than in a group, it must be more dramatic in a bone than in an individual. Again, this is due to differences in timing.

This approach can be extended further. Long bones have epiphyseal zones at each end. It can be asked whether the spurt in elongation of a long bone is synchronous at the two ends. The changes at each end can be measured using natural bone markers — for example, trabecular patterns, or growth arrest lines (Roche 1965). Measurements in a subsample of the Fels children[1] showed a variable sequence of spurts between the two ends. These variations were not related to differences between the skeletal-maturity levels of the two ends. This implies that the spurt at one end of a bone is more dramatic than the spurt in the whole bone.

It is interesting biologically that spurts in different bones occur in various orders in individuals. These spurts result from a single central-nervous-system trigger mechanism acting on the endocrine system to cause increased levels of circulating hormones. In turn, these hormones act on the epiphyseal zones of the long bones. Presumably, these zones do not differ in the hormones to which they respond, but they must vary in their thresholds.

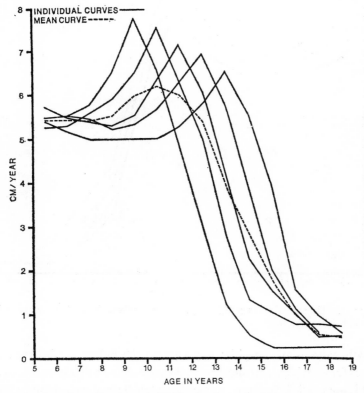

Figure 10. Data from Shuttleworth (1937), showing annual increments in stature for five girls differing in age of peak height velocity. The interrupted line shows mean increments for the group

[1] A group of white Ohioans, studied longitudinally over several decades by the Fels Research Institute of Yellow Springs, Ohio, United States of America.

BIOLOGICAL AGE

It is difficult to overemphasize the point that increments for a population do not match mean increments for individuals. Data from Shuttleworth (1937) show annual increments in stature for five girls differing in the ages at which they reached PHV (see Figure 10). The spurt was abrupt in each girl, but a mean for the group would follow the dotted line and would not match the growth pattern of any girl. The data for these girls can be graphed in relation to a biological age — for example, age in relation to PHV (see Figure 11). This markedly reduces the differences between the

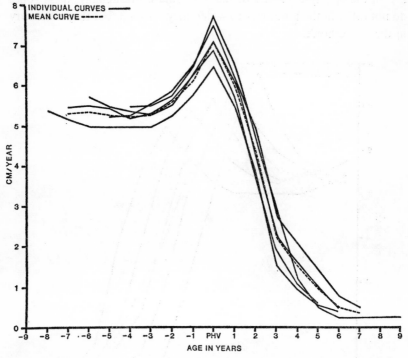

Figure 11.   The same data as in Figure 9, with the time base changed to age in relation to peak height velocity

growth patterns of the girls; and because the differences between the curves for individuals are now small, the mean reflects them reasonably.

It is appropriate to return to the subject of skeletal age. Between birth and maturity, changes occur in the radiographic appearances of bones that are independent of bone size. The original cartilaginous model is replaced by bone (see Figure 12, A-D), and the bone ends develop secondary centers of ossification, or epiphyses (see Figure 12, E), that remain

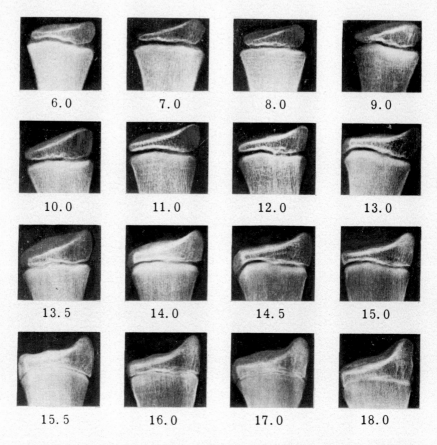

6. 0   7. 0   8. 0   9. 0

10. 0   11. 0   12. 0   13. 0

13. 5   14. 0   14. 5   15. 0

15. 5   16. 0   17. 0   18. 0

Plate 1. Modal radiographs of the distal end of the radius in boys, showing changes in levels of maturity at annual intervals from six to eighteen years. Note that the cartilage between the secondary center of ossification and the shaft is replaced gradually

separate from the major part of the shaft (diaphysis) for a long period. Most elongation occurs at the cartilaginous junctions between these secondary centers and the shafts.

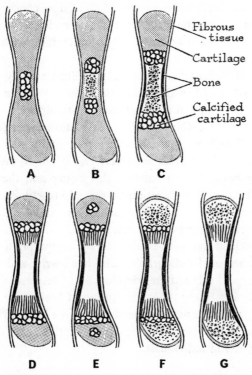

Figure 12. Diagrammatic representation of the maturation of a long bone. The approximate age scale is: A, six weeks prenatal; B, seven weeks prenatal; C, eight weeks prenatal; D, ten weeks prenatal to two years; E, two to six years; F, six to sixteen years; and G, adulthood (from Roche 1967)

The features used to grade skeletal maturity are mainly alterations in the secondary centers, in the zones between these centers and the shafts, and in the ends of the shafts. Some bones, however — for example, those of the wrist — do not develop secondary centers. Their maturity is graded from alterations in the shapes of the articular surfaces. The secondary centers (see Figure 12, E) enlarge during childhood and pubescence, and come to replace almost all the cartilage at the end of the bone and to resemble it in shape. The hyaline joint cartilage remains over the end of the bone and there is some cartilage between the secondary center and the shaft. While the latter cartilage remains, the bone has a potential for elongation. After this cartilage has been replaced by bone, further elongation of the bone cannot occur (see Figure 12, G). At this stage, it is said that the secondary center of ossification has fused with the shaft (epiphyseo-diaphyseal fusion) and the bone is adult. This final stage of skeletal maturation could be suggested as the end point of adolescence, but problems would arise. These include the sparsity of data concerning the ages at which fusion occurs, the fact that it occurs earlier at some sites than others, and that it would be necessary to radiograph each child to see whether he were mature.

Some stages of skeletal maturation can be illustrated by modal radiographs of the distal end of the radius (see Plate 1). These show typical levels of maturity at annual intervals from six to eighteen years in boys, with size kept constant. The secondary ossification center (epiphysis), in the upper part of each photograph, enlarges gradually, and the space between it and the shaft becomes narrower. This is due to the replacement of cartilage by bone. Fusion between this center and the shaft begins at seventeen years with obliteration of the gap (cartilage) between the two pieces of bone. Only a radio-opaque line remains at eighteen years to indicate the level of the previous junction.

Typically, skeletal maturity is assessed by comparing a standardized radiograph with modal radiographs. The hand-wrist and the knee are assessed commonly, using atlases developed in Cleveland (Greulich and Pyle 1959; Pyle and Hoerr 1969). In a group of Melbourne children, the median differences between the skeletal ages of the hand-wrist and of the knee were close to zero (see Table 5). However, these ages differed by as much as 1.22 years in individuals.

Table 5.   Differences (knee less hand) in boys between the skeletal ages of the knee and hand-wrist (year) (Roche and French 1970)

Chronological age	n	Centiles			Maximum
		25	50	75	
12	27	-0.04	0.06	0.15	-0.97
13	42	-0.05	0.06	0.17	1.22
14	41	-0.04	0.02	0.16	0.34
15	21	-0.04	0.04	0.20	0.29

This directs attention to another aspect of human variability. The bones of an individual mature at different rates, even when assessments are made by comparison with modal standards. This system of assessments does, of course, remove systematic differences in levels between bones. Data from the Fels Longitudinal Sample (Garn, et al. 1961) show the percentage of children with particular differences in timing between fusion at the proximal end of the tibia and the completion of fusion in the hand-wrist (see Figure 13). Within individuals, these events differed in timing by as

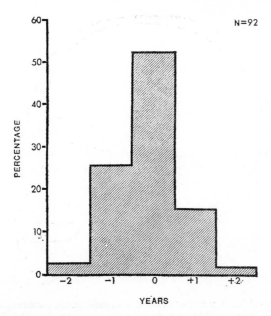

Figure 13.   The relative differences in timing between fusion at the proximal end of the tibia and the completion of fusion in the hand-wrist (data from Garn. et al. 1961)

much as two years in each direction. Even within the hand-wrist area, the maturity levels of particular bones differ within an individual (Roche 1962). Consequently, assessments of skeletal maturity are not exact. It is impractical to radiograph the whole skeleton, and it is not possible to select, in advance, an area that is representative. These assessments are inexact, also, because the mean interobserver and intraobserver differences are about three months, even for well-trained and experienced observers (Roche, et al. 1970; Johnson, et al. 1973).

CRANIAL BASE ELONGATION

This aspect of adolescent growth is a more detailed one. Measurements were made between midline points on standardized lateral radiographs of the cranial base. The recorded measurements were adjusted to compensate for their known radiographic enlargement. Basion (Ba) is the most posterior point on the basiocciput, sella (S) is the midpoint of the pituitary fossa, and nasion (N) is the junction between the frontal bone and the nasal bone (see Figure 14).

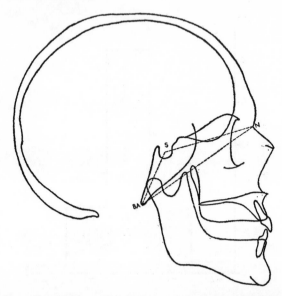

Figure 14.　An outline drawing of a lateral head radiograph, indicating the points on the cranial base between which measurements were made. Ba = basion, S = sella, and N = nasion

The median annual increments for Ba-N, S-N, and Ba-S, in groups of boys and girls from the Fels Longitudinal Sample (Lewis and Roche 1972, 1974; Roche and Lewis 1974) show that growth spurts occurred in each sex for each length (see Figure 15). As would be expected, these occurred much earlier in the girls than in the boys, and they were much more marked in the boys, with the possible exception of spurts in Ba-S. These spurts were both preceded and followed by decelerations. Growth in these three lengths, at the median level, was continuing at seventeen and a half years in the boys, but in the girls, at the median level, it had ceased at about sixteen and a half years.

These spurts were small. The mean sex-specific difference between annual increments during the spurts and those during the immediately preceding intervals ranged from 1.0 to 2.0 millimeters for the three lengths. However, the mean interobserver and intraobserver differences in these measurements were small also (about 0.1 millimeters). There is little doubt

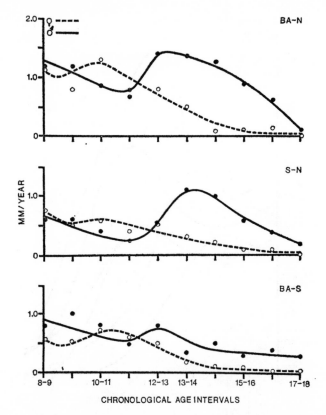

Figure 15.   Median increments (millimeters/year) in boys and girls for Ba-N (basion-nasion), S-N (sella-nasion), and Ba-S (basion-sella)

that the spurts observed were real. This is attested by their earlier occurrence in early-maturing children within a sex, and their earlier occurrence in girls than in boys.

Stature increments were analyzed in the same children. The spurts in stature, at the median level, were greater in the boys than in the girls (see Figure 16). As for the cranial base, there were decelerations before these spurts in each sex, but those for the girls occurred earlier than the age range of Figure 16.

In interpreting the data for the cranial-base lengths, it should be noted that S-N and Ba-N have a terminus at nasion. Nasion is on the external surface of the cranium and, strictly, is not in the cranial base at all. Elongation of these two distances may reflect apposition of bone at nasion that need not be associated with elongation in the cranial base. Consequently, more attention will be paid to Ba-S, which is completely within the cranial base. Spurts do occur in Ba-S. At the tenth centile level, there

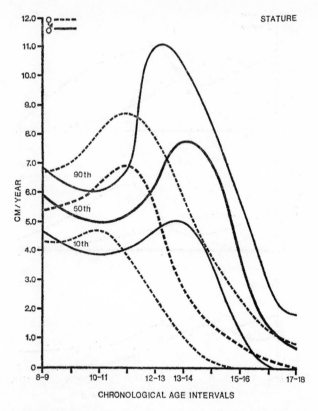

Figure 16. Centiles for increments in stature (centimeters/year) in the same children whose cranial base increments were analyzed

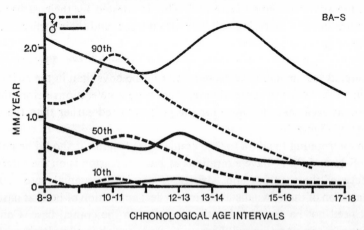

Figure 17. Centiles for annual increments (millimeters/year) in Ba-S (basion-sella) in boys and girls

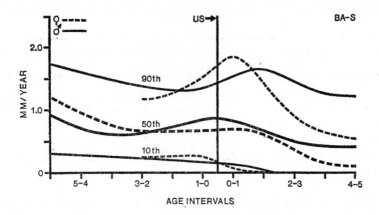

Figure 18.   Centiles for annual increments (millimeters/year) in Ba-S (basion-sella) in boys and girls, considered in relation to intervals before and after ulnar sesamoid ossification

was little elongation for any interval in either sex (see Figure 17). At the fiftieth centile level, however, there were definite spurts in each sex that were more marked at the ninetieth centile level. These spurts occurred about two years later in the boys than in the girls. In boys, at the fiftieth centile level, elongation was still occurring at about 0.4 millimeters/year at seventeen to eighteen years. Elongation continued until about eighteen years in boys and fifteen and a half years in girls (median levels).

These spurts in Ba-S can be considered in relation to a biological age instead of a chronological age (Figure 18). The biological age chosen was age in relation to the onset of ossification in the ulnar sesamoid. This is a small bone in a tendon near the metacarpophalangeal joint of the thumb. On this time basis, at the median level, spurts tended to occur slightly earlier in boys than in girls; this sequence was reversed at the tenth and ninetieth centile levels. The major effect of using a biological instead of a chronological age was to remove almost all sex differences in timing.

In these cranial-base studies, a pubertal spurt was defined as an increase in elongation rate that was approximately a doubling of the previous median age-specific rate. In boys, spurts were considered present only when the increase between successive increments was at least 0.75 millimeters per year. The corresponding figure for girls was 0.5 millimeters per year. Spurts were almost equally common in the two sexes and occurred in most children for each length. They were more common in Ba-N than S-N, and least common in Ba-S (see Table 6).

Table 6.   Incidence and size (in millimeters) of cranial-base elongation with reference to first pubertal spurts (Roche and Lewis 1974)

| Length | Percentage incidence | | Mean increments | | | | | |
| | | | before | | during | | after | |
	Boys	Girls	Boys	Girls	Boys	Girls	Boys	Girls
Ba-N*	93.1	95.1	0.5	0.6	2.5	2.0	1.5	0.8
S-N*	86.2	85.3	0.2	0.2	1.5	1.2	0.9	0.4
Ba-S*	79.3	68.3	0.3	0.3	1.8	1.4	0.6	0.4

* Ba = basion, N = nasion, S = sella

The mean increments during the spurts for each length were slightly greater in the boys than in the girls. When the differences in mean increments during the spurts were related to the sizes of the mean increments before the spurts, it was clear that considerable relative increases had occurred. For example, in Ba-N in boys, the mean increments increased from 0.5 to 2.5 millimeters per year — an increase of 400 percent.

In some children, two spurts were noted. If the increase between the increments in two successive annual intervals exceeded 0.5 millimeters in a girl, this change was accepted as a spurt. If there was a similar increase between two later successive annual intervals, this was accepted as a second spurt. The first pubertal spurts in each child occurred about 1.4 to 1.7 years earlier in the girls than the boys (see Table 7). However, there

Table 7.   Mean ages of occurrence of first pubertal spurts (years)(Roche and Lewis 1974)

| Length | Chronological age | | Interval before PHV* | | Interval after US† | | Interval before menarche |
	Boys	Girls	Boys	Girls	Boys	Girls	Girls
Ba-N‡	12.8	11.4	0.8	0.3	0.3	0.9	1.5
S-N‡	13.3	11.5	0.3	0.3	0.7	1.0	1.4
Ba-S‡	13.0	11.3	0.5	0.5	0.4	0.8	1.6

* peak height velocity
† onset of ossification in ulnar sesamoid
‡ Ba = basion, N = nasion, S = sella

was little difference in timing between the sexes with respect to years before PHV. When timing of the first pubertal spurts was analyzed in relation to the interval after ossification occurred in the ulnar sesamoid, it tended to be slightly later in the girls. These spurts occurred about one and a half years after menarche. These findings — that the use of a biological age removed most of the sex differences in timing — help substantiate the fact that the phenomena observed were real.

The fact that these spurts were real and that they were not due to an error of measurement at one age can be demonstrated by serial cranial-base measurements for two boys (see Figure 19). One was an early-maturing boy (Number 026) and the other a late-maturing boy (Number 197). The findings for Ba-N are typical of those for the three lengths. The early-maturing boy had the shorter Ba-N distance until twelve years, when he was experiencing a pubertal spurt. At that time his Ba-N distance became the larger and remained so until about seventeen years. At this age, the late-maturing boy was having his pubertal spurt and his Ba-N distance became the larger.

The occurrence of pubertal spurts in the cranial base and the continued elongation of the cranial base until about seventeen and a half years in boys and sixteen and a half years in girls has little practical application to orthodontia, because orthodontic appliances do not affect cranial-

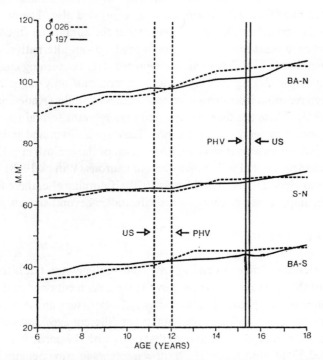

Figure 19.   Distance graphs of cranial-base lengths in an early-maturing (Number 026) and a late-maturing (Number 197) boy. US = age at onset of ossification in the ulnar sesamoid; PHV = age at peak height velocity

base growth. However, there are biological implications, some of which can be considered in answering the question, "Does the foot fit the shoe?" If the cranial base elongates, what happens to the brainstem, which is in contact with the cranial base?

The distance from sella to nasion increases during and after puberty. Some of this would be due to apposition at nasion (Björk 1955. 1968; Ford 1958; Koski 1960; Enlow 1968), but deposition does not occur on the internal surface of the frontal bone where the S-N line crosses it (Enlow 1968). Consequently, it is reasonable to assume that during puberty and adolescence there is an increase in the distance from the pituitary gland, which lies close to the sella point, and the frontal pole of the cerebral cortex. Similarly, the elongation in Ba-S implies an increase in the distance from the pituitary gland to the lower border of the medulla oblongata. This increase occurs despite slight posterior repositioning of sella due to apposition on the anterior aspect of the pituitary fossa and resorption on its posterior aspect (Busch 1951; Acheson and Archer 1959; Baume 1961; Latham 1972).

It is reasonable to assume that since the "shoe" (the cranial base) has elongated, the "foot" (the brainstem) has elongated also. The only other possible explanation would be to assume that the dura mater (the "sock") has thickened markedly, but this could apply, as an alternative, only to the elongation in S-N. There are no reported data concerning changes in dural thickness during puberty or adolescence, and only slight changes have been reported from cross-sectional studies of adults (Anderson 1910; Todd 1923). These are the first reported data relevant to brainstem elongation during puberty or adolescence. They are indirect and inferential, but the inferences are reasonable. Elongation of the brainstem is likely to reflect changes in glial cells rather than in neurons (Winick 1968; Winick and Rosso 1969; Dobbing and Sands 1970). If nothing else, these findings show the importance of carrying growth studies beyond sixteen years.

MUSCLE STRENGTH

If adolescence is defined as ending when one becomes adult, it is tempting to regard this as occurring when growth stops. As mentioned earlier, this criterion must be specific, because various body tissues and organs cease their growth (in size or functional ability) at different ages. Increases with age in muscle strength cease at ages that differ with the particular strength measured. Data from Jones (1949) show increases in grip strength, in both boys and girls, until at least seventeen years, but pull-and-thrust strength ceases earlier, particularly in girls (see Figure 20).

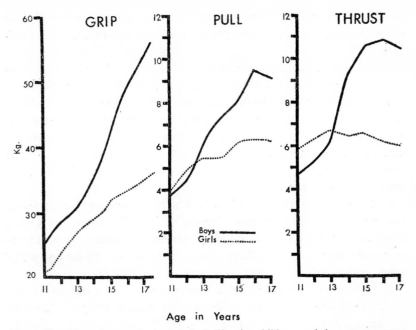

Age in Years

Figure 20.   Means for muscle strength in Californian children aged eleven to seventeen years (from Jones 1949)

The sex differences in these three types of muscle strength increased markedly after thirteen years. This could be due to sex differences in circulating hormones or in the response of cells with XY as opposed to XX sex chromosomes; or it could be a socially determined difference, reflecting activity related to sport.

Most experimental work has been on rats, in which the postnatal muscle changes differ basically from those in man (Cheek 1968). Muscle growth in children is due mainly to increases in cell NUMBER, which may reflect an effect of growth hormone. In rats, muscle growth depends much more on increases in cell SIZE (Cheek 1968; Cheek, et al. 1965; Gordon, et al. 1966). Nevertheless, some experiments on rats are of direct interest. In these animals, exercise increases the cell size rather than the cell number (Steinhaus 1955, 1962), without increasing the number of myofibrils per muscle fiber (Holmes and Rasch 1958).

Studies in man are of two types. Some have been based on anthropometric data (e.g. arm circumference) or work physiology (e.g. maximum oxygen intake) in groups before and after training programs, or in trained and control groups (Malina 1969). These studies indicate increases in muscle mass and, presumably, cell size, with training. These effects last for about six months after training. They occur in each sex to similar proportionate extents. This indicates that, inasmuch as participation in these programs is socially determined, they may accentuate the sex differences.

Other studies in man relate to muscle biopsies. These have been restricted to cross-sectional observations of muscle cell number and size in the gluteus maximus and rectus abdominis muscles (Cheek 1968). In boys, the increase in cell number is more rapid after ten and a half years than before. There is a fourteenfold increase from two months to sixteen years, and a doubling from ten to eighteen years. In girls, the increase is linear from six to seventeen years; the cell number is about two-thirds that of boys at the latter age.

Cell size increases in a linear fashion in boys to seventeen years (at least), but in girls there is no increase after ten and a half years. At early ages, the cells are larger in girls than in boys, but this is reversed at about fourteen and a half years. Girls have doubled their cell size by ten and a half years, and boys have done so by fourteen and a half years.

In boys, muscle strength increases more rapidly in the legs than in the back (see Figure 21; Brookes 1929), and the increase in leg strength does not decelerate up to twenty-three years.

Right-grip strength differs markedly between prepubescent and postpubescent boys within the same chronological age group (Figure 22).

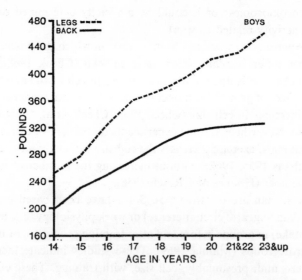

Figure 21.   Means for muscle strength in the legs and back of boys (from Brookes 1929)

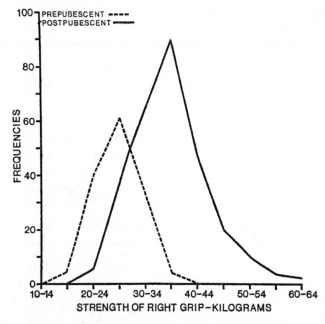

Figure 22.   Means for right-grip strength in boys aged 14.0 to 14.49 years, separated into prepubescent and postpubescent groups (from Crampton 1944)

STAGES OF PUBERTY

Particularly during pubescence and early adolescence, children may be grouped according to their level of pubertal development. Often this requires more than merely recording secondary sex characters. Such records are inappropriate at early ages when these characters are undeveloped, or later when they are developed completely, although at these early and later ages, also, children should be separated into maturity groups. When only cross-sectional data are available, this separation can be done effectively using skeletal age. If serial data are available, other biological ages can be used — for example, years before or after PHV, onset of ossification in the ulnar sesamoid, and menarche.

There are methodological problems in classifying children on the basis of the development of secondary sex characters and other pubertal events. Some authors refer to particular children as being in "puberty stage 2," for example, which is meaningless and misleading. A diagrammatic representation of the pubertal spurt in boys and in girls, and the mean timing of some events in relation to these spurts illustrates some of the problems (see Figure 23). Menarche, of course, comes after the peak of

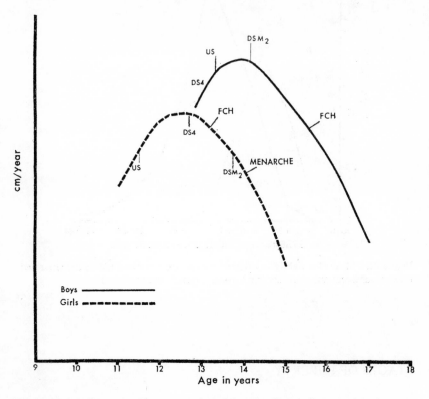

Figure 23.   A diagrammatic representation of the mean timing of some pubertal events in boys and girls in relation to the spurt in stature (data from Björk and Helm 1967; Deming 1957). US = onset of ossification in ulnar sesamoid; DS4 = all permanent canine teeth completed; FCH = fusion of capitellum of humerus to the shaft; DSM$_2$ = all permanent second molar teeth erupted

the spurt in girls. Onset of ossification in the ulnar sesamoid (US) precedes PHV in both sexes, but is closer to it in boys than in girls. DS4 is a stage of dental development when all permanent canine teeth have erupted. This occurs near the apex of the spurt in girls, but markedly before it in boys. Furthermore, this follows US in girls, but precedes it in boys. DSM$_2$ is the stage of dental development at which all permanent second molar teeth have erupted. This occurs just after the apex of the spurt in boys, but considerably after it in girls. FCH (fusion of the capitellum of the humerus) occurs after the apex of the spurt in each sex, but is further removed from it in boys than in girls.

Not only does the sequence differ between the sexes, but there are sequence variations within a sex. This would be expected, because the age

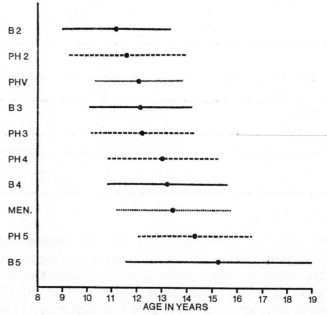

Figure 24. Means, ± 2 standard deviations, for ages of occurrence of pubertal events in girls (data from Marshall and Tanner 1969). B2, 3, 4, 5 are stages of breast development; PH2, 3, 4, 5 are stages of pubic hair development; PHV = peak height velocity; MEN = menarche

of reaching each pubertal stage is markedly variable, while the differences between the mean ages, within a sex, are comparatively small (see Figure 24; Marshall and Tanner 1969, 1970).

The occurrence of variations in sequence is clear from data concerning the number of girls who had reached particular pubic hair and breast stages at PHV and menarche (see Table 8). At PHV, girls may be in breast stage 2, 3, or 4. At menarche, they may be at breast stage 2, 3, 4, or 5. There are similar wide ranges of pubic hair stages at PHV and at menarche. Nevertheless, these events are associated. At PHV, both breast and pubic hair are likely to be in stage 3. At menarche, the breasts are commonly in stage 4 and pubic hair in stage 3.

This considerable variability is illustrated also by relationships between pubic hair and breast stages (Marshall and Tanner 1969), as shown in

Table 8.   Number of girls who had reached particular pubic hair and breast stages at PHV and menarche (Marshall and Tanner 1969)

Breast stage	Number of girls at PHV	at menarche	Pubic hair stage	Number of girls at PHV	at menarche
1	0	0	1	9	1
2	10	1	2	11	3
3	20	21	3	14	15
4	9	50	4	5	50
5	0	9	5	0	11

Table 9.   Number of girls who had reached particular pubic hair and breast stages (Marshall and Tanner 1969)

Pubic hair stages	Breast stages				
	1	2	3	4	5
2	14	43	24	7	0
3	3	21	46	22	1
4	2	4	44	46	6
5	0	1	9	39	31

Table 9. If there were a monotonic relationship between pubic hair and breast stages, almost all the girls would be grouped on a diagonal running downwards across the table from left to right. Although there is a concentration along this diagonal, there is also considerable variability. At pubic hair stage 3, any breast stage from 1 through 5 may be present. Alternatively, at breast stage 3, any pubic hair stage from 2 through 5 may be present.

Because pubic hair development, breast development, PHV, and menarche are not fully interrelated in timing, a girl should not be classified as being in "puberty stage 2," for example. Similar considerations apply to boys. It is necessary to record separate stages for each system or organ. Thus, a girl could be classified as follows: pubic hair stage 2, breast stage 3, has not reached menarche, reached PHV six months ago, ulnar sesamoid ossified, and skeletal age of twelve years. There is some redundancy in this information, and in an educational setting often some data will be lacking. In a clinical setting, they should be available.

CONCLUSION

This rapid survey will be concluded by emphasizing several points. Usually social scientists regard those who measure stature and weight as having clean, accurate data. Some of the problems with such data have been demonstrated. Secondly, there is a widespread concept that serial data are better than cross-sectional data, perhaps because they are more difficult to obtain, are uncommon, and therefore are assigned a scarcity value. This is unfortunate. Serial data are essential for some purposes, but cross-sectional data are adequate for many others and, for some, they are likely to be better.

Some scholars, on the other hand, consider that serial studies are unrewarding — that research workers collect mountains of data and do not know what to do with them. There was some justification for this view before multivariant and time-based statistics were developed, and before computers were available. These criticisms are no longer justified. Two important present aims are to identify significant problems that can be answered using existing serial data and to obtain the essential financial support for such study. But new serial data are needed, also, because of changing interests and methodology, and because most growth studies are terminated before the children have stopped growing. There is a lack of information about growth during adolescence, and very few collections of relevant serial data are left that have not already been analyzed. Yet it is precisely during adolescence that children and their parents are most concerned about their growth.

Finally, it is urgent that physical parameters be recorded in large-scale or intensive studies of adolescent behavior, that these be recorded accurately, and that, from the beginning, careful consideration be given to the timing of data collection and the way in which these data will be used.

REFERENCES

ACHESON, R. M., M. ARCHER
1959 Radiological studies of the growth of the pituitary fossa in man. *Journal of Anatomy* 93:52–67.

ANDERSON, J. H.
1910 The proportionate contents of the skull as demonstrated from an examination of forty Caucasian crania. *Journal of the Royal Anthropological Institute of Great Britain and Ireland* 40:279–284.

ANDERSON, M., S.C. HWANG, W. T. GREEN
1965 Growth of the normal trunk in boys and girls during the second decade of life, related to age, maturity, and ossification of the iliac epiphyses. *Journal of Bone Joint Surgery* 47A:1554–1564.

ANSON, B. J., T. H. BAST, E. W. CALDWELL
1948 The development of the auditory ossicles, the otic capsule and the extracapsular tissues. *Annals of Otology* 57:603–633.

BAUME, L. J.

1961   Principles of cephalofacial development revealed by experimental biology. *American Journal of Orthodontia* 47:881–901.

BJÖRK, A.

1955   Cranial base development. *American Journal of Orthodontia* 41:198–225.

1968   The use of metallic implants in the study of facial growth in children: method and application. *American Journal of Physical Anthropology* 29:243–254.

BJÖRK, A., S. HELM

1967   Prediction of the age of maximum pubertal growth in body height. *Angle Orthodontia.* 37:134–143.

BLIZZARD, R. M., A. JOHANSON, H. GUYDA, A. BAGHADASSARIAN, S. RAITA, C. J. MIGEON

1970   "Recent developments in the study of gonadotropin secretion in adolescence," in *Adolescent endocrinology.* Edited by Felix P. Heald and Wellington Hung. New York: Appleton-Century-Crofts.

BOCK, R. D., H. WAINER, A. PETERSEN, D. THISSEN, J. MURRAY, A. ROCHE

1973   A parameterization for individual human growth curves. *Human Biology* 45:63–80.

BROOKES, F. D.

1929   *The psychology of adolescence.* Boston: Houghton Mifflin.

BÜCHI, E. C.

1950   *Änderungen der Körperform erwachsenen Menschen. Eine Untersuchung nach der Individual-Methode.* Vienna: Ferdinand Berger.

BUSCH, W.

1951   Die Morphologie der Sella turcica und ihre Beziehungen zur Hypophyse. *Virchow's Archives of Pathological Anatomy* 320:437–458.

CHEEK, D. B.

1968   *Human growth: body composition, cell growth, energy, and intelligence.* Philadelphia: Lea and Febiger.

CHEEK, D. B., G. K. POWELL, R. E. SCOTT

1965   Growth of muscle cells (size and number) and liver DNA in rats and Snell Smith mice with insufficient pituitary, thyroid, or testicular function. *Bulletin Hopkins Hospital* 117:306–321.

CRAMPTON, C. W.

1944   Physiological age as a fundamental principle. *Child Development* 15:1–52.

DAVENPORT, C. B.

1930   "Physical growth in the second decade," in *Physical and mental adolescent growth.* Proceedings of the Conference on Adolescence, Cleveland, Ohio.

DAY, R., W. A. SILVERMAN

1952   Growth of the fibula of premature infants as estimated in roentgen films: a method for assessing factors promoting or inhibiting growth. *Études Neonat* 1:111–114.

DEMING, J.

1957 Application of the Gompertz curve to the observed pattern of growth in length of forty-eight individual boys and girls during the adolescent cycle of growth. *Human Biology* 29:83–122.

DOBBING, J., J. SANDS

1970 Timing of neuroblast multiplication in developing human brain. *Nature* 226:639–640.

ENLOW, D. H.

1968 *The human face. An account of the postnatal growth and development of the craniofacial skeleton.* New York: Harper and Row.

FORD, E. H. R.

1958 Growth of the human cranial base. *American Journal of Orthodontia* 44:498–506.

GARN, S. M., C. G. ROHMANN, B. APFELBAUM

1961 Complete epiphyseal union of hand. *American Journal of Physical Anthropology* 19:365–373.

GORDON, E. E., K. KOWALSKI, M. FRITTS

1966 Muscle proteins and DNA in rat quadriceps during growth. *American Journal of Physiology* 210:1033–1040.

GREULICH, W. W., S. I. PYLE

1959 *Radiographic atlas of skeletal development of the hand and wrist* (second edition). Stanford: Stanford University Press.

HOLMES, R., P. J. RASCH

1958 Effect of exercise on number of myofibrils per fiber in sartorius muscle of rat. *American Journal of Physiology* 195:50–52.

JOHNSON, G. F., J. P. DORST, J. P. KUHN, A. F. ROCHE, G. H. DAVILA

1973 Reliability of skeletal age assessments. *American Journal of Roentgenology* 118:320–327.

JONES, H. E.

1949 Motor performance and growth: a developmental study of static dynamometric strength. *University of California Publications on Child Development* 1(1):1–182.

KOSKI, K.

1960 Some aspects of the growth of the cranial base and the upper face. *Sartryck ur Odontologisk Tidskrift* 68:344–358.

LATHAM, R. A.

1972 The sella point and postnatal growth of the human cranial base. *American Journal of Orthodontia* 61:156–162.

LEWIS, A. B., A. F. ROCHE

1972 Elongation of the cranial base in girls during pubescence. *Angle Orthodontia* 42:358–367.

1974 Cranial base elongation in boys during pubescence. *Angle Orthodontia* 44:83–93.

MALINA, R. M.

1969 Exercise as an influence upon growth: review and critique of current concepts. *Clinical Pediatrics* 8:16–26.

MARESH, M. M.

1972 A forty-five year investigation for secular changes in physical maturation. *American Journal of Physical Anthropology* 36:103–110.

MARESH, M. M., J. DEMING
1939   The growth of the long bones in eighty infants: roentgenograms versus anthropometry. *Child Development* 10:91–106.

MARSHALL, W. A., J. M. TANNER
1969   Variations in pattern of pubertal changes in girls. *Archives of the Disorders of Childhood* 44:291–303.
1970   Variations in pattern of pubertal changes in boys. *Archives of the Disorders of Childhood* 45:13–23.

MELLITS, E. D.
1965   "Estimation and design for intersecting regressions." Unpublished Ph.D. dissertation, Johns Hopkins School of Hygiene and Public Health, Baltimore.
1968   "Statistical methods," in *Human growth: body composition, cell growth, energy and intelligence.* Edited by D. B. Cheek. Philadelphia: Lea and Febiger.

PYLE, S. I., N. L. HOERR
1969   A radiographic standard of reference for the growing knee (second edition). Springfield, Illinois: Charles C. Thomas.

ROCHE, A. F.
1962   Lateral comparisons of the skeletal maturity of the human hand and wrist. *American Journal of Roentgenology* 89:1272–1280.
1965   The sites of elongation of human metacarpals and metatarsals. *Acta Anatomica* 61:193–202.
1967   The elongation of the mandible. *American Journal of Orthodontia* 53: 79–94.
1972   The elongation of the human cervical vertebral column. *American Journal of Physical Anthropology* 36:221–228.
1974   Differential timing of maximum length increments among bones within individuals. *Human Biology* 46:145–157.

ROCHE, A. F., G. H. DAVILA
1972   Late adolescent growth in stature. *Pediatrics* 50:874–880.

ROCHE, A. F., N. Y. FRENCH
1970   Differences in skeletal maturity levels between the knee and hand. *American Journal of Roentgenology* 109:307–312.

ROCHE, A. F., A. B. LEWIS
1974   Sex differences in the elongation of the cranial base during pubescence. *Angle Orthodontia* 44:279–294.

ROCHE, A. F., C. G. ROHMANN, N. Y. FRENCH, G. H. DAVILA
1970   Effect of training on replicability of assessments of skeletal maturity (Greulich-Pyle). *American Journal of Roentgenology* 108:511–515.

SCAMMON, R. E.
1927   The first seriatim study of human growth. *American Journal of Physical Anthropology* 10:329–336.
1930   "The measurement of the body in childhood," in *The measurement of man.* Edited by J. A. Harris, C. M. Jackson, D. G. Paterson. Minneapolis: University of Minnesota Press.

SCHEFFER, V. B., F. WILKE
1953   Relative growth in the northern fur seal. *Growth* 17: 129–145.

SHUTTLEWORTH, F. K.
1937 Sexual maturation and the physical growth of girls age six to nineteen. *Monograms in Social Research and Child Development* 2(5):1–253.

STEINHAUS, A. H.
1955 Strength from Morpurgo to Muller — a half century of research. *Journal of the Association for Physical and Mental Rehabilitation* 9: 147–150.
1962 "Lectures on the physiology of exercise." Reprinted in *Toward an understanding of health and physical education* (third edition). Edited by A. H. Steinhaus, 83–104. Dubuque, Iowa: William C. Brown.

TANNER, J. M.
1962 *Growth at adolescence* (second edition). Oxford: Blackwell Scientific Publications.

TODD, T. W.
1923 Dura volume in the male white skull. *Anat. Rec.* 26:263–273.

TROTTER, M., G. C. GLESER
1958 A reevaluation of estimation of stature based on measurements of stature taken during life and of long bones after death. *American Journal of Physical Anthropology* 16:79–123.

VAN DER LINDEN, F. P. G. M.
1970 The interpretation of incremental data and velocity growth curves. *Growth* 34:221–224.

WINICK, M.
1968 Changes in nucleic acid and protein content of the human brain during growth. *Pediatric Research* 2:352–355.

WINICK, M., P. ROSSO
1969 Head circumference and cellular growth of the brain in normal and marasmic children. *Journal of Pediatrics* 74:774–778.

Late Adolescent Changes in Weight

ALEX F. ROCHE, GAIL H. DAVILA, and E. DAVID MELLITS

Within individuals, little is known about changes in weight after the age of peak height velocity. There is, however, marked interest in related questions, such as whether children maintain similar centile levels for weight across age (Mossberg 1948; Asher 1966; Eid 1970). The present analysis has shown that the rates of growth in weight in individuals alter at about the ages when growth in stature ceases and that these ages differ markedly between individuals. The ages at which changes occur in the rates of growth in weight, together with the total increments in weight after particular growth and developmental landmarks, should interest not only research workers but all those responsible for the professional care of adolescents and young adults.

Boothby, et al. (1952) reported annual weight increments, with large sample sizes, to about 18 years in males and 21 years in females. At all ages with adequate sample sizes, the means for the males markedly exceeded those for the females. Mean annual increments exceeding one kilogram occurred to 20 years in the males and 17 years in the females. Von Verschauer (1954) reported the weights of twins measured at two ages separated by about eighteen years. The total increments in weight between the two measurements were calculated for the first listed of each pair of monozygous twins and for each dizygous twin. The mean increments, from about 19 to 37 years, were 8.7 kilograms (s.d., 7.91) in 11 males and 6.6 kilograms (s.d., 7.13) in 27 females.

A national probability sample of the adult United States population was studied in the Health Examination Survey. These data were

This work was supported by Contract 72-2735 and Grants HD-03472 and HD-04629 from the National Institutes of Health, Bethesda, Maryland.

weighted to provide estimates for the total noninstitutionalized United States population (Stoudt, et al. 1965). Consequently these cross-sectional data allow estimates of median increments for males (21-30 years, 5.4 kilograms; 30-40 years, 0.9 kilograms) and females (21-30 years, 1.8 kilograms; 30-40 years, 3.2 kilograms).

MATERIAL AND METHODS

The present data were derived from southern Ohio white children (118 boys; 111 girls) in The Fels Longitudinal Sample. They were weighed serially from 1 month to at least 22 years, and, in some cases, to ages exceeding 40 years. The mean ages of the last weights were 30 years in each sex. These measurements were made at visits scheduled five times in the first year and then six-monthly, except after 18 years when they were scheduled at biennial intervals.

The weights were measured to the nearest 0.1 kilograms with the subjects wearing standard light indoor clothing. Data recorded during pregnancy were excluded. The statures of these children were used to obtain six-monthly increments (Roche and Davila 1972). The midpoint of the interval with the largest increment in stature was recorded as the age of peak height velocity (PHV). When two successive increments were equally the largest, the midpoint of the combined interval was Consideration was given to combining successive six-monthly stature increments to annual increments, thus reducing seasonal effects. ture increments to annual increments, thus reducing seasonal effects. This was not done because PHV would be determined less reliably, and this was not justified by the small seasonal variations in increments in a subset of the children. Furthermore, PHV should be considered the midpoint of the largest increment regardless of the factors, seasonal or otherwise, that are responsible for the changes in the rates of growth.

Age at menarche was obtained by six-monthly inquiry at appropriate ages. The ages at which the distal end of the femur and the proximal end of the tibia became mature were recorded as those of the first radiographs in which the corresponding epiphyseal lines were completely obliterated. Children were excluded from this part of the study if the interval between this radiograph and the immediately preceding radiograph of the knee exceeded 1.7 years. The mean ages at which PHV and menarche occurred (Table 1) were similar to those in other healthy American children (Frisch and Revelle 1971; Maresh 1971). Hand-wrist skeletal age was recorded as the mean of bone-specific

Table 1. Centiles for ages (years) of achieving developmental landmarks

	N	10	50	90
PHV boys	115	12.7	13.7	15.2
PHV girls	101	10.2	11.7	13.2
Menarche	104	11.5	12.8	14.6

skeletal ages obtained using the Greulich-Pyle atlas (1959).

Applying the method of Mellits (1965, 1968), two polynomial lines were fitted to all available weight data for each individual, recorded after the age of PHV. This procedure was applied in 57 boys and 58 girls; in the remainder there were too few data points at later ages. This procedure assumes a discontinuity exists between data pertaining to earlier and later ages.

Piecewise regressions are calculated to locate the junction between these earlier and later data subsets for the individuals. The method fits the most precise estimates for the two polynomials considered together. A 2-degree polynomial was fitted to the earlier data and a 1-degree polynomial was fitted to the later data. This junction was accepted as an age at which the rate of growth in weight changed in each individual.

Statistical tests showed that these polynomials were more appropriate than higher order ones. The choice appears appropriate from a biological viewpoint also. During the earlier period, weight is decelerating; this reflects a nonlinear multiplication process rather like the second part of a sigmoid growth curve. In the later period, growth in stature has ceased and the changes in weight are approximately constant across time.

When two or fewer data points were later than the junction at which the goodness of fit was maximized, the junction with the second-best fit was chosen. This was done in 12 boys and 7 girls. In some individuals, the goodness of fit, for the two polynomial lines combined, varied only slightly between some junctions. In addition, after 18 years, the data points were at intervals of at least two years. Consequently, it was impossible to determine precisely the age at which the rate of growth in weight changed in each individual.

Due to the mathematical form of the equations when combined 2-degree and 1-degree polynomials are fitted to a set of data points, there may be two junctions between these polynomials within the age range covered by the data. When this occurred, the earlier junction was used in the analysis because the second has no biological meaning. Also, it is possible that the polynomials will not actually intersect. However, in these cases, the most precise estimates of the two lines will indicate points of discontinuity between the two junctions.

These discontinuities are essentially "intersections." In 11 of the children studied, this was in fact the case. For convenience, the junction between the early and late data subsets at which the fit was best will be referred to as the "intersection" although there were two intersections in some children and none in others. Essentially the same group of children was included in a corresponding analysis of stature (Roche and Davila 1972).

RESULTS

Completely longitudinal data from 118 boys and 111 girls were used to obtain six-monthly increments for weight from 12.5 to 18 years (Figure 1). The medians for the boys exceeded those for the girls at all ages and the patterns of change differed between the sexes in ways that reflected the timing of pubertal growth spurts. The median increments increased with age in the boys until 14-14.5 years but decreased later; in the girls they decreased fairly regularly throughout the whole period. The median increments in the girls were less than 1 kilogram for each interval after 14.5-15 years but only for the interval 17.5-18 years in the boys. The ranges from the tenth to the ninetieth centiles were larger in the boys than the girls for each interval.

The median ages of intersection of the polynomial lines fitted to the earlier and later data subsets were 21.1 years in the boys and 18.4 years in the girls. These ages varied markedly with ranges of more than 8 years from the tenth to the ninetieth centile in each sex (Table 2).

Table 2. Centiles for ages of intersection of polynomial lines for weight in 57 boys and 58 girls

	10	50	90
Chronological age (yr) — boys	16.9	21.2	25.1
Chronological age (yr) — girls	15.8	18.4	24.6
Years after PHV — boys	4.0	8.2	11.5
Years after PHV — girls	3.5	7.3	12.8
Years after menarche	2.5	5.6	11.8
Years after SAa 13 years — boys	3.9	8.4	12.3
Years after SAa 11 years — girls	4.3	7.3	14.0

a SA = skeletal age.

The median ages at which the two lines intersected were 8.2 years after PHV in the boys and 7.3 years after PHV in the girls.

The median difference between age at menarche and age at the

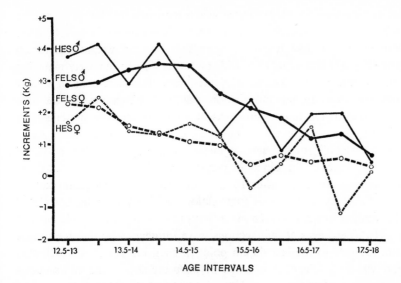

Figure 1.   Median six-monthly increments for weight in the present sample (Fels) and in the United States Health Examination Survey (HES). The latter data are from Hamill, et al. (1973)

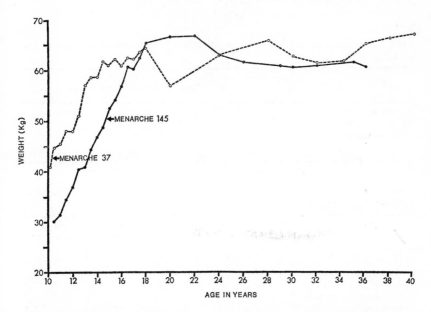

Figure 2.   Graphs of weight against age for two girls differing markedly in age at menarche. The girl with menarche at 10.2 years (No. 37) gained more weight after menarche than the girl with menarche at 14.8 years (No. 145)

intersection was 5.6 years. There was a tendency for age at menarche to be associated negatively with the total increment in weight after menarche (r = – 0.42, n = 75). Figure 2 shows serial weight data for an early (No. 37) and a late (No. 145) maturing girl. In the early maturing girl, the intersection was at 22.4 years and the increment in weight from menarche to the intersection was 18.5 kilograms. In the late maturing girl, the intersection was at 19 years and the increment in weight from menarche to the intersection was 15.5 kilograms.

The variability of the ages at intersections, as judged by the range from the tenth to the ninetieth centile, was similar for chronological age, and the intervals after PHV, menarche, and particular skeletal ages (Table 2). The ages at intersections were significantly correlated with weights at the intersections in boys (r = + 0.37, p < .01) but not in girls. These ages at intersections were influenced by the age ranges from the first to the last datum point in each individual. In each sex, there was a significant association between the ages at the intersections and the ages when the last weights were recorded, although the ages of the last weights were not associated significantly with the slopes of the 1-degree polynomials. In each sex, the ages at the intersections for weight were significantly correlated with the ages at PHV (r = + 0.38, p < .01 in boys, and r = + 0.26, p < .05 in girls).

Table 3. Centiles for total increments in weight after some chronological ages (in kilograms)

	To intersection				To last weight			
	N	10	50	90	N	10	50	90
16 years — boys	57	1.3	7.5	19.3	93	4.1	14.0	27.5
16 years — girls	58	–2.2	1.6	4.2	76	–2.6	3.9	13.8
18 years — boys	57	–2.4	3.2	12.5	93	–0.2	7.9	20.2
18 years — girls	58	–5.0	–0.3	2.7	76	–2.9	2.5	11.8

Table 4. Centiles for total increments in weight after growth and developmental landmarks (in kilograms)

	To level of intersection				To last weight			
	N	10	50	90	N	10	50	90
PHV — boys	57	15.7	24.2	34.0	90	14.8	28.0	39.3
PHV — girls	57	11.1	15.5	26.0	73	10.3	18.5	33.2
Menarche	58	3.5	10.4	16.7	75	5.7	11.2	25.2
Femur mature — boys	24	1.2	5.5	15.1	29	3.0	14.2	29.7
Femur mature — girls	24	–5.0	0.7	5.4	28	–2.4	3.4	13.3
Tibia mature — boys	26	0.1	6.1	13.8	31	3.1	13.2	26.1
Tibia mature — girls	25	–4.0	0.7	5.5	29	–1.7	5.2	11.7

The total weight increments after particular chronological ages were considerably larger in the boys than the girls whether the increments considered were to the levels of the intersections of the polynomials or to the last weights available (Table 3). For example, the median increments from 18 years to the last weight were 7.9 kilograms in the boys but only 2.5 kilograms in the girls. The corresponding values for increments to the levels of the intersections of the two polynomials were 3.2 kilograms for the boys and -0.3 kilograms for the girls. A sex difference remain if the increments in girls after 16 years are compared with those in the boys after 18 years, although this comparison compensates for the two-year sex difference between the median ages for PHV (Table 1). The median increments after 16 years were markedly larger than those after 18 years, in both boys and girls.

The data in Table 4 show the total increments in weight after some phenomena of growth and development. These were markedly variable in each sex whether calculated to the ages of intersection of the polynomial lines or to the last weights recorded. The increments were markedly larger in boys than in girls after PHV, after the femur was mature, and after the tibia was mature. This sex dichotomy was relatively greater after the completion of maturation in long bones than after other chronological and developmental landmarks. It was reflected in the slopes of the 1-degree polynomials that were fitted to the late data subset (Table 5). The slopes were more commonly positive and tended to be steeper in the boys than the girls. As expected, from the generally positive slopes of the 1-degree polynomials, the median increments to the last recorded weights were consistently greater than those to the intersections.

Table 5. Centiles for the slopes of the 1-degree polynomials that were fitted to the later data (57 boys; 58 girls)

	Centiles		
	10	50	90
Boys	−0.40	0.48	1.14
Girls	−0.40	0.23	1.01

DISCUSSION

The median ages of intersection for weight are almost the same as those reported for stature in boys but are about one year later in girls (Roche and Davila 1972). As for stature, the variability of the ages at intersection for weight is similar whether considered in relation to chronological age, PHV, menarche, or skeletal age, indicating that these ages have little relationship to rates of maturation in individuals.

These ages of intersections are much more variable in timing than those for stature. Growth in stature is more regular than growth in weight and, at the intersections, the minimum variances tended to be higher for weight than for stature. Precise ages for individuals, at which the rates of growth in weight changed, could not be determined due to the nature of the available data. However, the ages obtained in this analysis were shown to be reasonable by checking against the original data.

There are few reported data with which the present findings can be compared. The six-monthly increments indicate considerably lesser rates of gain than those reported by Boothby, et al. (1952). They are, in general, similar to national estimates for the United States (Hamill, et al. 1973) but the present data show more regular trends. Presumably, this reflects the longitudinal nature of the present data.

The total increments after 18 years are similar to those reported by von Verschauer (1954) for males but they are markedly less than the values he reported for females. On the other hand, the present total increments from 18 to 30 years are slightly higher than recent national estimates for the United States for the age interval 21-30 years (Stoudt, et al. 1965). These differences are proportionately similar in each sex and probably are due, in large measure, to differences in the age ranges considered.

The present median values show sex-associated differences in the patterns of weight change during adolescence. The girls reached PHV about two years before the boys and were about two years younger than the boys when the median six-monthly increments became less than 1 kilogram. Nevertheless, the intersections of the polynomials occurred about three years earlier in the girls than the boys. The marked tendency for boys to exceed girls in total weight increments after the femur or the tibia became mature probably reflects sex differences in the growth of the length and circumference of the trunk during late adolescence (Anderson, et al. 1963; Hansman 1970).

The sex differences in increments are not due entirely to variations in rates of maturation. This can be seen in comparisons between increments for ages differing by two years and by comparisons between increments after PHV. Furthermore, the total weight increments after menarche were only moderately associated with age at menarche.

The intersections located with this statistical approach indicate that changes occur in the rates of growth in weight. However, these points of intersection are only moderately reliable guides to the ages at which these changes occurred. These ages were influenced by the age ranges of the available data and, necessarily, their reliability was limited by the infrequency of the examinations after the age of 18 years. The present data do, however, provide new knowledge of growth during the poorly documented period between late childhood and early adulthood. They should help define the nutritional needs of adolescents and assist the management of children in whom weight levels or the patterns of change in weight are unusual.

REFERENCES

ANDERSON, M., W. T. GREEN, M. B. MESSNER
  1963   Growth and predictions of growth in the lower extremities. *Journal of Bone and Joint Surgery* 45-A: 1–14.
ASHER, P.
  1966   Fat babies and fat children; the prognosis of obesity in the very young. *Archives for Diseases of Childhood* 41:672–677.
BOOTHBY, E. J., M. A. GUY, T. A. L. DAVIES
  1952   The growth of adolescents. *Monthly Bulletin, Great Britain Ministry of Health* 11:208–223.
EID, E. E.
  1970   Follow-up study of physical growth of children who had excessive weight gain in first six months of life. *British Medical Journal* 2: 74–76.
FRISCH, R. E., R. REVELLE
  1971   Height and weight at menarche and a hypothesis of menarche. *Archives for Diseases of Childhood* 46:695–701.
GREULICH, W. W., S. I. PYLE
  1959   *Radiographic atlas of skeletal development of the hand and wrist* (second edition). Stanford: Stanford University Press.
HAMILL, P. V. V., F. E. JOHNSTON, S. LEMESHOW
  1973   *Height and weight of youths, 12-17 years, United States.* National Health Survey, Vital and Health Statistics, Series 11, Number 124. Washington, D.C.: U. S. Government Printing Office.
HANSMAN, C.
  1970   "Anthropometry and related data, anthropometry skinfold thickness measurements," in *Human growth and development*. Edited by R. W. McCammon. Springfield, Illinois: Charles C. Thomas.
MARESH, M. M.
  1971   Single versus serial assessment of skeletal age: either, both or neither? *American Journal of Physical Anthropology* 35:387–392.
MELLITS, E. D.
  1965   "Estimation and design for intersecting regressions." Unpublished M. D. thesis, Johns Hopkins University School of Hygiene and Public Health.

1968   "Statistical methods," in *Human growth; body composition, cell growth, energy and intelligence.* Edited by D. B. Cheek. Philadelphia: Lea and Febiger.

MOSSBERG, H.-O.
1948   Obesity in children; clinical-prognostical investigation. *Acta Paediatrica Scandinavia* 35, supplement 2.

ROCHE, A. F., DAVILA, G. H.
1972   Late adolescent growth in stature. *Pediatrics* 50:874–880.

STOUDT, H. W., A. DAMON, R. MC FARLAND
1965   *Weight, height, and selected body dimensions of adults, United States — 1960–1962.* National Health Survey, Vital and Health Statistics, PHS Publication 1000, Series 11, Number 8. Washington, D.C.: U. S. Government Printing Office.

VON VERSCHAUER, O. F.
1954   *Wirksame Faktoren im Leben des Menschen; Beobachtungen an ein- und zweieiigen Zwillingen durch 25 Jahre.* Wiesbaden: Franz Steiner Verlag GMBH.

Growth and Development Patterns and Human Differentiation in Papua New Guinean Communities

L. A. MALCOLM

The widely varying ecosystems which have developed in New Guinea have, over the centuries, imposed widely differing stresses on biological man and may have led to both the natural selection of those human characteristics most fitted for survival and also to the molding of the individual in his growth from conception to maturity. Variation has been preserved by social and geographic barriers, and as a consequence human differentiation found in New Guinea is as diverse as the environmental situations in which man is found. To what extent differentiation may be attributed to dissimilarity among initial immigrants or to the development of variation *in situ* remains speculative, but genetic studies to date tend, if anything, to support the latter as a more probable source of observed variation.

The growth of a child is a dynamic process, which at any stage is the result of a number of competing influences. Tanner (1962) states that growth is genetically programmed, that the genotypic growth pattern is determined at conception, and that only the most potent of environmental influences are capable of deflecting the growth pattern from its programmed course.

This paper examines the way in which molding by environmental pressures, natural selection, and the genotype may influence the observed growth pattern among New Guinean children, and the relationship between this growth pattern and human physical variation in New Guinean populations.

Growth begins at conception. The earliest stage at which we can normally measure the child, however, is at birth, by which time certain crucial events in child development have already occurred. Figures for

New Guinean birth weights from different populations (Malcolm 1970a) are shown in Table 1. Already wide variation in size is apparent, and the weight of Lumi infants (Wark and Malcolm 1969) and Inanwantan infants in West Irian (Oomen 1961) is lower than in any other world situation. Even in the most favored New Guinean situation, mean weights remain below those regarded as normal for developed countries.

Table 1. Birth weights of New Guinean infants from some populations

Population	Weight	Source
Chimbu Station	3.27	Barnes 1963
Chimbu Village	3.00	Barnes 1963
Rabaul	2.96	Scragg 1955
Lae Town	2.91	Malcolm 1970a
New Ireland	2.64	Scragg 1955
Lumi	2.40	Wark and Malcolm 1969
Inanwantan	2.32	Oomen 1961

Birth weight, from nutritional surveys, appears to be related to the varying nutritional circumstances of the populations concerned. Recent work on factors determining the growth of the fetus suggest that environmental influences are of much greater significance than the genotype. While it is certain that the fetus receives a greater degree of protection in its intrauterine environment than after birth, the assertion that it is a parasite which normally has a complete priority on maternal resources has recently been strongly challenged (Bergner and Susser 1970). Birth weight is sensitive to factors related both to the intrauterine environment, such as weight of the mother, parity, mother's weight gain during pregnancy, maternal but not paternal size, and also to factors in the wider maternal environment, e.g. smoking, malaria, nutrition, and socioeconomic change. The main determinant of maternal size is the nutritional environment in which the mother herself was reared. Birth weight may therefore reflect the maternal nutritional past rather than the present.

GROWTH OF THE PRESCHOOL CHILD

The early growth of the Papua New Guinean child (Malcolm 1970b) (Figure 1) follows a pattern typical of developing countries in that the rate of increase in size up to three to four months after birth either parallels or exceeds that of children in more privileged societies: most infants double their birth weight in three months. This has been attributed to a number of factors, including the unregimented feeding

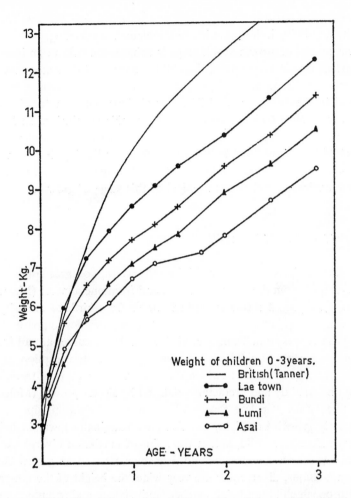

Figure 1. Weight from 0–3 years of some Papua New Guinean children compared with British children (Tanner, et al. 1966)

schedule and outstanding lactational output. One may well speculate on the part natural selection has played in favoring the survival of those infants whose mothers were genetically endowed with larger than average breast size and better lactational performance. However, this early rapid growth is not sustained, and a sharp break in the continuity of the curves occurs in all groups. A progressive divergence from the European norm results after four to six months even in the most favored societies, while rates of growth for the Asai child are lower than reported in any other world population. This change is associated in most populations with a decline in the adequacy of the breast to provide the total nutritional needs of the infant and the inadequate quality and delay in introduction of supplementary feeding.

The control of growth at this stage is being taken over to an increasing extent by the genotype of the child. Tanner (1962) states that the maternal uterine control of growth is replaced by the fetal genotype control in the early years of life. Correlations obtained for this age group from New Guinean children support this conclusion. In Bundi children (Malcolm 1970a), significant correlations between both parents and child have developed by the age of three, indicating that a limited genetic control is being exercised, although heavily overlaid with the intense environmental stresses typical of this stage of growth.

GROWTH TO MATURITY

Growth rates in New Guinean children after the age of three continue to diverge, both from the European norm and from one another (Malcolm 1970a, c). Figure 2 shows smoothed curves from birth to maturity of New Guinean children of both sexes in different societies compared with European curves from Tanner, et al. (1966). These curves are all based on measurements of children of known age, with the exception of the curve for the Asai children, which is based on the eruption of teeth, this being only slightly and predictably delayed by slower growth (Malcolm and Bue 1970). The Lae town child, however, despite his apparently slow early growth in weight, remains only marginally lower in height than the European child, and at the point of maximum divergence the height-age is only one year behind. For the slower-growing New Guinean populations, divergences are very wide, the height of the ten-year-old European child not being reached until sixteen and seventeen years with Bundi and Asai children respectively. While these latter groups are aiming for a lower target adult stature, the tendency to underestimate age when such estimates are based on European standards is obvious. Despite these wide divergences, patterns typical of European growth curves are preserved; male-female differences remain, although the crossover prior to the adolescent spurt tends to be earlier with slower growth, while the adolescent spurt, which also begins at around the point of the crossover, is, if anything, slightly earlier in onset but much more prolonged than in the European child. Maximum growth velocity is lower and occurs later with slower growth.

Sexual development is closely related to the overall growth rates and is markedly delayed in the slower-growing populations (Table 2). In

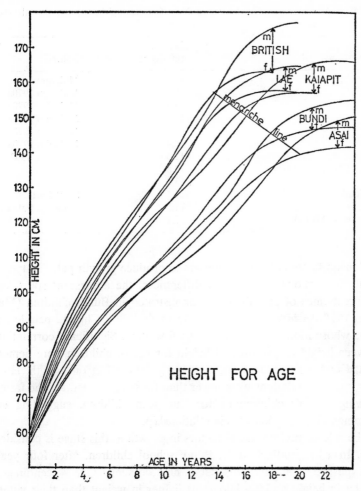

Figure 2. Growth in height from birth to maturity of children from some Papua New Guinean populations compared with British children (Tanner, et al. 1966)

Lae urban children, menarche occurs at a mean of 13.8, but in Bundi and Lumi children it occurs around 18.0 years (Malcolm 1970a, i.p.), a figure later than that reported for any other world population. The "menarche line" across the graph (Figure 2) gives, at its intersection with the female curve of a population, the mean age of menstruation for that population. This indicates not only the delay in menarche with slower growth and the high correlation between these characteristics, but also the decreasing stature attained when menarche occurs, which varies from 96 to 98 percent of the adult female height, compared with 95 percent in the European child.

Table 2.   Age of menarche in Papua New Guinean girls compared with some other populations

Population		Mean age (in years)	Source
Lae urban		13.8	Malcolm i.p.
Megiar		15.5	Malcolm 1970a
Kaiapit		15.6	Malcolm 1970a
Chimbu		17.5	Malcolm 1970a
Bundi		18.0	Malcolm 1970a
Lumi		18.4	Malcolm 1970a
Hong Kong	Rich	12.5	Lee, et al. 1963
	Average	12.8	
	Poor	13.3	
England		13.1	Scott 1961
Nigeria		14.1	Tanner, et al. 1962
Hutu (East Africa)		17.1	Hiernaux 1964

Genetic factors obviously operate to produce growth patterns typical of all populations, e.g. the sex differences, the adolescent spurt, etc. Different rates of growth were demonstrated in Bundi children (Malcolm 1970a) whose mothers were from the taller Chimbu people and those whose mothers were local Bundi women. Significant correlations between height of parents and height for age of children were demonstrated in Bundi children, indicating a genetic effect on growth. However, these correlations were lower than those calculated for the faster-growing Kaiapit children or for European children, suggesting environmental depression of this relationship.

The role of environmental factors in growth at this stage is considerable. In a longitudinal study, Bundi school children, after four years of exposure to a boarding-school environment, were 4 centimeters shorter in height and 2.5 kilograms lighter in weight than their village counterparts (Malcolm 1970a). After eight years at school, they had advanced to the normal size of the village child. This change is probably related to a number of factors, in particular the quality and frequency of school meals. A supplementary protein feeding program using skim-milk powder resulted in an acceleration of growth with a rapid initial catch-up phase, to a continuing rate of growth equal to that found in European children (Malcolm 1970b). After four years, these children are now 7.3 centimeters taller and 3.1 kilograms heavier than village children of the same age (Figures 3 and 4). These findings demonstrate the lability of the growth rate in the presence of exposure to differing environmental influences. The growth performance of Lae urban children whose protein intake is substantially higher than that of

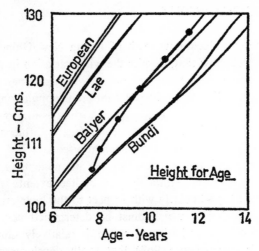

Figure 3. Height changes with supplementary feeding in Bundi school children

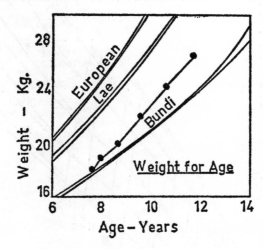

Figure 4. Weight changes with supplementary feeding in Bundi school children

village children (Malcolm i.p.) demonstrates that the New Guinean child has a potential for growth which is not being realized in the village and tends to minimize the possible role of genetic factors in the slow growth rate of the village child.

One may conclude, therefore, that the genotype operates in preserving the patterns of growth, but in a nutritionally deprived environment this plays a comparatively minor role in the tempo of growth.

DENTAL DEVELOPMENT

Eruption times for deciduous teeth of Papua New Guinean children
(Malcolm 1970c) show that, despite the wide variation in growth rates
for the child under three years old, there is no significant variation in
the deciduous eruption times between different populations. Variation
within populations, however, is correlated with rates of growth, suggesting that this characteristic is under strong genetic influence and is almost completely resistant to environmental effects.

On the other hand, the eruption times of permanent teeth (Malcolm
and Bue 1970) do vary, although to a limited extent, with rates of
growth (Figure 5), particularly with respect to the later erupting teeth.
However, this variation, which must be determined very largely by
environmental effects, as indicated above, is relatively small and supports Tanner's conclusion (1962) that tooth development is under

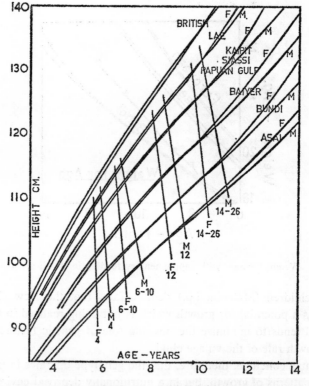

Figure 5. Effect of rate of growth on eruption times of teeth in Papua New
Guinean communities (vertical lines at the intersection of the growth curve indicate
the mean age at which a certain number of teeth are erupted)

strong genetic control and that environmental effects on growth only influence to a minor extent the development of the upper part of the body. Eruption times of teeth for Lae urban children are earlier than for any previously reported populations, particularly for the premolars and molars.

SKELETAL DEVELOPMENT

The maturation of the skeleton in Papua New Guinea children as determined from hand and wrist X rays (Malcolm 1970a) is markedly delayed, in comparison with European children: throughout the whole growth period the skeletal age is, on the average, 75 percent of that of European standards at any given age. Bone formation in slow-growing children, particularly cortical width, is much reduced, with a tendency to vacuolation in the medullary shafts.

The response to supplementary protein described above suggests that an increased protein intake accelerates the growth of bone in linear dimensions, but information is as yet not available to establish whether bone maturation is concomitantly accelerated. There is a high correlation between skeletal age and height age (0.6 percent), suggesting that this delay in skeletal age is, as might be expected, largely due to environmental effects.

THE MATURE ADULT

What are the consequences for the adult — the end-product of these various influences operating both pre- and post-natally and throughout childhood?

Table 3 shows the range of stature and weight for young, mature adult males from a number of New Guinean populations (Malcolm 1970a, i.p.). Figures for young adults have been selected where these have been available, as a progressive decline in both height and, particularly, weight is a feature of all Papua New Guinean communities. The stature of the male adult ranges from 150.4 centimeters in the short Asai people of the Madang Highlands to 173.5 centimeters for the young men of Butibum village near Lae, who may be regarded as having been urban dwellers for some 20 to 25 years. It is of considerable interest that the young Butibum male is some 7 centimeters taller than the older adult, a difference which can only be accounted for by a marked secular change in this society. The difference in the female height, however, is much less, there being only 2 centimeters difference between younger and older women.

Table 3.   Mean height and weight for male adults in some New Guinean populations

Population	Height (in centimeters)	Weight (in kilograms)	Source
Asai	150.4	45.3	Malcolm 1970a
Bundi	156.3	54.6	Malcolm 1970a
Lumi	157.1	52.5	Malcolm 1970a
Chimbu	158.7	53.6	Malcolm 1970a
Baiyer R.	159.0	—	Freedman and MacIntosh 1965
Kaiapit	166.1	59.6	Malcolm 1970a
Butibum	173.5	62.4	Malcolm i.p.

The Butibum male, however, is now reaching the mature height predicted from the growth rate of the male child in that village, who on average is some 2 to 3 centimeters taller than the average Lae urban child.

The adult stature in traditional New Guinean societies is closely related to the rate at which children in that society have grown. Figure 6 shows the height of male and female children at four and twelve years from different New Guinean societies, plotted respectively against the mean male and female adult height of that society. A close correlation is present in all traditional societies. However, a wide discrepancy exists in urban children, whose rate of growth greatly exceeds that which would be predicted from the height of their parents, indicating the presence of a marked secular change towards more rapid growth.

The ultimate stature reached by the Lae town children may be substantially greater than that of their parents, most of whom were reared in the village. But the number of children, with the exception of those from Butibum, who have lived throughout their growth span in the urban environment is at present insufficient to establish whether this will be so, although the small number of children who have reached mature height are some 2 to 3 centimeters taller and 1 to 2 kilograms heavier than the average of their parents.

In view, therefore, of the close relationship between the rate of growth and adult height, and the apparently small influence of the genotype on the rate of growth, it would seem most probable that adult height and presumably certain other adult characteristics are determined to a very large extent by intensity and duration of environmental

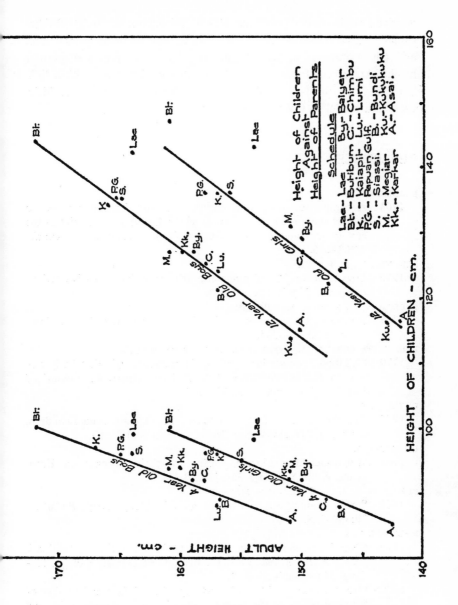

Figure 6.   Height of male and female children at four and twelve years from different New Guinean societies plotted against the mean male and female adult height of that society

influences throughout the growth period.

It has been suggested that slow growth might be derived from natural selection, slow growers being better fitted for survival in a nutritionally deprived environment (Malcolm 1970a; Frisancho, et al. 1970). Presumably, as a consequence of the obvious link between growth rates and adult stature, this would lead to selection of adults of shorter height. At present there appears to be little evidence for such a link, but it may be that specifically designed animal experiments could be used as a model to test this possibility.

REFERENCES

BARNES, R.
  1963 A comparison of growth curves of infants from two weeks to twenty months in various areas of the Chimbu sub-district of the eastern highlands of New Guinea. *Medical Journal of Australia* 2:262–266.

BERGNER, L., M. SUSSER
  1970 Low birth weight and prenatal nutrition: an interpretative review. *Pediatrics* 46:946–966.

FREEDMAN, L., N. W. G. MAC INTOSH
  1965 Stature variation in western highland males of East New Guinea. *Oceania* 35:287–304.

FRISANCHO, ROBERTO A., STANLEY M. CARN, WERNER ASCOLI
  1970 Childhood retardation resulting in reduction of adult body size due to lesser adolescent skeletal delay. *American Journal of Physical Anthropology* 33:326–336.

GATES, R. E.
  1964 Eruption of permanent teeth of New South Wales school children, parts I and II. *Australian Dental Journal* 9:211, 380.

HIERNAUX, J.
  1964 Weight-height relationship during growth in Africans and Europeans. *Human Biology* 36:273–293.

LEE, M. M. C., K. S. F. CHANG, M. M. C. CHAN
  1963 Sexual maturation of Chinese girls in Hong Kong. *Pediatrics* 39:389–398.

MALCOLM, L. A.
  1970a *Growth and development in New Guinea: a study of the Bundi people of the Madang district.* Institute of Human Biology, Madang. Monograph Series 1.
  1970b Growth, malnutrition and mortality of the infant and toddler of the Asai valley of the New Guinea highlands. *American Journal of Clinical Nutrition* 23:1090–1095.
  1970c Growth of the Asai child of the Madang district of New Guinea. *Journal of Biosocial Science* 2:213–226.
  1972 Anthropometric, biochemical and immunological effects of protein supplements in a New Guinean highland boarding school. *Ninth International Congress of Nutrition, Mexico*, September 1972.

i.p. Health and nutrition, growth and development of children in urban Lae, Papua New Guinea.

MALCOLM, L. A., A. BUE
1970 Eruption times of permanent teeth and the determination of age in New Guinean children. *Tropical and Geographical Medicine* 22:307–312.

OOMEN, H. A. P. C.
1961 The Papuan child as a survivor. *Journal of Tropical Pediatrics* 6:103.

SCOTT, J. A.
1961 *Report on the heights and weights (and other measurements) of school pupils in the County of London in 1959.* London County Council.

SCRAGG, R. F. R.
1955 Birth weight, prematurity and growth rate to thirty months of the New Guinea native child. *Medical Journal of Australia* 1:128–132.

TANNER, J. M.
1962 *Growth at adolescence* (second edition). Oxford: Blackwell Scientific Publications.

TANNER, J. M., B. O'KEEFE
1962 Age at menarche in Nigerian school girls, with a note on their heights and weights from age 12 to 19. *Human Biology* 34:187–196.

TANNER, J. M., R. H. WHITEHOUSE, M. TAKAISHI
1966 Standards from birth to maturity for height, weight, height velocity and weight velocity for British children, 1965. *Archives of Diseases of Childhood* 41:454, 613.

WARK, LYNETTE, L. A. MALCOLM
1969 Growth and development of the Lumi child in the Sepik district of New Guinea. *Medical Journal of Australia* 2:129–136.

Physical Growth and the Social Environment: A West African Example

D. K. FIAWOO

The hypothesis that Euro-American children have better growth performance than their African counterparts and that such a difference is due primarily to nutrition is no longer new to educators and clinicians in Africa. The few scattered investigations on the continent seem to prove the hypothesis.[1] But beyond this, we know very little about the physical growth patterns of the African child. Only a few figures, even of heights and weights, can be found in the published literature that go beyond the formative period. We need to know what local factors promote and retard growth. The specific objectives of this paper are as follows:

1. to give figures on heights and weights of Ghanaian children;
2. to examine the relative growth patterns of boys and girls; and
3. to compare the heights and weights of children from different environmental situations in Ghana.

METHODS

The height and weight measurements of 4,585 primary-middle school children and 715 Achimota (secondary) school students were collected between 1966 and 1968. The children, wearing uniforms but without

[1]   See the references, especially Waddy (1956), Deane and Geber (1964), and Welbourne (1951). The only published material on height and weight growth in Ghana comes from Waddy's survey of children from the Northern Territories. Although the sample is quite large, the limited age range of six to twelve for boys and girls tends to hamper analysis in terms of the development cycles and the relative growth of boys and girls.

shoes, were measured with the help of trained undergraduates of the Department of Sociology of the University of Ghana at Legon. Data were regrouped into bivariate frequency tables and analysis was by the regression technique.[2]

By far the most important factor in the analysis of heights and weights of African children is the problem of accuracy of age. Exact age was calculated for each child from the date of birth and the date of measurement. Unusual care was taken to ensure accuracy. The schedules for the measurements required details of information on age, including evidence of age. Such evidence included inspection of birth certificates, school records and the interviewing of teachers and of parents where necessary. In the villages where recorded ages were few, all the available techniques were used in the assessment of age.

Subjects and their Social Environment

Five groups of Ghanaian children, plus a small sample of expatriate non-African children, representing different social environments in Ghana were selected for study. With the exception of the international schools, all the Ghanaian children in the selected schools were weighed and measured. Of the former, only half the total number in school were randomly selected.

a. Achimota school students: This was the only group of secondary school students. Measurements were taken by the medical department of the school.[3] Included in this sample were 227 girls and 488 boys.

Very high standards of secondary school education obtain in the country generally; nevertheless, Achimota School, founded in 1925, has since its foundation enjoyed the reputation of an elite school. Being a residential school with a tradition of good discipline, it was expected that the students would have more than average growth performance.

b. "Privileged" urban children: These were Ghanaian children attending various expensive international schools at Accra during the period of this study. They included the Accra International School at the Cantonments, Christ the King and the Ridge Church School. These are highly rated schools and very much in demand among the elite Ghanaian families. They are mostly operated by expatriates and the large

---

[2]   The author is grateful to Dr. Kpedekpo of the Institute of Statistics, Legon, for statistical advice.
[3]   I am grateful to the headmaster and the medical officer-in-charge for their permission to analyze these data and to incorporate them in this study.

majority of teachers are expatriate graduates or holders of high professional certificates.

The results of their Common Entrance Examination[4] from year to year, and their high standard of discipline are said to justify the exorbitant fees paid. The children who patronize these schools tend to come from relatively wealthy or highly educated Ghanaian homes. Included in this sample were 223 girls and 213 boys.

c.   Other urban children: These children were drawn from various government and City Council primary-middle schools in the heart of Accra. Their parents live at Accra and the children enjoy the amenities of West African urban life. There were 735 girls and 756 boys in this group.

d.   Suburban children: Like the group above, these children were attending various government-approved primary-middle schools, but at the outskirts of Accra, or in suburban areas. All the settlements featuring in this study were within a radius of five to ten miles from the heart of Accra and included Apenkwa, Anumle, Achimota (village) and Alogboshie on the Accra-Nsawam Road.

Large numbers of children attending these schools were drawn from nearby villages of Kisseihma and Christian's Village situated between Legon and Achimota. Apart from Anumle which represents a planned settlement,[5] all these are very primitive communities with the barest minimum of social amenities. The parents of the children are mostly wage earners who commute to Accra, Legon and Achimota School. Only a tiny fraction are full-time farmers. There were 408 girls and 593 boys in this sample.

e.   Rural school children: These were attending various Local Authority and Mission Schools in the Tonu (Tongu) Lower Volta District. The selected villages included Tefle, Sogakofe, Sokpoe, Vume and Kpotame. All the villages lie on the main trunk road from Accra to Lome in the Togo Republic. The men are mostly farmers and fishermen; the women assist the men but are also petty traders in their own right (Fiawoo 1961). This group comprised 651 girls and 1,005 boys.

f.   Expatriate children: This group was made up mostly of Euro-American children attending the same international schools as the privileged urban children discussed above. Their parents held key positions in international organizations, in government, education, commerce and the diplomatic fields. They included children of university

[4]   This is an examination conducted by the West African Examinations Council for admission to approved secondary schools.
[5]   Anumle represents the staff village of Achimota School.

professors and lecturers, and Syrian-Lebanese children whose parents were very successful traders in Ghana. The sample included 146 girls and 156 boys.

From these group characterizations, the following deductions were made:

1. Families in the urban area are probably wealthier than those in the rural area and the suburbs.

2. Urban parents who send their children to expensive international schools are probably better off economically than those who send their children to normal government schools.

If it is further postulated that the physical growth of the child is closely related to parental socioeconomic status, then the following hypotheses are relevant:

1. Privileged urban children will grow taller and heavier than their normal counterparts in the city.

2. Other urban children will have better growth performance than their rural and suburban counterparts.

RESULTS

Among 2,568 primary-middle school boys aged between five and eighteen, there is a marked degree of correlation between age and height, the correlation coefficient being 0.99: the older the boy the taller he grows. The highest point of acceleration is at age fourteen to fifteen which falls within the Ghanaian pubertal age range of thirteen to fifteen.[6] At age eighteen boys are still growing; the mean is 65.6 inches and the range between 57 and 73 inches.

Among 2,017 primary-middle school girls there is almost perfect correlation between age and height ($r = 0.98$), the highest point of acceleration being at age ten to eleven. The curve rises sharply between ages ten and thirteen (see Figure 1). This is not different from the Euro-American pattern, where the highest point of acceleration for girls is between eleven and thirteen (Cole and Morgan 1961). At age fifteen growth declines appreciably and is hardly noticeable at seventeen to eighteen. The mean height at eighteen is 63.4 inches and the range is between fifty-nine and sixty-eight inches.

---

[6] From various studies conducted at Accra and the Sogakofe district of the Volta Region (unpublished materials).

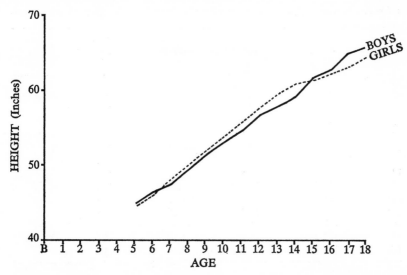

Figure 1. Relative rates of growth of boys and girls in primary-middle schools

Table 1. Primary-middle schools: distribution of weight according to age — boys

Age	Mean weight	Standard deviation	Standard error of mean	Total number of boys
5	43.4	3.3	0.63	27
6	43.6	5.1	0.50	104
7	46.0	7.1	0.46	242
8	50.9	7.4	0.47	248
9	55.7	8.4	0.52	261
10	61.0	10.5	0.69	235
11	64.8	8.4	0.57	220
12	71.7	10.4	0.71	214
13	76.3	11.9	0.82	214
14	81.1	10.2	0.72	198
15	92.6	15.0	1.05	203
16	97.9	16.7	1.28	169
17	109.0	15.7	1.32	142
18	114.8	14.4	1.51	91

Relationship between Age and Weight

In Table 1 are shown the features for weight for boys. There is a positive correlation between age and weight ($r = 0.98$). The highest point of acceleration is at age fourteen to fifteen — the same as for height. The annual gain remains significant at seventeen, and at eighteen the

Table 2.   Primary-middle schools: distribution of weight according to age — girls

Age	Mean weight	Standard deviation	Standard error of mean	Total number of girls
5	44.8	4.5	0.90	25
6	45.2	6.9	0.71	95
7	48.0	5.3	0.36	215
8	52.0	9.8	0.59	272
9	57.2	11.1	0.71	243
10	63.5	12.1	0.74	268
11	69.5	10.5	0.70	224
12	78.0	15.4	1.25	151
13	86.6	15.1	1.25	146
14	91.8	13.5	1.22	123
15	100.8	13.2	1.25	113
16	108.2	9.4	1.08	76
17	113.4	13.2	1.86	51
18	117.4	8.0	2.07	15

boys are still growing. At eighteen the mean is 114.8 pounds and the range between 79 and 148 pounds. This wide range is probably suggestive of the varying socioeconomic groups of children featuring in this study.

The growth features for girls are expressed in Table 2. Once again, there is a marked degree of correlation between age and weight (r = 0.99). Except for age fourteen, the curve rises sharply between twelve and sixteen years. At eighteen the weight curve is still rising. There is no marked difference between growth in height and growth in weight for girls except that ages fourteen and fifteen (followed closely by age thirteen) stand out as the highest point of acceleration in weight growth, whereas in height, growth begins to decline at this age. This might suggest that growth in weight declines less rapidly than growth in height. The mean weight at eighteen years is 117.4 pounds and the range between 96 and 140 pounds.

Relative Rates of Development for Boys and Girls

Contrary to the Euro-American pattern, Ghanaian girls are heavier and taller than the boys for a considerable part of their growing period, including the elementary school years. In height, boys and girls are almost at par between the ages of five and six — the boys lead by only a tiny fraction of an inch. Between six and seven years the girls catch up with the boys and outdistance them at seven. They maintain the

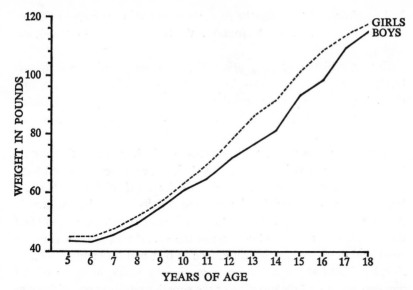

Figure 2. Relative rates of weight increase of boys and girls in primary-middle schools

lead from seven until fourteen. The boys overtake them at fifteen and maintain the lead for the rest of adolescence.

In weight, the female superiority is even more striking; girls are heavier than boys throughout the growing period, i.e. from five to eighteen (Figure 2).

These represent significant departures from the Euro-American norms where the growth trend shows a tendency for boys to exceed girls in height and weight from birth through the preschool and elementary school years. The girls become physiologically mature two years sooner than boys and thus attain adolescence earlier. This has the effect of carrying them ahead of the boys between eleven and thirteen. By fifteen, however, the boys are back in the lead "when their greater and probably more sustained adolescent spurt begins to take effect" (Tanner 1967: 18). This male superiority is true of height and weight growth. It is significant that the Ghanaian expatriate group is parallel to the Euro-American standard in the relative growth of boys and girls. The Ghanaian rural, suburban and urban groups are well behind this standard.

While there is some physiological explanation for the superiority of girls over boys between preadolescence and early adolescence, there seems to be no such explanation for the overall superior growth performance of boys in the Euro-American pattern. Similarly, one can find no biological basis for the superiority of girls over boys in Ghana. Perhaps the answers may be found in the Ghanaian social and cultural setting.

Since nutrition may be a prime factor in the superior growth performance of Euro-Americans over Africans, one may conclude that Chanaian girls have more appetite than boys. In traditional Chanaian homes, it is customary fo rgirls to assist with the domestic chores of their mother, including the preparation of food.

It is not improbable that this nearness to the hearth affords them an advantage over boys in feeding. This desire to eat more, nurtured from the home, is probably carried over to the residential schools. This hypothesis is supported by the extreme obesity of market women in Accra, who apparently eat more than their male counterparts, but exert themselves less, and thus burn less of the stored fat (energy). Hence a combination of quantitative difference in diet and differential occupational roles of the sexes appears to tip the scales in favor of the females. But the whole question of the superior performance of females needs further study.

Individual Group Performance

The Ghanaian growth pattern delineated above represents the average performance of the groups of primary-middle school children discussed above in the introduction. It does not include Achimota School. To a large extent, each group typifies this growth pattern, especially in the case of the relative growth of boys and girls. In the following paragraphs, I examine each group in relation to the others and to the total pattern. It should be borne in mind, however, that each part of the whole is relatively small and that statistical errors are possible in the reckoning of individual group mean.

Tables 3 and 4 show the mean height growth for boys and girls. In the former, Achimota shows a trend of marginal superiority to rural, suburban and urban groups, the differences being mostly between one and two inches. Compared to privileged urban and the expatriate groups, however, Achimota shows consistently inferior performance at eleven to thirteen years, the only age groups where data are comparable. The height growth for girls shows a fairly similar trend.

In weight growth, the pattern is strikingly similar to height: Achimota is generally inferior to the urban "privileged"-expatriate group, but is clearly superior to the rural-suburban-urban group. In weight, how-

Table 3.   Achimota and primary-middle schools: distribution of height according to age — boys (mean height, inches)

Age	Rural	Suburban	Urban	Privileged urban	Achimota	Total boy	Expatriate
5	—	—	42.0	45.0	—	27	44.8
6	45.2	43.5	44.6	48.1	—	104	46.3
7	47.1	45.5	46.5	49.2	—	242	48.8
8	49.2	48.0	48.4	51.2	—	248	52.1
9	51.0	49.4	50.3	53.7	—	261	54.4
10	52.0	51.0	52.3	55.4	—	235	55.2
11	53.6	53.7	53.6	57.1	55.5	226	58.1
12	55.9	55.1	56.0	58.4	58.2	242	58.9
13	57.2	56.7	57.4	59.0	58.9	268	59.0
14	58.4	57.9	59.1	—	61.5	278	—
15	60.5	61.9	60.9	—	62.9	291	—
16	62.4	62.1	61.8	—	65.1	239	—
17	64.1	64.4	63.7	—	65.9	201	—
18	65.2	64.7	65.1	—	65.3	147	—

Table 4.   Achimota and primary-middle schools: distribution of height according to age — girls (mean height, inches)

Age	Rural	Suburban	Urban	Privileged urban	Achimota	Total girls	Expatriate
5	44.5	43.0	—	44.5	—	25	44.7
6	44.5	43.9	45.9	46.7	—	95	45.9
7	47.1	46.0	48.2	48.4	—	215	49.1
8	49.7	47.4	49.7	51.4	—	272	51.7
9	51.1	48.9	51.3	53.7	—	243	53.3
10	52.7	51.3	53.5	56.0	52.5	269	55.3
11	55.0	53.8	55.6	58.2	58.9	235	59.1
12	56.7	55.0	58.2	61.5	59.7	176	60.7
13	58.8	57.7	59.7	62.7	61.3	181	—
14	59.4	59.0	61.9	—	61.5	182	—
15	61.0	60.8	61.3	—	62.4	140	—
16	62.7	61.5	62.1	—	61.8	104	—
17	61.8	62.3	63.4	—	62.1	74	—
18	63.9	61.5	64.5	—	62.7	25	—

ever, the gap between Achimota and the rural-suburban-urban group is very wide compared to the urban "privileged"-expatriate group.

When the privileged urban is compared with the expatriate the results are very close indeed. In height growth for girls aged five, seven, eight, and eleven the expatriate group has the edge; the Ghanaian privileged urban group is dominant at ages six, nine, ten, and twelve. For the boys, the privileged urban group takes the lead from five to ten. The expatriate group catches up and outdistances it at eleven and maintains the lead up to age twelve. At thirteen the privileged urban group catches up and both groups remain at par.

The same dramatic performance characterizes weight development (Tables 5 and 6). For the boys, the Ghanaian group takes the lead at

Table 5.   Achimota and primary-middle schools: distribution of weight according to age — boys (mean weight, pounds)

Age	Rural	Suburban	Urban	Privileged urban	Achimota	Total boys	Expatriate
5	—	—	35.0	45.9	—	27	45.5
6	40.7	37.9	40.6	51.9	—	104	50.4
7	45.4	42.2	44.0	57.7	—	242	59.4
8	50.5	47.7	48.4	62.2	—	248	66.0
9	55.0	51.1	53.9	69.5	—	261	69.4
10	57.8	54.4	60.2	75.0	—	235	71.7
11	63.5	63.2	63.1	83.2	76.4	226	87.7
12	71.2	68.9	71.3	86.1	85.6	242	91.5
13	76.1	73.5	77.1	88.0	90.4	268	91.0
14	81.1	78.0	83.8	—	102.6	278	—
15	88.7	99.2	92.0	—	109.4	291	—
16	99.2	96.7	102.5	—	122.5	239	—
17	109.9	108.5	111.3	—	125.5	201	—
18	114.8	118.2	121.0	—	124.9	147	—

Table 6.   Achimota and primary-middle schools: distribution of weight according to age — girls (mean weight, pounds)

Age	Rural	Suburban	Urban	Privileged urban	Achimota	Total girls	Expatriate
5	41.5	40.0	43.0	45.7	—	25	44.4
6	40.7	38.2	45.7	49.6	—	95	48.7
7	45.0	41.3	49.7	55.8	—	215	56.6
8	51.6	41.3	52.1	64.1	—	272	65.8
9	53.6	45.9	57.2	72.7	—	243	67.1
10	60.8	54.9	62.6	78.2	67.0	269	74.5
11	67.2	62.9	69.8	88.6	87.9	235	89.7
12	73.4	68.3	83.0	95.5	94.4	176	94.3
13	78.1	81.3	91.1	99.0	108.7	181	—
14	85.0	87.3	99.2	—	111.7	182	—
15	96.3	99.0	103.8	—	116.3	140	—
16	104.5	106.2	109.8	—	121.8	104	—
17	106.8	116.0	118.5	—	120.5	74	—
18	114.7	115.0	127.0	—	122.0	25	—

five and six; it is overtaken by the expatriate group at seven and eight. The privileged urban group recovers the lead at nine and maintains it until ten, when it is again overtaken by the expatriate group which maintains the lead from eleven to thirteen. The same general features characterize the growth for girls.

In height and weight growth for boys and girls, the urban group shows complete superiority over the suburban. But there is an interesting development when urban is compared with rural. While the urban girls are consistently taller and heavier than the rural girls, the rural boys are taller than the urban boys — except for the postpubertal period of seventeen and eighteen; in weight, the rural boys are superior between six and eleven; the urban boys seize the lead from twelve to eighteen.

In effect, urban superiority over rural is not a *fait accompli*; it is questionable in places. The superior development in height among the rural boys is probably due to open-air activities which contribute to a better growth of the long bones.[7] Correspondingly, strenuous farm activities on the part of the rural boys may lead to the burning of much of the stored fat (energy).

Factors Promoting and Retarding Growth

In terms of aggregate growth performance, the six groups featuring in this study may be ranked as follows:

1. expatriate,
2. urban privileged,
3. Achimota,
4. urban,
5. rural, and
6. suburban.

The first three groups show better-than-average growth performance. The children are taller and heavier than the last three.

There is considerable evidence that children from both expatriate and privileged urban groups belong to the highest socioeconomic strata. Their parents are highly educated and hold status positions with corresponding earning power. Such well-to-do parents are better able to afford the balanced diet necessary for growth than their less affluent urban counterparts.

[7] Personal communication from Dr. Oracca-Tetteh, a biochemist at Legon.

Achimota school has long ceased to be the preserve of the elite as a result of the fee-free educational policy of the Ghana Government. The selection of students from the "common entrance" pool ostensibly gives a fair chance to all Ghanaians; nevertheless, an unobtrusive selective process operates whereby the students — usually the cream of the pool — tend to come from the well-to-do homes with a relatively long tradition of education.[8] Secondly, Achimota is a residential school with a tradition of good feeding and good discipline. These combined factors tend to encourage better-than-average growth performance.

The urban group represents a heterogeneous body. It includes the middle-range stratum of Ghanaian society and the "working classes." Obviously, some of the children in this group would have excellent growth opportunities, and others would be far less fortunate because of varying parental socioeconomic status. It would be desirable in future growth research to break this group down into two or three discrete components. The results would probably show that the higher the parental socioeconomic status, the better the growth performance in the urban area.

Rural performance in this study reveals that the natural environment, the geographical setting, as well as the occupation dictated by these surroundings, may contribute to physical growth.

Finally, the poor suburban growth performance is a clear reflection of the effects of unsanitary surroundings, economic poverty, and gross illiteracy.

SUMMARY AND CONCLUSIONS

The following major conclusions have emerged from this study:
1.   The highest point of acceleration in height and weight growth for boys is at age fourteen to fifteen, and for girls at ten to thirteen.
2.   Girls are bigger and taller than boys for a considerable part of their growing period.
3.   In terms of individual group performance, it has been shown that the higher the socioeconomic group of the child's parent, the better the growth performance. For example:
   a.   "Privileged" urban children perform as well as expatriate children in Ghana and are taller and heavier than the average Ghanaian urban child;

[8]   See Foster (1965: Chapter 7) for a fuller discussion on the relationship between school attendance and parental socioeconomic status.

b.   urban children have better growth performance than their sub-urban counterparts; and

c.   rural children perform better than suburban children; and some-times as well as urban children.

Some of these conclusions, especially the differential growth per-formance of children of different socioeconomic groups, are already familiar in the Euro-American context where periodic measurement of the height and weight of school children has become a regular feature of educational research. While the social strata are less clearly defined in Ghana — and in Africa generally — than in Europe or America, one can safely distinguish between the urban elite and the average urban dweller in terms of education and/or earning power.

Similarly, the distinctions between urban and rural, urban and sub-urban are almost clearcut in the African context. One is likely to find a higher standard of education with a stronger earning power in the urban area. It is the relationship between rural and suburban which needs further study. The relatively permanent village settlement adja-cent to a major road and with clearly defined means of sustenance is certainly superior to a suburban community where members have to eke out an existence; it may even offer a challenge to the urban settle-ment as this study reveals.

Thus, the various groups in this study represent defined socio-economic groups in the African context. The study further reveals that there is some relationship between these groups and the growth per-formance of the children.

The conclusions relating to the growth spurt as well as the superior growth performance of girls over boys need further study.[9] These con-clusions need to be treated as hypotheses which must be tested and retested by successive investigations. The final picture will probably emerge only after years of painstaking field work.

Finally, it is important to stress that the data analyzed in this paper have been collected only from southern Ghana. How far they reflect Ghana as a whole will depend upon future investigations.

---

[9]   Note that in his study of Baganda children in the vicinity of Kampala, Wel-bourne (1951) observed that girls up to nine years were taller and heavier than the boys, but from twelve to fourteen years they were shorter and lighter. He was unable to comment on the significance of this pattern because of an alleged un-certainty concerning the ages of his subjects.

REFERENCES

COLE, L., J. J. B. MORGAN
  1961   *Psychology of childhood and adolescence.* New York: Holt, Rinehart and Winston.
DEANE, R., M. GEBER
  1964   The development of the African child. *Discovery* 25:1, 14–19.
FIAWOO, D. K.
  1961   *Social survey of Tefle, Ghana.* Child Development Monograph (mimeograph).
  1972   "Puberty and adolescence in Ghana." Unpublished manuscript.
FOSTER, PHILIP
  1965   *Education and social change in Ghana.* Chicago: University of Chicago Press.
GRANT, M. W.
  1951   "The technique for the analysis of heights and weights." Mimeographed manuscript. Applied Nutrition Unit, London School of Hygiene and Tropical Medicine.
GRANT, M.W., G. R. WADSWORTH
  1959   The height, weight, and physical maturity of Liverpool schoolgirls. *The Medical Officer* 102:303–306.
JELLIFE, D. B.
  1962   The African child. *Transactions of the Royal Society for Tropical Medicine and Hygiene* 46:13.
ROBERTS, D. F.
  1960   "Effects of race and climate on human growth as exemplified by studies on African children," in *Human growth.* Edited by J. M. Tanner. Oxford: Pergamon Press.
TANNER, J. M.
  1967   *Education and physical growth.* London: University of London Press.
WADDY, B. B.
  1956   Heights and weights of children in the northern territories of the Gold Coast. *The Journal of Tropical Medicine and Hygiene* 59:1, 1–4.
WELBOURNE, H. F.
  1951   The growth of Baganda children in the vicinity of Kampala. *East African Medical Journal* 28:428.

Medical Care of Adolescents in a Suburban Community

I. R. SHENKER

Modern Western society views adolescence as a period of physical, mental, and emotional development occurring between childhood and adulthood. It is a transitional phase through which each individual is expected to enter and leave after having successfully completed its tasks. It is a period of life characterized by its fluidity and rapid changes. Internal and external upheavals occur which may produce confusion, uncertainty, and anxiety in even the most "healthy" youngster. It is a period of life when grossly abnormal behavior may be considered not deviant. Its changes, to say the least, are complex both biologically and psychologically, and no two adolescents are completely alike. This view of adolescence is reflected in recent medical practice in the United States.

The age of onset of adolescence is as difficult to determine as is the age of becoming an adult. Certainly medical factors may be less important in this determination than cultural ones. In general, adolescence may be said to begin sometime after ten years of age and end about age twenty. The onset of puberty coincides with the onset of adolescence, while the completion of puberty occurs well before the completion of adolescence. Adolescents are essentially a healthy group, but prior to twenty years ago in the United States, they had been neglected medically. With the establishment of the first adolescent clinic in the United States at the Boston Children's Hospital in the early 1950's, the discipline of adolescent medicine has been emerging. It can be stated that, in fact, at this point in time adolescent medicine is in its own late adolescence. Within the last ten years, however, this interest in age-group medicine, which provides specialized care for adolescents, has increased significantly. It is noteworthy that the recognition of the need for specialized facilities to treat adolescents really preceded the explosion of adolescents in terms of their numbers and the specific medical concerns of youth today, such as drug abuse and the sexual revolution and its resultant problems.

The kind of patients served within various clinics throughout the country varies with the localities of the specific sponsoring institutions, their sources of financial support, the needs of the particular target groups of adolescents to which one directs his attention, or infact may be skewed by particular disease entities of interest to personnel working within various settings. It is logical, however, that the development of the discipline of adolescent medicine stems from pediatrics, which was the first age-group-related specialty in medicine to be established. To be sure, there has been a significant lowering of infant and childhood mortality within the last fifty years in the United States. It thus seemed reasonable to redirect some dedication and research orientation, which developed pediatric care to exemplary levels, toward the adolescent population.

Medical care of adolescents, heretofore, was largely forsaken since this group of patients traditionally has a relatively low morbidity and a low mortality for physical illness. This remains true even today. The mortality rate will doubtlessly not be affected significantly during our lifetime unless we are able to define the etiology of, and reduce the number of, motor vehicle accidents and until medical advances in disease-oriented or organ-system specialties produce a cure or prevention for neoplasms, since accidents and neoplastic disease are the two major causes of mortality in the adolescent age group. The morbidity of adolescents, however, is a much more complex situation. Although this is a relatively healthy period of life, the number of adolescents seeking medical care is increasing at a rapid pace. It is indeed fortunate that the model of comprehensive care which will be described has been able to respond to changing needs of adolescents throughout this 20-year span. This comprehensive adolescent clinic model has been utilized around the country and has been adopted and modified to provide care for large numbers of children in comprehensive child and youth projects. To some extent the comprehensive model is now being established and fostered by the United States government in Health Maintenance Organizations (HMO) for large numbers of population groups.

Stemming from a recognition that adolescents were not receiving adequate care in clinics oriented to deal with specific diseases, several comprehensive adolescent clinics were originally developed. It was, in fact, the pediatric cardiologist who was one of the first to recognize the need to become involved with total patient care rather than with specific disease problems. It was apparent to the observant clinician that adolescents were uncomfortable in pediatric clinic settings, where they could not identify with younger patients and were resentful of being treated as children, when in fact a major problem which aggravated their primary medical conditions could often be traced to adolescent adjustment problems which were frequently ignored. For example, it makes little sense to write prescriptions for penicillin tablets in the prophylaxis of rheumatic fever if the adolescent does not take them. It is important for the physician treating the patient for the prophylaxis of recurrent rheumatic fever to understand the adolescent's aversion to taking daily medication, from a psychological point of view, so that he may more effectively deal with his adolescent patient to accomplish his medical goal while fostering the patient's emotional growth. Similar relationships in the treatment of diabetes, epilepsy, or other chronic diseases become apparent.

American teenagers may be viewed as people in the process of completing four tasks: one, the emancipation from parental dependency; two, establishment of personal and sexual identity; three, development of personal moral and ethical codes; and four, selection of a career and lifestyle. Physical illness represents a threat to successful completion of these tasks. The teenager who is undergoing the development of an adult body needs to adapt to a new self-image. A relatively homeostatic organism is suddenly disrupted by physiological events, the heightened awareness of peers, and a need for acceptance by both the same and the opposite sex, needs which often conflict with a desire to draw back to the security of childhood. It is in this charged state of emotional development that the onset of physical illness, upsetting normalcy, tends to promote dependence at a time when independence is so vital. Any real or imagined threat to the body image during adolescence can be more traumatic and difficult to cope with than at any other time of life.

It is this type of patient to whom we address ourselves in the care given at the adolescent clinic of our institution. This clinic was established in 1964 with a grant from the Children's Bureau of the Department of Health, Education and Welfare. This federal department has subsequently been moved and is now within the Child Health Service of the Health Services and Mental Health Administration of the United States Public Health Service. Ours is a comprehensive, multidisciplinary clinic, and we are charged with providing total medical care for adolescents and with demonstrating a model program which would provide a wide variety of services and meet a variety of medical needs of this age group. In addition, the institution has an 18-bed inpatient adolescent unit which was opened in August of 1970. A specialized atmosphere is provided, geared toward the needs of adolescents. The pathology seen in the inpatient unit

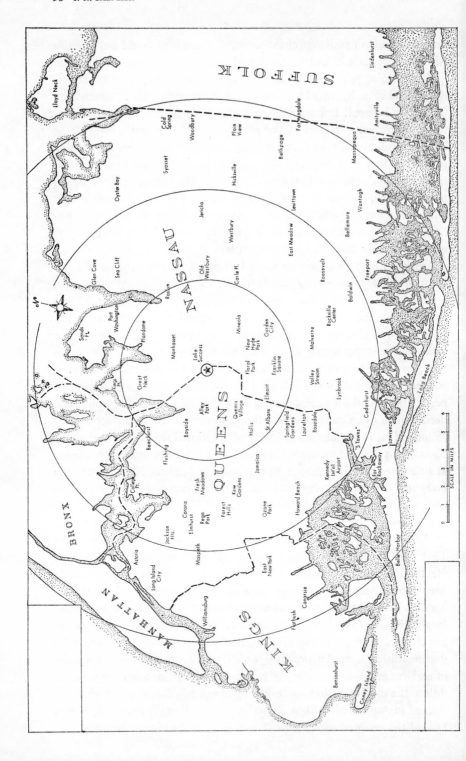

is a varied one. All patients admitted to the hospital between the ages of 13 and 18, with some overlap on either end of the age range, are admitted to the adolescent unit. The population of this unit would typically consist of one or two patients with malignant diseases; several patients with traumas following automobile accidents; patients undergoing various surgical procedures both elective and acute, such as appendectomies, cosmetic surgery, or orthopedic surgery; patients with inflammatory bowel disease or cystic fibrosis; diabetics; and youngsters admitted because of self-inflicted overdose of medication. Our population may be somewhat skewed towards youngsters with malignancies and cystic fibrosis because of the large number of patients who come to the institution with these conditions. Although we are a community hospital, we are also a regional center for some specialized conditions.

The outpatient population, however, is more representative of the pathology occurring in the general community. The reputation of the institution is such that it does draw patients from a wide variety of areas in Queens and Nassau Counties of New York, in addition to significant numbers of patients from further east on Long Island (see Figure 1). We are essentially in a suburban community. Since we are a federally funded clinic we do not discriminate against any patients regardless of their income category. This includes high-income families as well as low-income ones. However, the majority of our patient population could be characterized as middle to lower middle class. Under 10 percent of our patient population would be considered upper income while under 20 percent would be low-income or medicaid-eligible (government-supported) patients.

Our clinic structure is similar to that of several other clinics throughout the country and consists of a team (see Figure 2). The clinic team includes

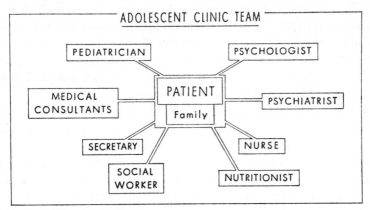

Figure 2.   Adolescent clinic team

a pediatrician, social worker, nurse, nutritionist, psychologist, psychiatrist, and other medical consultants who focus on the patient and his family. Not all members of the team are involved with each patient, but these varied services are available when needed and indicated. Each patient has his own physician during his stay in the clinic, and every effort is made to provide for continuity of this relationship. This is done by providing a nucleus of pediatricians who have been with the clinic for several years. Patients who are seen by rotating house staff officers or medical students are also introduced to one of the permanent members of the staff who then becomes the patient's primary physician when the trainee's period is completed on the service. An effort is made to make all patients known to either the nurse coordinator or social worker, as well as to the primary care physician. Although clinic hours are three afternoons weekly, it is important that adolescents have access to the clinic personnel or the institution at all times. This is done through the use of the full-time staff.

The clinic tries to provide individual physician relationships while parental support, guidance, and counseling is frequently delegated to ancillary personnel, such as the social worker. Her task also includes working with parent groups for counseling in order to provide support for those parents who are having difficulty in coping with their adolescents. In recent years, this has been a major task. Coping with teenagers seems to have become a more difficult and challenging problem for more and more families.

Approximately one-third of our patient population is seen for one or two visits by the psychiatric consultant at the pediatrician's request. Fifteen percent of our patients are seen by the psychologist for evaluation. This is often an aid to school or other referral sources and also helps to clarify cases with more complex emotional problems. The psychologist is not required to provide identical services for all patients. In an evaluation session she may elect to do short-term counseling, a full psychological inventory, or several specialized tests. The services provided are individualized.

The simultaneous availability of the team members during clinic hours allows for some immediate consultation in many areas so that the number of clinic visits for each patient can be reduced and communication maintained amongst those members of the team with a particular interest in a patient's problem. This comprehensiveness is a recognized major asset of such clinic settings. It is interesting to note that private physician referrals often occur in difficult diagnostic and management situations of adolescents, since it is recognized that in a comprehensive care facility it is easier to obtain all needed services in a less fragmented manner than would be possible from an individual private physician. Illustrative of this would be a youngster seen for short stature and poor school performance. The relationship of these complaints may be intimate or alien. However, a comprehensive adolescent clinic can seek to establish the etiology of short stature, concern itself with any learning problems the youngster is exhibiting, inquire into the family background and influences, investigate nutritional factors, and outline a treatment plan as a result of a consultation and discussion at a team meeting. The patient is able to receive all his care in one facility and may receive long-term follow-up and guidance.

It is important to note that prior to the establishment of a specific adolescent clinic within the hospital very few adolescents were seen in the outpatient department. The clinic has also aided in providing follow-up care for adolescents seen episodically in the Emergency Room and has reduced the inappropriate use of the Emergency Room by adolescents. There is a greater tendency on the part of the community to utilize the Emergency Room as a primary care facility. This inappropriate use of such services leads to episodic, fragmented care — to the ultimate detriment of the patient. The adolescent has to have a facility within the institution in which he feels comfortable, in which his needs are known and in which an attempt is made to satisfy these needs. When the adolescent feels comfortable with the source of his medical care he will seek help earlier for any significant medical conditions, and this will ultimately result in better total health for the adolescent.

It is also important to realize that adolescents need help in "negotiating the system." They seek care in many settings. This has resulted in the establishment of many free clinics, hot-lines, store-front facilities, etc. To be sure, these all have their place in the total system of delivery of health care to the adolescent. However, such facilities must have adequate back-up services available. We have recently been approached by two different community groups wishing to locate a clinic in shopping malls. These malls have become the congregating place for adolescents in suburbia. They have replaced the corner candy store of urban America as a place for socialization of teenagers. We anticipate soon becoming affiliated with one or several of these units to more effectively reach larger numbers of youngsters, by establishing outreach clinics. It is important, however, that such facilities do not consider themselves primary medical care deliverers for adolescents with the potentially serious illnesses that may be portended by common symptoms of abdominal pain, headaches, dizziness, etc. Close medical supervision and affiliation with clinics in major hospital settings are mandatory. Rap sessions, peer counseling, and groups are adjuncts to medical care, not a replacement for it.

During the academic year July 1972 through June 1973, our clinic serviced 957 patients. Of these, 579 were new to the clinic. I think it is intere sting to review the presenting problems and subsequent diagnoses of these new patients. Why do they seek care? What are their concerns? And are they unique to this group patients, or may some generalizations be made?

Table 1.   Presenting problems and subsequent diagnoses of new patients in the Adolescent Clinic, 1972–1973

ABDOMINAL PAIN   18

Abdominal epilepsy	2
Emotional problems of signifi-	
cance	3
Functional complaints	7
Peptic ulcer	3
Intestinal virus	3

ALBUMINURIA   2

ALLERGIES   30

Asthma	9
Allergic rhinitis	15
Atopic dermatitis and eczema	4
Chronic pharyngitis	2

ANEMIA   2

Iron deficiency	1
Gaucher's	1

BIRTH CONTROL PHYSICALS   13

Pathology uncovered

No pathology	4
Hyperthyroidism	1
Recurrent kidney infection	1
Trichomonas and monilia	6
Peptic ulcer	1

CHEST PAIN AND RESPIRATORY
PROBLEMS   15

Pneumonitis	2
Allergies	4
Functional complaints	5
Upper respiratory infection	4

DERMATOLOGIC DISORDERS   40

Acne	15
Eczema	6
Moniliasis	2
Psoriasis	3

Seborrhea	3
Alopecia	3
Urticaria	2
Emotional problems	6

DIABETES MELLITUS   6

FUNCTIONAL FATIGUE   6
FREQUENT COLDS AND
SORE THROATS   13

Allergies	6
Tonsillitis	4
Pharyngitis — recurrent	3

HEADACHES, DIZZY SPELLS,
WEAK SPELLS   24

Tension	5
Migraine	4
Allergies (nasal)	6
Functional	9

HEARING PROBLEMS   7

Congenital deafness	3
Ear infections	4

INFECTIOUS HEPATITIS   1

INFECTIOUS MONONUCLEOSIS   1

MULTIPLE COMPLAINTS   9

Functional complaints	3
Emotional problems	3
Multiple handicaps — retarded,	
deaf	3

NEPHRITIS   3

NOSEBLEEDS   1

OBESITY   46

ORTHOPEDIC DEFORMITIES   30

Coxa valga	1
Scoliosis	8

Chest assymetry	1
Osteopetrosis	1
Osgood-Schlatters disease	7
Sacroiliac symptoms-disc	2
Arthritis	3
Functional pain and emotional problems	6
Torn cartilage	1

PARONYCHIA 1

PARESIS — (hysterical) 2

PILONOIDAL CYST 4

PREGNANCY TESTS 92

Negative	47
Positive	45

PRIMARY PSYCHIATRIC PROBLEMS 6

Schizoid personality	2
Passive-aggressive personality	2
Psychosis	2

ROUTINE EXAMINATION 47

No significant pathology	15
Adjustment reactions	3
Brain damage — minimal brain damage	2
Depression	1
Poor school performance — underachieving	6
Visual screening	6
Obesity	6
Sickle cell trait	2
Dysmenorrhea	4
Scoliosis	2

ROUTINE GYNECOLOGY 24

Irregular menses	7
Vaginal discharge	3
Dysmenorrhea	6
Secondary amenorrhea — low carbohydrate intake	3
Secondary amenorrhea — Turner's mosaicism	2

"SCHOOL PROBLEMS" 55

Hyperactivity	7
Deficient IQ	4
Depression	1
Acting-out behavior	7
Personality disorder	8
Minimal brain damage "organicity"	19
Specific learning disability	4
Adjustment reactions	4
Postencephalitic sequelae	1

SEIZURES 8

SHORT STATURE 21

Familial or delayed adolescence	13
Concomitant emotional problems	8

THYROID AND ENDOCRINE 4

TUMORS 23

Gynecomastia	3
Cervical adenopathy	4
Warts	2
Ovarian	1
Lipoma	1
Nevi	3
Ganglion cyst	2
Keloids	3
Hernias	2
Sebaceous cyst	2

URINARY INCONTINENCE 7

Enuresis	6
Stress incontinence	1

VENEREAL DISEASE TESTING 30

Gonorrhea	2
Non specific urethritis	2
No venereal disease	26

VEGETARIANS — FOR DIET THERAPY 3

WEIGHT LOSS 3

Depression	1
Anorexia nervosa	2

Table 1 presents an analysis of presenting problems and subsequent diagnoses of new patients in the Adolescent Clinic during the past year. It is a frequent occurrence that the complaint presented may have little relevance to the subsequent diagnosis. We have made some attempt in these listings to organize various categories so that one may obtain an impression of this group of patients, rather than simply placing each patient into a specific diagnostic category. Although patients may frequently have more than one diagnosis, I have not considered secondary diagnoses to be of little clinical significance. It must be kept in mind that the patients who present themselves for medical care are already a selected group and are not necessarily characteristic of the general adolescent population, if one were to survey such a group. Our clinical experience in general is such that we tend to see a significant number of patients with severe emotional problems. It is in fact true that some of our patients have psychiatric pathology that may be covertly much more severe than may be seen in an adolescent psychiatric clinic. In the latter type of facility there has already been a recognition on the part of the patient or family that the adolescent suffers from a serious emotional disorder. In a medical-clinic population, those problems of a severe emotional nature may be somaticized and repressed to such a degree that they are overtly denied. Personnel dealing with adolescents in this setting must be cognizant of this and help adolescents and their families appreciate lack of organic pathology. This should not be construed, however, as advocating that every patient with a somaticizing illness be confronted with a diagnosis of emotional or psychiatric nature and a prescription for psychotherapy. However, it is one of our functions to work with certain patients until such time as they become more amenable to accepting this type of recommendation.

Eighteen patients were seen for abdominal pain, and the breakdown of the various reasons for such pain is given. One can see we have listed functional complaints for 7 patients and emotional problems of significance for 3 patients. These 10 patients, well over 50 percent of the total, did not have organic pathology. Abdominal pain represents a common symptom in childhood, but this is a less pervasive and more transient symptom in childhood than it is during adolescence and interferes little with total function. It is interesting to note that in an earlier review of the records of all 450 patients seen in the clinic between September 1964 and January 1966, we found that 60.7 percent of the 56 patients with headaches and abdominal pain had symptoms which were functional in origin. This figure is almost identical to our current data (Scheldkrout and Shenker 1968).

One might comment on the numbers of ulcers that we discovered, since peptic ulceration is felt to be another disease of anxiety or stress to some degree, and since it is clearly apparent that the close interrelationship between organic symptomatology and emotional pathology in this group of patients is highly significant.

Albuminurea is occasionally discovered on routine examinations for various purposes, and an occasional patient is sent in for evaluation of a laboratory finding or for a physical finding discovered on some routine examination elsewhere. It is our function, then, to evaluate these objective findings, confirm or deny them, and try to establish their etiology. In the case of albuminurea, this frequently turns out to be a condition known as orthostatic albuminurea, which is a benign, transient condition of little clinical significance.

Allergies are a frequent complaint of patients entering into the clinic. We utilize a weekly adolescent allergy clinic to treat and evaluate these patients after they are initially screened by their primary care physician. Patients in this group range from very mildly ill to the very severely ill who require ongoing therapeutic intervention by many members of the clinic team. For example, a severe asthmatic may be seen on a weekly basis for desensitization treatment, may find himself in the hospital for acute episodes, may require long-term social service support for the family, may require psychiatric and psychological evaluation and treatment, etc. This is not an uncommon occurrence for a small number of very seriously ill adolescents. Our allergist is continually impressed by the multifactorial nature of the disease and an almost uniform reluctance on the part of many youngsters to give up pets which may be a contributory factor to the production of their symptomatology.

Although iron deficiency anemia is not an uncommon occurrence in our society, the tendency for many youngsters to be influenced by advertisements for medications, vitamins, etc. may be one reason why only one patient was found to have this. Iron deficiency anemia in adolescent males is an extremely rare disease, and sources of blood loss should be sought before attributing lack of intake as an etiology. Gaucher's disease is a storage disease of congenital etiology and it is extremely rare.

The next category, birth control physicals, is worthy of comment. Thirteen patients came to us specifically for birth control devices. These do not include other patients already known to the clinic who are given birth control information during the year. It seems highly significant that of the small number of 13 patients seen, only 4 were found to be completely free of pathology. An extremely interesting girl is the one with hyperthyroidism who presented herself to the clinic because she was having sexual relations with a boyfriend and was anxious to be placed on birth control pills. It is our policy that no patient is given birth control pills or other birth control devices without a complete physical examination and basic laboratory data. On physical examination, this girl was found to have an enlarged thyroid gland, an obvious facial tremor and bulging eyes, and was clearly in a state of active hyperthyroidism. Laboratory data confirmed this diagnosis, and the patient was advised that she was not a candidate for birth control pills at this time and, more importantly, required medical or surgical intervention for her hyperthyroid condition. This patient was extremely adamant in not involving her family in her care. However, the potentially serious nature of her condition was made known to her, and after counseling and discussion the patient agreed to approach her family. The patient had previous poor experience with receiving proper medical care and sympathy from her parents, who continually stated there was nothing wrong with her and she was imagining all her ills. The patient came from a rather well-to-do family and had to connive to have her parents take her to their family physician, since she refused to tell her parents she had come to our clinic. Once in the private physician's office she was able to tell him of our findings and he readily appreciated and concurred with us. He then arranged to have this patient hospitalized. She was hospitalized in a neighboring hospital and received further diagnostic evaluation and treatment for her condition.

After discharge from the hospital this patient returned to our clinic, without her family's knowledge, because she still wished to receive birth control devices. We elected to offer this girl a diaphragm, which she accepted, and she is continuing to take antithyroid medication. This is an important patient from a learning point of view. One cannot go about providing birth control measures of one type to every patient. Every patient must be evaluated individually and her needs assessed. It is also apparent that the lack of birth control devices is rarely a hindrance to youngsters who wish to engage in sexual intercourse. It therefore seems obvious that adolescent clinics must educate and provide services of this type if unwanted adolescent pregnancies are to be prevented and abortions are to be eliminated as a method of contraception.

Acne in the adolescent population, certainly one of the traditional, almost universal, complaints of young people, should receive some comment. Here again our approach is not simply to write a prescription for medication, be it creams, ointments, or pills, etc., but to explore with the adolescent the reason he or she is having this problem, the outlook for it, and how he can best cope with it. It is often difficult to convince youngsters that what they read in popular magzines or have been told over the years is untrue. For example, there is no evidence whatsoever that diet has any relationship to the development of acne. It is interesting to note youngsters' reactions to this fact. It is also important to stress the lack of relationship of acne to such habits as masturbation.

Six new diabetics were admitted to the clinic during the year. Diabetes mellitus during adolescence is often a difficult disease to control. During the adolescent growth spurt caloric requirements increase at a rapid rate and insulin requirements vary considerably with increased caloric requirements, exercise, etc. There is often a denial of illness on the part of the teenager, which may result in his manipulating the taking of insulin for the secondary gain which the adolescent hopes to receive on a conscious or unconscious level. Fatigue, frequent colds and sore throats, headaches, dizzy spells, weak spells, etc. can be lumped into one general category in which it is frequently difficult to make a specific diagnosis. It is important however to ascertain whether or not one is dealing with a migraine syndrome since the treatment of this disorder may be directed towards its vascular etiology with specific therapy. You will note that of the 24 patients with headaches, dizzy spells, and weak spells, if one eliminates the 10 with allergies and migraine as etiology, one is left with 14 in the functional or nonorganic category, and here again the 60 percent figure is not too far wrong.

There are a few medical conditions which occur only during adolescence. These should be recognized. Patients presenting with joint pains require careful investigation. Of 19 of these, 7 were found to have Osgood-Schlatter's disease, a specific aseptic necrosis of the anterior tibial tubercle which occurs only during adolescence. Other conditions to be cognizant of during adolescence are juvenile round back or juvenile epiphysitis, slipped capital femoral epiphysis, and rheumatoid arthritis, although the latter is not limited to adolescence, but may begin during adolescence.

Forty-six patients were seen because of a chief complaint of obesity. Obesity remains a challenge and an enigma to the physician. Its etiology is varied and its treatment more so. It is a difficult problem to deal with and requires many devoted hours of care for what are often very few tangible results. During this past year, obesity represented under 10 percent of our admission complaints. However, in previous years it has run between 15 and 20 percent of the presenting patients. In other clinic settings it is often a most frequent presenting diagnosis. One could discuss obesity in the adolescent for many hours. Suffice it to say that it is a frustrating condition. We have much research information available on a theoretical level but our therapeutic modalities are limited to diet, counseling, persuasion, and nutritional guidance. The latter is the most important element in the treatment of obesity, and although its effects may not be readily appreciated, in the long term, it is possible that one can alter eating patterns for a long range beneficial result. From the physician's standpoint, the results are uniformly bad. From the nutritionist's standpoint, they are more optimistic. From the psychiatric standpoint, one may effect some changes within the personality and the patient's adaptation; however, little weight loss has occurred as a direct result of psychotherapy.

Two patients presented with hysterical paresis. This is an extremely rare phenomenon, where a partial paralysis has occurred for emotional reasons. This is a severe conversion reaction, and, although unusual, we continually see a few patients a year who present with this condition. It is frequently impossible to delineate a specific emotional event or trauma which causes this, and these patients frequently seem on the surface to be rather well-adjusted psychologically. It is felt that perhaps the emotional etiology of this condition is so painful that it is repressed subconsciously and protected from revelation. We have been able, by utilizing more superficial techniques such as suggestion and prophecy that the condition would improve, to help these patients gradually improve. These patients should be observed for a long period and one should be prepared to deal with any psychopathology that manifests itself.

Ninety-two patients presented for pregnancy tests; of these tests, about half proved positive and half negative. The patients who had negative pregnancy tests were encouraged to receive birth control counseling and medication or devices. Those with positive pregnancy tests are dealt with on an individual basis by the social worker and nurse, and a plan of treatment is decided upon. Most of these girls sought abortions and in New York State readily received them. Patients are encouraged to involve their parents in these decisions, and, although this is not always possible, it is somewhat surprising that in the majority of instances they are able to do so. Certainly, prior to the legalization of abortion in early pregnancy, medical personnel were in a difficult situation in regard to adequately helping these youngsters. As a clinic in a community voluntary hospital, we were relatively impotent in helping adolescent girls who sought abortions prior to 1971.

Of 47 patients seen for routine examinations, only 15 were found to have no significant pathology. Here again the pathology uncovered or elucidated varied. Complaints of irregular menses, vaginal discharge, dysmenorrhea, etc. are common in adolescence. School referrals numbered 55. The request for neurological evaluations is frequent to substantiate the diagnosis of minimal brain damage or organicity. By the time the youngster is in adolescence, the mode of treatment often remains rather uniform and directed toward therapy and remediation rather than drugs. We have utilized drugs such as dexedrine and ritalin for some of these adolescents with minimal results, in contrast to their often excellent results in younger children.

Thirty patients were seen for venereal disease testing. Of these, 26 were completely normal, 2 had gonorrhea and 2 had nonspecific urethritis.

In looking at the entire picture, it becomes quite obvious that although we are dealing with many organic conditions in this group of patients, at least one-half have some emotional pathology for which they require help. It is also interesting to note that we had no patients directly presenting to our clinic with a specific complaint of drug abuse, although we can elicit drug-use history in many patients. I have not specifically studied this in our clinic population this year, but two years ago we surveyed two local high schools in regard to drug use and found that about 17 percent of the student population could be considered drug abusers. The hospital maintains several specific programs for drug-abusing youngsters, and, as such, these different programs will see patients directly. We utilize these drug centers as direct referral sources, and a close liaison is maintained between our general clinic and them. The clinic provides all backup medical services for patients in the daycare drug abuse centers of which there are two. However, the patterns of drug abuse are constantly changing so that it is difficult to extrapolate even one's own data. The experience in our own day centers is that, whereas we had anticipated the centers serving about 100 patients a year, they are serving fewer patients for a longer period of time. It has become quite obvious in the last year or two that patients who are drug abusers have serious emotional pathology requiring long-term therapeutic treatment. The model of the ex-drug addict being able to treat most drug abusers is not tenable in our population.

In summary, I have presented the origins of adolescent medical care in the United States, described our clinic structure as representative of this model, and discussed the pathology seen in a group of 579 patients from essentially middle-class suburbia. The strong interrelationships between physical and emotional illness are emphasized. The concern with pregnancy, venereal disease, and birth control is a phenomenon of recent years in this group of patients.

REFERENCES

SCHELDKROUT, M., I. R. SHENKER
1968 Headaches and abdominal pains in adolescents. *Clinical Pediatrics* 7(1): 55–58.

Psychotherapy in Adolescents

JORGE G. GONZÁLEZ

Day by day, youth wishes to influence to a greater extent the orientation and development of a world which they find outdated in some respects, unstable in others. Indications of this wish are the assorted juvenile movements that have arisen in the last two decades and have progressively made themselves felt in different social fields, obliging educators, psychologists, politicians, anthropologists, and psychiatrists to reevaluate the concept of the pathological problems of adolescence.

Today we, as psychiatrists, must go outside our field to distinguish which problems are pathological and which are not. The period of adolescence is affected by a number of factors, biological, psychological, sociological, and cultural; thus, a simple definition of adolescence is impossible. Only a holistic approach will enable us to understand and to treat the adolescent.

Psychiatrists accept the fact that the adolescent period falls between the ages of twelve and twenty. It is obvious, however, that chronological age is not a valid index of development; neither is somatic growth or emotional maturity. That is why adolescence cannot be defined in purely medical or psychiatric terms. Normal adolescence does not necessarily imply tumultuous phenomenology, since many young people reach adulthood without turmoil.

Adolescent behavioral problems that have been augmented in the last few years are indisputedly influenced by social factors. These, as well as the cultural factors involved, subsume such extensive variables that it is difficult to define what is normal and what is abnormal.

In Latin America, the subject of adolescence has increasingly interested psychologists and social scientists during the last few years. More than half of the present population in the countries belonging to the Third World is under twenty years of age. The thinking and activities of young people are more and more taken into account in our changing, unstable, and unequal world. Such collective phenomena as the adoption of repressed behavior, unusual and bizarre patterns of social and sexual modes, the use of hallucinogens and other drugs, and individual and group violence have been identified, almost invariably, with the youth.

The Latin American adolescent has to contend with a double disadvantage: he not only finds himself on the borderline between childhood and adult life, but he is also affected by the disturbing circumstances that characterize the developing societies. For him, the minimal conditions for survival are sometimes barely present.

Studies attempting to clarify the pathology and therapy of the psychosocial disorders affecting Latin American adolescence are few. In psychiatry there are many different approaches to adolescence: psychological theories alone number at least eight, psychodynamic theories more than five.

The points of reference from which I focus upon the psychotherapy of adolescence are two: psychoanalysis and child psychiatry. Historically, psychoanalysis concerns neurotic adults and views patients of all ages in terms of an established personality structure and the fundamental aspects of childhood. Psychoanalysis uses techniques designed to modify the personality structure and not merely to deal with specific symptoms. The treatment is based on the knowledge of one's self.

Child psychiatry begins with the child as the center of attention and focuses on the nature of his growth and development from childhood to adulthood. Child psychiatry notes the special dependence of the child on parental care. It examines the internal and external factors that influence his growth. The treatment is directed toward what the individual is capable of doing. The parents are used as part of the therapeutic process, since the goal is to aid in the development of the child. In other words, child psychiatry strives to help the child to achieve maturity at all stages of development.

I consider Anna Freud's definition of adolescence to be the most accurate in conveying the enigma and paradox of the adolescent process:

Adolescents are excessively egoistic, regarding themselves as the center of the universe and the sole object of interest, and yet at no time in later life are they capable of so much self-sacrifice and devotion. They form the most passionate love relations, only to break them off as abruptly as they began them. On the one hand, they throw themselves enthusiastically into the life of the community and, on the other, they have an overpowering longing for solitude. They oscillate between blind submission to some self-chosen leader and defiant rebellion against any and every authority (Freud 1968).

In addition, adolescents are selfish and oriented toward materialism at the same time that they are tremendously idealistic. They may be aesthetic at times, yet they are capable of expressing the most primitive instincts without control. They display wide variations in outlook, ranging from optimism to extreme pessimism. On some occasions they will work diligently and enthusiastically, while at other times they are apathetic and lazy.

In the technical application of psychotherapy during adolescence some basic concepts and trends may be observed: the flexibility of the approach, with special focus on the actual problems; the STRENGTHEN-ING of the ego; the decreasing emphasis on the psychodynamic analysis of the biographical past, due to its therapeutic unproductiveness; a stimulus toward the development of objective criteria, stable and substantial, allowing an effective management of the real situation; a comprehension of new realities determined by the changes that accompany sexual maturity; a shorter duration in therapy than in the case of adults. A dynamic, economical, psychogenetic, and adaptive comprehension is necessary on the part of the therapist, as well as an awareness of the role assigned to him.

While it is not necessary to stress here the details of the therapeutic process, it is important to point out that the psychotherapy of adolescence is an arduous and passionate undertaking which requires time, patience, and even a personal gift. It is highly motivating and demands a fundamental respect for the adolescent and a constant control of the mechanism of countertransference. Most important, the existing difficulties in the diagnosis of problems and in the therapeutic approaches to psychotherapy in the adolescent require that we, as psychiatrists, enlist the support of anthropologists in clarifying what is and what is not pathological in the youth of today. We must develop new techniques for the understanding and treatment of the young in a world which is changing at a pace that defies adaptation.

REFERENCES

BALSER, B. H.
  1960 *Psicoterapía del adolescentes.* Buenos Aires: Ediciones Horme.
COBOS, F.
  1970 *Psiquiatría infantil.* Colombia: Imprenta Nacional.

CORREAL, G.
1972 "Adolescencia y sociedad." Paper read at the XII Congreso Nacional de Psiquiatría, Cali, Colombia.

FREUD, A.
1968 *The ego and the mechanisms of defence* (revised edition). London: Hogarth Press.

GARCIA, H.
1972 "Hospitalización en psiquiatría." Ponencia Official, XII Congreso Nacional de Psiquiatría, Cali, Colombia.

JOSSELYN, J. M.
1952 *The adolescent and his world*. New York: Family Service Association of America.

LEON, C. A.
1956 Psicoterapía adaptiva. *Revista Colombiana de Psiquiatría* 7(4).

MARTINE, A.
1966 Las psicoterapías. *Revista Colombiana de Psiquiatría* 6. *Manual Diagnóstico y Estadístico de Trastornos Mentales*. Translation of *Diagnostic and statistical manual of mental disorders* (second edition) of the American Psychiatric Association. Buenos Aires: Acta.

MAY, A. R., J. H. KAHN, HOLIN. B. CRONH
1971 *Mental health of adolescents and young persons*. Geneva: World Health Congress.

MONTANO, H.
1972 "Estudio nosologico predominante en una muestra del Instituto Colombiano del Sistema Marvioso, Clinica Monserrat." Paper read at the XII Congreso Nacional de Psiquiatría, Cali, Colombia.

POLATIN
1966 *A guide to treatment in psychiatry*. Philadelphia, Montreal: J. B. Lippincott.

ROSSELLI, H.
1969 Psicoterapía — alcances y limitaciones. *Revista Colombiana de Psiquiatría* 6.

WARREN, W.
1971 "The psychiatry of adolescents," in *Modern perspectives in child psychiatry*. Edited by J. G. Howells. New York: Bruner Mazel.

WEYNER, J. B.
1970 *Psychotherapy, psychological disturbances in adolescence*. New York: John Wiley and Sons.

Transcultural Aspects of Mental Illness Among Puerto Rican Adolescents in New York

MARIO RENDON

For several decades the migration of Puerto Ricans to the United States has been increasing. If we add Puerto Ricans by birth and by parentage, the total for 1960 was 892,513. Almost three-quarters (72 percent) were in New York State; of those in New York State, 95 percent were in New York City. It has been reported that during the last decade this migration has reversed itself: a growing number of Puerto Ricans are returning to their homeland. Also, there has been increasing dispersal from New York State. Although the significance of these last trends remains to be established, it is encouraging: Puerto Ricans pay a high price for their transculturation in terms of mental health.

Malzberg (1956, 1965) has shown that Puerto Ricans in New York State show an unusually high incidence of mental disease, as measured by hospitalization rates. This observation seems to have been corroborated by the Midtown Manhattan Study (Srole, et al. 1962). Here I examine this phenomenon as seen in the Puerto Rican adolescent in New York.[1]

In 1960, 46.3 percent of the Puerto Rican population in New York was under twenty years of age. The corresponding number for non-Puerto Ricans was 33.6 percent. The Puerto Rican population of New York continues to include a large percentage of young people. This reflects the fact that birthrates are much higher in Puerto Rico, and, therefore, families come to New York with more children. Thus, the Puerto Ricans are a group with relatively more children and adolescents than

---

[1] Fitzpatrick and Gould (n.d.) have already suggested that this may be due to an intercultural misunderstanding.

the rest of the population of New York. This age composition of the Puerto Rican population affects the economic structure of the group: a smaller segment of the population is economically productive, adding to the characteristic illiteracy, crowding, and poverty.

Although in 1960 Puerto Ricans constituted only 3.8 percent of the total population of New York, they accounted for 4.5 percent of all first admissions to all mental hospitals; of the first admissions diagnosed as schizophrenic, the Puerto Ricans accounted for 8.3 percent. Table 1 presents some of the characteristics of this tendency of Puerto Ricans to suffer from mental illness. As we can see from the average annual standardized rates per 100,000, nonwhite Puerto Ricans are most likely to be hospitalized (611.4). United States-born Puerto Ricans (320.9) are more likely to be hospitalized than the Puerto-Rican-born (221.1). And males (287.0) are more vulnerable than females (192.9).

The age composition of the mentally ill Puerto Rican group is shown in Table 2. Those over seventy rank first, presumably because of organic and senile diseases. After the aged, adolescents are the next most vulnerable. In average annual rate of admissions, late adolescents (ages fifteen to nineteen) outrank any other age group up to age seventy. Their rate per 100,000 (279.8) is more than double that of the corresponding group of non-Puerto Rican adolescents (113.0). In contrast, the non-Puerto Rican adolescents have the lowest rate of all non-Puerto Rican age groups except children under fifteen. This

Table 1. Mental illness in New York State among Puerto Ricans, non-Puerto Ricans, and Puerto Rican subgroups, 1960–1961 (source: Malzberg 1965)

	Average annual standardized rate (per 100,000)
Mental illness among:	
Puerto Ricans	239.0
non-Puerto Ricans	184.1
Puerto Rican males	287.0
Puerto Rican females	192.9
white Puerto Ricans	225.2
nonwhite Puerto Ricans	611.4
Puerto Rican-born Puerto Ricans*	221.1
United States-born Puerto Ricans*	320.9
non-Puerto Rican nonwhites	312.4
Schizophrenia among:	
Puerto Ricans	95.3
non-Puerto Ricans	50.0

* Ages fifteen to forty-four only.

Table 2. First admissions to all hospitals for mental disease in New York State, 1960–1961, classified according to age and origin (source: Malzberg 1965)

Age (years)	Of Puerto Rican birth or parentage					Of non-Puerto Rican origin				
			Total		Average annual rate (per 100,000)			Total		Average annual rate (per 100,000)
	Males	Females	Number	Per cent		Males	Females	Number	Per cent	
under 15	199	54	253	12.0	52.5	958	332	1,290	2.9	14.7
15–19	201	118	319	15.1	279.8	1,350	992	2,342	5.2	113.0
20–24	207	124	331	15.7	259.9	1,612	1,303	2,915	6.5	167.4
25–29	178	115	293	13.9	222.4	1,666	1,651	3,317	7.4	173.1
30–34	156	108	264	12.5	231.7	1,697	1,889	3,586	8.0	162.0
35–39	119	82	201	9.5	223.0	1,745	1,862	3,607	8.1	154.4
40–44	66	54	120	5.7	188.4	1,552	1,731	3,283	7.3	147.2
45–49	42	36	78	3.7	148.0	1,402	1,582	2,984	6.7	136.8
50–54	31	23	54	2.6	149.2	1,354	1,456	2,810	6.3	133.3
55–59	27	29	56	2.7	198.4	1,312	1,346	2,658	5.9	144.7
60–64	18	22	40	1.9	208.6	1,249	1,246	2,495	5.6	156.2
65–69	13	9	22	1.0	183.9	1,294	1,408	2,702	6.0	202.9
70–74	14	12	26	1.2	344.9	1,438	1,546	2,984	6.7	306.6
75 and over	18	35	53	2.5	757.1	3,240	4,545	7,785	17.4	745.8
Total	1,289	821	2,110	100.0	164.2	21,869	22,839	44,758	100.0	138.7

is intriguing: why are Puerto Rican adolescents most vulnerable, while non-Puerto Rican adolescents are least vulnerable to mental disease, as measured by hospitalization? What makes the Puerto Rican adolescent more prone to mental illness and hospitalization?

Schizophrenia is the most frequently diagnosed mental disease, particularly among Puerto Ricans. Puerto Rican admissions with a diagnosis of schizophrenia are 31.9 percent of all admissions; non-Puerto Rican are 27.0 percent. According to Malzberg (1965), Puerto Ricans exceed their expected quota by 118 percent, whereas the number among non-Puerto Ricans is significantly lower than expected. Insofar as age is concerned, schizophrenia appears predominantly between fifteen and forty-four; thus, it starts in late adolescence. Again, there is a remarkable contrast between Puerto Ricans and non-Puerto Ricans.

How can we understand these abnormally high rates among Puerto Ricans as compared with other groups in New York? In attempting to account for the difference, there are many factors to consider. Puerto Ricans come to New York because they are in distress. They think ahead to the economic possibilities that the metropolis offers them. They dream of abundance, freedom, and a new life. When they reach New York, they find themselves at the bottom of the socio-economic structure. Very often they face the disintegration of their cultural values. Both poverty and migration have been shown to be directly related to the incidence of mental disease (Hollingshead and Redlich 1958; Degaard 1932). Moreover, it is known that social class often influences the diagnosis, the kind of treatment, and, therefore, the prognosis of any disease (Mishler and Scotch 1963; Carkhuff and Pierce 1967).

Language, an important ego function, is a source of stress for the Puerto Rican. Often the children arrive in the States without any command of English, and they are placed in a school that functions in English. How such children manage to survive this situation is remarkable. A frequent phenomenon among Puerto Rican families is the bilingual family in which the children and their parents converse in two different languages: parents address the children in Spanish; the children answer in English. That children adapt to the language and habits of the new culture faster than their parents has many psychological implications. Among other things, it may reinforce their questioning of the authority of the parents.

The Puerto Rican family is structured differently from the U.S. family. The Puerto Rican family is an extended family with strong ties, in which several generations may share one household and live closely together; the American family is nuclear. In the Puerto Rican family the children often stay at home until they get married; in the American family adolescents often leave for college or jobs. The Puerto Rican family is strongly complementary in its roles, and more patriarchal, in the sense that the man has more authority and more privilege; the American family is more symmetrical in its roles, with a tendency for greater equality for the mother and children. The fact that American women more often work, and that education is more available, seems to account for this. That the Puerto Rican children become more adapted to the new culture than their parents often makes their parents dependent on them, especially for contacts in the outside community. This role reversal may take place when the child is quite young and may burden the child with the responsibility for mothering the uprooted parents. The child's natural tendency for growth and separation-individuation may threaten the parents' roles. This conflict involves the child's assumption of roles and values that are alien to the parents' tradition and the old culture.

Aggressiveness is valued in American culture. In order to survive in New York City, a person must be competitive and aggressive. "Be aggressive," often the motto of American parents, reflects a socio-economic structure based on competition and "free enterprise." This core value of American society runs counter to the main Puerto Rican family principle, *respeto* [respect, reverence, regard, consideration]. This conflict of values may be expressed as expansiveness versus self-effacement, an inner conflict for the adolescent groping towards his identity (Horney 1950).

Sexuality is another area of value conflict which is culturally determined. Virginity at marriage is still preached in the Puerto Rican family. Many adolescent Puerto Rican girls make sure during the first interview to tell us that they are virgins. Some are very proud of it. In some of these families chaperons are still an institution to ensure that the growing girls are closely watched. Some Puerto Rican mothers check the sanitary napkins of the adolescent girl every month for evidence of nonpregnancy. The mother's worry, of course, sometimes has a paradoxical effect since it often involves a double message in which the latent content is much stronger than the manifest one. While the parents worry at home, the adolescents get an opposite message from their peers and the outside culture, in which early sexual experimentation is frequent and there is free access to contraception. This cultural conflict adds another burden to the natural generational conflict of Puerto Rican adolescents.

How do Puerto Rican adolescents deal with these conflicts? Is there a style determined by their culture? Can this be discerned in the way they respond to this compounded stress?

To achieve a sense of identity — the main task of adolescence — is difficult when opposite, sometimes antagonistic sets of roles and values are at work, when what is praised at home is not regarded in the same way outside the home. Although this is true for all adolescents, it is compounded when the gap is widened by cultural factors, as in this case. Thus, Puerto Rican adolescents in New York are under greater stress than other adolescents, and this may partially explain their vulnerability to mental disease.

The Puerto Rican adolescent responds to this conflict predominantly with a typical defense mechanism: dissociation. In my experience, dissociation is common among Puerto Rican adolescents. Although I think that dissociation is more frequent among adolescents in general than among adults, Puerto Rican adolescents dissociate as a matter of culturally determined style.

In a way, dissociation is a phenomenon common to all mental disease, but there are two main syndromes in which dissociation is paramount: schizophrenia and hysteria. Distinguishing between the two in diagnosis, as stated by Bleuler (1950), is often very difficult. There are, however, some features that can help. In hysteria, dissociation has the following characteristics: it is total, useful, and socially learned — often validated by others and sometimes shared. The dissociative episode is total: often it entails a complete, lengthy, dramatic happening, entirely dissociated from consciousness and often covered by amnesia. In schizophrenia, the dissociation is partial: perception, motor activity, thinking, affect, do not correspond. There is also fragmentation of thinking, fragmentation of affect, etc. The flatness or narrowing of affect in schizophrenia has to be differentiated from the histrionic indifference of hysteria. Hallucinations in dissociative hysteria patients are usually visual, while in schizophrenics auditory hallucinations predominate.

A second characteristic of hysterical dissociation is its usefulness: the dissociative episode occurs when there is an overwhelming situation or task at hand, when strong emotions are involved in the areas of aggressiveness and sexuality. Many Puerto Rican boys go into a dissociative episode when they have to fight, while many of the girls have their sexual experiences within a dissociative episode. These tasks are sometimes difficult, and they require a degree of mastery of the motor apparatus, as well as coordination with other areas of behavior. Hysterical patients seem to use their dissociation in many ways. There are also many degrees of dissociation, starting with what appears as simple lying (pseudologia fantastica).

When I say that hysterical dissociation is socially learned, I mean that dissociation is usually an incorporated family pattern. Parents or their close relatives give a history of similar episodes; they also validate the patient's behavior or experience and confirm the patient's explanations of it. Sometimes it is difficult to ascertain who is the source of the story, as if the other person (relative, friend, witness) had induced the patient into the dissociative experience or *vice versa*. Hysterics are most vulnerable, and their hallucinations often seem to be shared by others.

Luz, a thirteen-year-old Puerto Rican girl was admitted because she had "a history of hallucinations." Upon admission, a diagnosis of schizophrenia was considered. Luz reported that she had been seeing the same tall and faceless woman, with long hair, a floor-length white dress, and a bouquet of flowers in her hands, who came to her repeatedly during the last two years. On one occasion the woman was limping, and on that same night Luz's grandmother had a stroke. Lately the woman had told Luz to kill herself. Just prior to admission, Luz had been found climbing the fence of a monument in a park, which was interpreted by Luz's friends as suicidal. A few hours earlier Luz had been reprimanded by her mother because she had accepted a gift from a certain boy. Luz's mother had known about Luz's "visions," but they did not concern her because Luz's grandmother and a female cousin had also seen the same woman. The father himself, the mother said, had seen "shadows."

Luz was a good, quiet girl at home; the parents had been concerned about her lately only because she seemed to be involved with a boy. This boy was said to be a member of a gang and to have connections with "junkies." The parents feared that Luz would "get married" too young (her mother had married Luz's father at the age of fourteen). To other adolescents in the hospital ward, Luz had said that she was planning to sleep with five boys in order to become a leader in her gang.

Behavior which to us appears bizarre and which, therefore, becomes decisive for the diagnosis, may be the outcome of ethnic peculiarities or of a specific attitude towards life. For example, the actions of hysterics who come from the Far Eastern countries sometimes appear as bizarre to us as the schizophrenics of our own country! (Bleuler 1950).

Bustamante (1968) has studied and described examples of schizophrenia-like hysteria in Cuba. It is very likely that the anthropological facts which, according to him, explain these syndromes, apply also to Puerto Rico and other Caribbean countries. He states that because of the intermixed religious background of the Spanish conquerors and African slaves, which led to a syncretic religious form called *santeria*, there is a socially accepted mixture of logical thinking in everyday life and magical thinking in religious practices. He has seen cases of hysteria or dissociative reactions with schizophrenic aspects that have been acute and short in duration and that have been described in Brazil, although there they have been diagnosed as schizophrenia.

Although the *espiritismo* [spiritism] of the Puerto Ricans in New York has not to my knowledge been fully studied, in my experience it lends itself to a considerable degree of magical thinking. Especially, it gives explanation and rationale to many dissociative episodes. It is my hypothesis, as I conclude this paper, that the incidence of schizophrenia among Puerto Ricans appears high partly because of lack of understanding of cultural phenomena. I submit (and this remains to be tested) that many hysterical dissociative episodes, especially among adolescent Puerto Ricans, have been misdiagnosed as schizophrenia.

SUMMARY

Epidemiological studies indicate that mental illness is quite high among Puerto Ricans in New York. Following older people with senile diseases, adolescents are the most widely affected group. This is in contrast with the relatively low incidence of mental illness among non-Puerto Rican adolescents. Besides poverty, crowding, illiteracy, lack of skill for qualified jobs, and other sources of stress, transculturation seems to explain this situation somewhat.

The transculturation of Puerto Ricans to New York involves learning a different language and adjusting to different roles and values. The structure of the family in New York differs from that prevalent in Puerto Rico. The two cultures follow opposite patterns in dealing with aggression and sexuality. This has particular significance for the Puerto Rican adolescent in his task of identity formation. Dissociation is the predominant defense in dealing with those conflicts, and dissociative phenomena may be misdiagnosed as schizophrenia because of lack of understanding of cultural differences.

REFERENCES

BLEULER, E.
　1950　*Dementia praecox of the group of schizophrenics.* New York: International University Press.

BUSTAMANTE, J. A.
　1968　Cultural factors in hysterics with schizophrenic clinical picture. *International Journal of Social Psychiatry* 14(2):113–118.

CARKHUFF, R. R., R. PIERCE
　1967　Differential effects of therapist race and social class upon patient depth of self-exploration in the initial clinical interview. *Journal of Consulting Psychology* 31:632–634.

DEGAARD, O.
　1932　Emigaion and insanity. *Acta Psychiatrica Neurologica* 4: Supplement 4.

FITZPATRICK, J. P., R. E. GOULD
　n.d.　"Mental illness among Puerto Ricans in New York: cultural condition or intercultural misunderstanding?" Task force paper prepared for the Joint Commission on Mental Health for Children, Chevy Chase, Maryland.

HOLLINGSHEAD, A. B., F. C. REDLICH
　1958　*Social class and mental illness.* New York: Wiley.

HORNEY, K.
　1950　*Neurosis and human growth.* New York: Norton.

MALZBERG, S.
　1956　Mental disease among Puerto Ricans in New York City, 1949–1951. *Journal of Nervous and Mental Disease* 123:262–269.

　1965　*Mental diseases among the Puerto Rican population of New York State, 1960–1961.* Albany, New York: Research Foundation for Mental Hygiene, Incorporated.

MISHLER, E. G., N. A. SCOTCH
　1963　Sociocultural factors in the epidemiology of schizophrenia. *Psychiatry* 26:315–351.

SROLE, L., T. S. LANGER, S. T. MICHAEL, M. K. OPLER, T. A. C. RENNIE
　1962　*Mental health in the metropolis. The Midtown Manhattan Study.* New York: McGraw-Hill.

PART TWO

The Cultural Context

Several Selves and Many Homes: Black Youth's Adaptation to Geographical and Cultural Mobility

EDWARD J. ECKENFELS

INTRODUCTION: ACTION RESEARCH IN THE RURAL SOUTH

For full-scale research projects to be truly successful in the black community, a new tradition of action research must be created which combines scientific rigor with community values as a method for community improvement. Such an approach was employed in conducting the Holmes County Health Research Project. Based on the premise that research is a process whereby the professional consultants and the local staff jointly discover how and what to learn (Friedlander 1970), sound working relationships were established early and impersonalization and detachment were avoided when dealing with subjects. The professionals taught the supervisors specific technical skills for training the local staff. Staff supervisory personnel, in turn, oriented the professionals to the staff's expectations and needs. Adequate time was taken to recast the research protocol in the framework of cultural values and local customs. The expertise of community residents was used at every stage of the research design and proved to be particularly valuable.

Since 1969 I have served as consultant to the Holmes County Health Research Project of the Milton Olive III Memorial Corporation, which has been investigating the biosocial correlates of intense out-migration in an impoverished, primarily rural, black community. The Milton Olive III Memorial Corporation, an organizational spinoff from the

Grant CH–00438–01, National Center for Health Research and Development, HEW (Principal Investigator, Mrs. Bernice Montgomery; Program Director, Mr. Eddie W. Logan).

civil rights movement and the Holmes County Freedom Democratic Party, is a nonprofit community corporation made up of representatives elected from the black communities of Holmes County, Mississippi.

This research grant is unique in that a community corporation is the grantee, with all operating responsibilities including financial control; a local leader rather than a visiting scientist is the principal investigator; all research, with the exception of a few tasks requiring specialized clinical expertise, is done by a staff of local community people; and a network of professional, unpaid consultants drawn from several academic and medical institutions (especially the University of Illinois, its medical school, and Rush Presbyterian-St. Luke's Medical Center in Chicago) committed themselves to the responsibility for staff training, research design, monitoring, analysis, and evaluation. The research emphasis on careful documentation of the current health problems of the black community and their relation to the demographic, cultural, and geographic features of the community was designed to lead to innovative health-care programs, the evaluation of which will be the topic for continuing research efforts.

As a consultant for social research, I participated in the training of the field staff and in the monitoring of their actions in a number of community-wide surveys, including a comprehensive household census of the black population and an investigation of their patterns of health utilization. In that capacity, I also worked closely with a small group of black youths, trying to find black residents of Holmes County who had migrated to Chicago. In all of these undertakings, I functioned not only as a data collector but as a participant observer immersed in the culture under study. It is on this combination of action research, data collection, observation, and personal involvement that this paper on the black adolescent in Holmes County is based.

The raw data were taken from my many conversations with black adolescents, which I have tried to relate to the everyday world in which they live.[1] Recollections of individuals responding to their environment over time and at different stages in their life span can produce human history that may illuminate an inquiry into the human response to

---

[1]   In his classic work, *Children in crisis* (1964), Robert Coles used what he called a clinical approach to finding out how people manage under stress and dangerous circumstances. Coles was not referring to a professional-client relationship, but rather to a simple and direct relationship in which the participant observer gets to know the human side of the people he is conversing with. Coles believed that in order to understand their humanness and see it in its everyday relationship to the world, it was necessary to bind the known and the seen in a sensible and tolerant conceptual system. In this sense, this report can be considered clinical.

social change. It is in this tradition and for these purposes that this presentation was undertaken. Let me begin with a brief demographic profile of the black community of Holmes County, Mississippi, followed by my account of experiences common to black adolescents, and concluding with a discussion of how identity is formed and shaped during this period of their lives.

A DEMOGRAPHIC SKETCH OF THE BLACK COMMUNITY OF HOLMES COUNTY, MISSISSIPPI

Holmes County is located in the central portion of Mississippi, around seventy-five miles north and slightly east of Jackson. It consists of a rather large geographical area, about 1,200 square miles. About one-fifth of this land is flat, rich delta soil and the rest is poor, eroded hill land. Holmes is a very rural county, with less than 20 percent of its inhabitants living in small towns and urban communities. Lexington and Durand are the only urban areas, with populations slightly more than 2,500 each. Lexington is the county seat, but Durant is the scheduled stop of the Illinois Central Railroad, a major artery to the urban North, especially Chicago. The county is predominantly agricultural, with cotton still the main crop; the delta section of the county is best characterized by its large cotton plantations. The increased mechanization of farming operations over the past twenty years has resulted in immense changes in the utilization of farm labor.

Our own comprehensive census of the black population (Shimkin and Rice 1971), undertaken just prior to the official 1970 United States Census, illustrates quite dramatically that the vast majority of these blacks live in a condition of grave social and economic deprivation. Some of the major findings may be stated as follows:

As of January, 1970, the black population of Holmes County was about 18,100, or 7 percent less than the 1960 population. The average household size was either four or five persons. About 54 percent of the population was female. The median age was between seventeen and eighteen, with 28 percent of the total population nine years of age or younger. Slightly more than 3,000 individuals, around 16 percent, were in their teens. This was broadly the same composition by age and sex as in 1960, but with a greatly intensified scarcity of men aged thirty to forty-nine because of heavy net out-migration.

Only two-thirds of all households consisted of husband-wife families. Nonetheless, almost half the families, both husband-wife and female-headed, were of the extended type. Yet nearly half the households, including 40 percent of the population, had no employed member.

The black population of Holmes County has been subject to intense migration since 1960: an exodus of some 6,000 persons, almost a third of the population, and a migration into the county of only about 1,500 persons. The out-migrants have been predominantly young workers, while children and the aged have predominated among in-migrants.

Despite increases in skill levels, only a third of the labor force of some 4,250 persons is fully employed in winter, about half in summer. The best educated, especially young women, have the poorest job opportunities. The median income for black families in 1970, according to the United States Census, was less than $ 1,000 annually.

About 4,500 persons, aged sixteen to seventy-four, are not in the labor force, including about 1,300 persons too disabled or sick to work. Almost a quarter of the entire population, aged thirty to forty-nine (the years of major family and social responsibility) are in this category. The effects of such disability and chronic illness on the intensification of poverty must be profound.

Adolescents make up about 18 percent of the total population and are one of the major groups of returning migrants. The average black Holmes Countian is of high school age. The very young median age of the population adds to the importance of black youth for the growth and development of their community.

MOBILITY AND STABILITY

Migration among members of minority groups is often considered to have an extremely disruptive effect on individuals' links with family, friends, and historical roots, to the point of behavioral disorganization (Brody 1968). In Holmes County it is not unusual to find that before black youths are out of their teens, they have lived in both the rural South and urban North; they have been in households in which they had both male and female authority figures; they have associated with the ghetto street-society, school-oriented children, and sharecroppers; and they have attended both segregated and desegrated schools. Despite all of this movement, one finds a sense of stability maintained for them through strong personal ties, emotional support, and intervention in times of crisis by an extended family network.

I would like to demonstrate the outcome of this mobility in three important settings: the household, the school, and the peer group, and show how each affects the personal growth and development of these youths with respect to their adaptation to the cultural stress of being black in this society.[2]

Households

It is not unusual for these young people to have experienced more than one stable family situation before they are out of high school. Let me illustrate what I mean by presenting an amalgam of experiences which form one pattern.

To begin with, an individual is quite often born into an extended family which provides him with a very sound, solid, social structure. He may be the third generation living in such a household on family-owned land. Before the child reaches school age, however, the father may feel he needs to go to Chicago to find work, planning to have his wife and children follow him after he gets a job.

When the mother and children arrive in Chicago, they often find they have to move a lot since the father, who is usually an unskilled worker, has little job security and is forced to change jobs frequently. Almost out of desperation, the mother must find a place where she can establish a more permanent household; and if she is at all fortunate, she may be able to get into the public housing projects. By this time, although the father is normally outside the family structure, he continues to provide money and maintains the hope that he will eventually be able to reunite his family. Very often, when the children reach the age of puberty, their mother begins to worry about their future and considers sending them back to Holmes County to live with their grandparents, aunts and uncles, or even friends.

One case I am familiar with follows this pattern quite closely. By the time James was ready to graduate from high school, he had experienced three very stable family situations. He was born and spent his early childhood on his grandfather's farm in the delta. During these early years, he was a member of a very large and close extended family. Before he was of school age, his father moved to Chicago to find work and his mother soon followed with James and his younger brothers and

---

[2]   Time constraints did not permit us the opportunity to investigate in any meaningful way the extremely important role religion plays in the lives of black people, especially those who are born and raised in the rural South. The significance of religion in shaping the identities of black Americans is well documented, but because it is a sensitive area of inquiry, we decided that the careful attention and detailed analysis that would be required should be the subject of another study.

sisters. In spite of difficult struggles, his mother kept her five children with her during all of her many moves within the city, and they experienced some of the excitement of the big city under her protection.

Shortly before James was ready to start high school, his grandmother died, and his mother was worried about how her father would manage the farm. But she was also concerned about the influences she felt the city was having on her son, and so she sent him back to Mississippi to live with his grandfather and his two maternal uncles, who were both close to him in age. At twelve he moved into a third family structure — an all-male, adult-oriented household which marked, for him, the end of his childhood.

By the time James reached adolescence, he had developed deep roots in two distinct but highly complementary households: one, the emotionally supportive and vital home of his mother in Chicago; the other, the quiet, hardworking environment of his grandfather's farm in Mississippi.

In many instances, having separate but related households has been advantageous for these youths born in rural poverty. Through this family network, they gain the variety of experiences that urban life can provide; but they also gain a sense of permanence by returning to the rural family scene they knew in their earliest years. The complementary quality of these two socialization processes has had the effect of enlarging their sense of identification and thereby improving their ability to cope with the stresses they encounter in later years.

Schools

Black adolescents from Holmes County who live in Chicago during their elementary school years usually attend many different schools. Occasionally, it may happen that they attend a desegregated school. But one adolescent told me that he found "integration" a very negative experience because there was blatant racism demonstrated by those in charge. And territorial boundaries were strictly laid out; contact with white children was artificial and generally unrewarding. I had the impression that, for this youngster, being in a desegregated school served only to curtail his freedom.

The high-school system for blacks in Holmes County plays an extremely important role in shaping adolescent aspirations. To begin with, there are actually two educational alternatives for black high-school students in Holmes County. Besides the public high schools, which, to all intents and purposes, are all black (the white community has dealt with school desegregation by withdrawing from the public school system and establishing its own academies), there is a privately owned, church-sponsored academy that is an elementary school, a high school, and a junior college. It is a special school for many reasons. It has a campus, dress code, boarding facilities, college preparatory courses as part of its high school curriculum, and a faculty shared by the high school and junior college. In the eyes of some educated blacks in the area, it offers the best education available to black students. But it is also the school where flunk outs and pregnant girls from the public school are sent, along with other students classified as special disciplinary problems. Therefore, in the view of some community residents, it is less a school than a kind of reformatory for misfits and drop outs.

If one compares the educational climate at the private school with that of the public school, one finds that the private school is more disciplined because of its strict behavior policies and strong religious norms as well as its greater supervisory control. Nevertheless, the private school seems to provide a more open learning environment, for it does not have to abide by the public school requirements regarding examination and promotion. Moreover, there is a greater opportunity for more individualized education at the private school, because the classes are smaller and very often taught by teachers who are of junior college caliber.

In the past, this private academy was the only black alternative to an essentially repressive public school system. As a private school, it did not have to abide by the rules and regulations imposed on blacks by the public school system. These regulations are the kind that made staying in school very difficult for blacks and, conversely, made forcing them out of the educational system and into the unskilled labor market very easy.

The situation at the public schools, however, seems to have improved rapidly in recent years. Now the public schools are literally in the hands of black administrators and teachers, who are taking the initiative to improve the overall educational environment. Furthermore, this situation has been facilitated by the students themselves, who have become more critical and vocal about the education they are receiving. With the changing atmosphere at the public schools, it is hard to determine which educational experience is more fruitful for black students.

Holmes County youths change schools more often when they are in Chicago than they do in Mississippi. But when a black teenager returns to Holmes County, he finds an educational opportunity with new meaning, because the high school system, both public and private, has become revitalized and highly motivated toward student achievement. Mothers who send their children back to Holmes County to avoid the dangers of adolescence in the city no longer have to sacrifice educational quality to do so.

Peer Groups

No discussion of adolescence can go very far without some reference to the critical role that peer groups play. As mentioned previously, a major concern of mothers who migrated to Chicago is the possibility that their children, especially the males, will become active participants in the street corner society of gangs, drugs, and crime. Our census demonstrated that the two largest groups of migrants returning to Holmes County were elderly people, primarily retired adult males, and young teenagers.

The common concern seems to be that, if it is at all possible, the children should be taken away and freed from the ghetto at least by the time they approach adolescence. But even after they return to Mississippi, the usual pattern is that they go back to Chicago for extended visits or entire summers. Hardly a black child grows up in Holmes County without spending some of his childhood years in Chicago and his adolescent years back in the South, with regular and occasionally protracted visits with his family in the North.

During their summers, these Holmes County youths acquire a certain sophistication in the city and return to Mississippi at the end of the summer with a strong individual awareness of urban lifestyle. The image of the docile, apathetic plantation youth is certainly not warranted in Holmes County. My impression of black teenagers is that they tend to be very up-to-date with respect to modern fads and fashions, subject only to the limitations of their economic situation.

These black youngsters are also comfortable in rural Mississippi, where they actually participate or feel free to associate with a variety of peer groups. By and large, these peer associations are dictated by the school situation and community of residence. I have observed a college-oriented crowd at both private and public schools. My impression, however, is that these groups are not as cliquish as those in white middle-class high schools because there is no residential community for maintaining or reinforcing these values outside of the family structure.

But on the small farms in the delta, there is a small number of teenagers, the children of sharecroppers, who have never left the county and who, because of economic deprivation, never finish high school. They follow the same living patterns as their parents and older brothers and sisters, picking cotton in the fields and doing other farm chores. Occasionally, they leave for the North, but their social deprivation is already too great to be overcome.

It is common, however, for the more mobile delta teenagers to be close friends with the sharecroppers' children, despite the extraordinary differences in their past experiences and their present goals. I know of one student at the private high school who associated freely with adolescent farm workers on the weekend when he was back in his local delta community. This individual, like so many other black adolescents I have met in Holmes County, demonstrated a magnificent ability to form attachments among a wide-ranging group of peers.

Adolescent behavior for many blacks in Holmes County can be characterized as a diversification of experiences, exemplified by the ability to move freely in the urban ghettos of Chicago and the rural communities of Mississippi. All of this movement does not have a disintegrating effect on their sense of self but rather an integrating effect which results in a character trait of ultimate importance: they develop the flexibility and resilience needed to survive.

I have had the rare opportunity of seeing that survival mechanism operate. In 1969, eighteen high school graduates from Holmes County were recruited as part of an open admissions policy for underprivileged blacks at a large midwestern university. Unfortunately, they were given no meaningful orientation or preparation about what to expect, and for most of them, it was their first full-fledged exposure to white society. Although the school was a state university, up until that time only about 2 percent of its enrollment had been black. These students experienced profound cultural shock when they found themselves in a completely hostile and alien environment. This climate seemed to permeate all aspects of their existence. In the dormitory there were restrictions that they perceived as being aimed against them: for example, when they played their kind of music, they were told it was obnoxious and loud, and they were threatened with punishment. But none of them felt free to make similar complaints about others.

Some of them felt that their only escape was to move into the black section of town. But the local blacks were hostile toward the university, which they believed accepted only middle-class blacks, and for the first time in their lives the students were rejected by other blacks. In spite of all this, there was some educational climate, some academic condition, under which these highly motivated youths could obtain an education. In fact, it is amazing to see how well they have done. For example, fourteen of them received their degrees, and at the present time four of them are in graduate or professional schools. They made the best of their situation by relying on their ability to be flexible, adaptive, and opportunistic when it was necessary. They got as much out of their education at the university as circumstances would permit.

SOME IMPLICATIONS FOR GROWTH AND DEVELOPMENT

Although the students admitted to the university program may be exceptional, certainly by Holmes County standards, their continuous success is worth some reflection. Most of those whom I have talked with have experienced some form of the mobility cycle I have described. They are members of large extended families, they have lived in both the urban North and rural South, and they graduated from high school in Holmes County. Undoubtedly, they were chosen by the community to be in the program because they were considered to have the greatest potential as college material.

Yet, regardless of this rare opportunity, they realized that they were black in a predominantly white society, and that acquiring the education and position that brings power can only be done within a cultural context that is maintained by the white majority. They also know that they will be judged more severely than their white counterparts. Moreover, most of them are not certain that success will guarantee them equal status in white society. But, they have learned to accept that reality and, in the final analysis, are grateful for it, because for them it is the resolution of the ultimate dilemma: how to gain power, position, and respect WITHOUT giving up their black identity. As cynical as this view of white society may sound, it echoes the social reality blacks know they must come to grips with if they are to obtain some of the social benefits that have traditionally been denied them. As Pierce (1968) has pointed out, white America applauds those who help themselves and those who are assertive enough to force their demands.

An increasing number of black adolescents in Holmes County are growing up with the belief that they do not have to settle for mediocrity because society has opened up and will continue to open up further. One of the things that the university students symbolized is that moving up can be easier when there are more avenues to educational attainment.

At the same time, however, the Holmes County students experienced the difficulties inherent in taking advantage of this chance to compete, as evidenced by the tension and anxiety they felt in the university setting. Through their sheer determination, however, they demonstrated that blacks do not have to settle for modest successes, but can aim for career choices that were formerly denied them.

One of the most serious problems that these young people struggle with is how they can become accepted and respected members of the major culture without facing retribution from those blacks who are left behind. Besides having to deal with recriminations of the white majority who believe they should "remain in their place," they are constantly aware of possible criticism from their own cultural group. Those black youths that I have talked with, however, have pointed out to me that throughout their lives their family and friends have helped them prepare for dealing with these conflicts. If anything, their loved ones have shown them that they have a vicarious positive feeling about their personal achievements, and that feeling will grow as they continue to share their accomplishments. My observations indicate that the university students were the pride of the black community.

If one reflects on the lives of these university students, one can see that their severest crisis occurred in the university setting, which, ironically, was supposed to be the realization of all their ideals. Many of them had been capable of handling all the other situations of potential confrontation in the urban ghettos of Chicago and the backward communities of Mississippi. But when the cultural shock became too much, when the personal crisis and the emotional tensions became overwhelming, they were able to rely, as they had in the past, on their immediate and extended families for support.

Throughout all this, the signs of identity seeking, including choice of occupation, are clearly evident. Some are even now engaged in postgraduate work. I have witnessed a magnificent integration of self taking place in many of these young people whose social and personal goals have merged and become one. Their sense of obligation follows a straight line from the development of a personal moral value system to a commitment to work in school and eventually in the black segment of society.

Perhaps the most amazing aspect of this story is the thread of stability in their personal growth and development in the face of grave deprivation. It is a stability that was derived from the hope, the love, and the confidence that was nurtured and sustained in so many places throughout the history of their young lives.

REFERENCES

BRODY, EUGENE B.
  1968 "Minority group status and behavioral disorganization," in *Minority group adolescents in the United States*. Edited by Eugene B. Brody. Baltimore: Williams and Wilkins.

COLES, ROBERT
  1964 *Children in crisis*. Boston: Little, Brown.

FRIEDLANDER, FRANK
  1970 Emerging blackness in a white research world. *Human Organization* 29.

PIERCE, CHESTER M.
  1968 "Problems of the Negro adolescent in the next decade," in *Minority group adolescents in the United States*. Edited by Eugene B. Brody. Batimore: Williams and Wilkins.

SHIMKIN, DEMITRI B., ANN RICE
  1971 "The black population of Holmes County, Mississippi: a statistical characterization as of January, 1970." Mimeographed manuscript, Urbana, Illinois.

Impact of Urbanization on Life Patterns of the Ga Adolescent

WILHEMINA KALU

In most African universities, departments of education have undertaken research on children in an African setting. Few, however, have focused specifically on adolescents, especially on the impact of rapid industrialization, urbanization, and the pressures of modernization on the traditional socialization processes. This study attempts to fill some of the gaps. It is based on the assumption that adolescence should not be treated as merely a phase of biological change in the course of growth. Needless to say, projects like this can best be carried out by micro, local studies. In the end, there may prove to be many similarities between the reactions of the Ga adolescent and those of adolescents in other parts of Africa to the pressures of urbanization. This is, first, because of the inherent nature of industrialization and the multicultural life patterns that prevail in the city and, second, because of the broad similarities in African culture.

At the outset, I discuss some of the main background features of the contemporary cultural milieu in which the Ga adolescent operates. These are (1) urbanization, (2) the population structure, and (3) educational changes. There is a description of the structure, roles, and functions of these three factors, inasmuch as the cultural pattern created by their complex interaction has an important effect on the mode of initiation of the adolescent into adulthood. There follows an introduction to the Ga people, whose geographical location, traditional social structure, and history are important to their contemporary situation. I then go on to discuss the broad phases of the emerging life patterns of the Ga adolescent within the context of these sociocultural changes.

It is germane to define the period of life considered as adolescence. In this paper, adolescence covers the ages nine to nineteen years, during which time there is considerable dependence on parents and kin, especially economically. Adolescence is divided into three broad phases: (1) early adolescence (nine to twelve years); (2) middle adolescence (thirteen to fifteen years); and (3) late adolescence (sixteen to nineteen years).

The discussion explores the functioning of what appear to be the three main institutions of socialization among the Ga people today: the family and kinship group — its structure, role and impact; the school — its varied roles, strengths, and influences, and the new dimensions of non-formal education; and the peer group — its varying structures and functions during various phases of adolescent life.

Each phase of adolescence is treated in some detail so as to bring out very many aspects of relevant sociocultural changes such as the following:

1. The different involvement of the institutions of socialization and the subsequent differentiation of adolescents at many stages
2. Dissemination of the cultural heritage — the continuities, discontinuities, and replacements, especially in socialization patterns and goals
3. The different relationships to parental figures and elders at each phase
4. The adolescent's involvement in family life and in the kinship group
5. Training in social behavior, interest in sex, and attitudes toward marriage
6. Adolescent recreational activities, facilities, and ideals
7. Differentiation of sex-behavior patterns in adolescence
8. Differences in life problems or difficulties facing the adolescent at each phase

It is hoped that this discussion will also highlight some of the adolescent's own perception and attitudes toward his life patterns and the definition of his responsibilities.

BACKGROUND FEATURES OF CULTURAL MILIEU

Urbanization

Urbanization in Africa has attracted considerable attention, especially in terms of demographic features. Density is often one of the main criteria in the definition of an urban settlement. According to the definition applied in the censuses of 1931, 1948, 1960, and 1970 in Ghana, a settlement of 5,000 or more population is considered urban. An urban settlement may be a town or a city. Ghana, like most African countries, is still predominantly an agricultural economy and is dependent on agricultural produce, of which cocoa is still the leading product, in spite of efforts at diversification. Industrialization has therefore been a relatively unimportant feature in defining urbanization in Ghana, at least until 1957. This contrasts with the concept of urbanization in Western countries. Before 1957, mechanized agriculture in Ghana, even for cash crops, was very limited in scale. Thus, industrialization was relatively absent until after the country achieved independence in 1957, when deliberate governmental policies set industrialization in motion (Addo 1971).

However, even in the pre-Independence period, rapid growth of urban settlements was already conspicuous. It was a result of cumulative government policies which expanded and established numerous social services, educational facilities, and commercial activities. These made living conditions in urban settlements more comfortable and enjoyable, provided numerous opportunities for employment, and offered some tangible share in the country's growing economy. A by-product of these policies was to keep the gap between urban and rural development wide and to ensure the migration of population from rural areas into the urban centers. In addition, the policies attracted large numbers of foreigners from Africa and other parts of the world to engage in skilled and unskilled labor. The foreign population of the country rose from 4.3 percent in 1948 to 12.3 percent in 1960 (Addo 1971, 1972). The 1960 census indicates that 18 percent of the total urban population in Ghana was foreign — foreigners tend to engage in urban-based economic activities — e.g. as chemists, surveyors, administrators, teachers, and traders. Thirty-five percent of the foreign population were born in Ghana, which indicates that this population tends to settle and stabilize (Addo 1972).

Accra is the capital of Ghana and therefore right in the center of these urban changes. However, Accra is also the home ground or area of geographical origin of the Ga people. Thus, the life pattern of the Ga youth comes to reflect both the features of growth and development of the country and an adjustment to its multicultural interrelationships.

The increase in urban population in the country accelerated to about 190 percent between 1948 and 1960, as compared with the 80 percent increase between 1931 and 1948 (Addo 1971). Accra and Kumasi, which before 1931 existed as towns, absorbed one-third of the total urban population increases between 1948 and 1960. Accra, however, remained in the lead in population increase. Its population of 133,192 in 1948 rose to 331,919 in 1960 and is still on the rise today.

Population Structure

The population structure of Ghana and Accra is another important factor in the life patterns of the Ga adolescent. Population studies in Ghana indicate that about 45 percent of the total population is under fifteen years of age. Young people between nine and nineteen years of age alone form 30 percent of the total population (Addo 1972). This pattern of a large segment of the population being of dependent age is fairly typical for the rest of Africa. However, children are still seen as an asset, and the kinship system is utilized to maximize this attitude. In 1960, 41 percent to 47 percent of children fifteen years old and older lived in towns (Addo 1971). The fertility rate, however, is lower in the larger towns or urban areas than in the rural areas of the country. The Ga tribe generally has a moderately high rate of fertility — about 5.4, as compared with the highest in the country, which is 7.2 for the central Togo tribes. Among the different ethnic and tribal groups of Ghana, the Ga had the highest percentage of urban concentration in 1960 — about 77 percent. Next highest was the group of Yoruba immigrants — about 47 percent (Engmann 1972a, 1972b).

Educational Changes

The drive for education has been described as one of the most inexorable forces at work in Africa today. Education is considered the "magic elixir" for the future of the continent. It is assumed that manpower with schooling will attract or ensure speedy economic development. In 1957, at the time of Ghana's independence, there were thirty-eight secondary schools, with 9,820 pupils, in a country of about five million population. Five years after Independence there were sixty-eight such schools. By 1967 there were 103 secondary schools, with a total of 42,276 pupils. Most of them mushroomed under the government's Educational Trust policies. Increase in primary schools, especially in the urban areas, proceeded along similar lines. At the higher level, where there had been a couple of colleges, three universities appeared, and a host of vocational institutes have followed. The trend in development of education was different from that during the years before 1957, when schools were being founded mainly by private and missionary bodies.

Education in Ghana today is often seen as an avenue of escape from the drudgery of subsistence agriculture to the security of gainful employment. It is the stepping-stone to economic security for the family unit and social insurance for the kinship group. It is the quickest way to get a significant share in the fruits of national development. The structure of the educational system itself, however, interferes with the effectiveness of schooling as a means for consistent and realistic integration with the economic, social, and political facts of the society. The schools tend to be the competitive arena for the best talents in the country. This feature is embodied in the common entrance examinations for the selection of entrants into the secondary educational system, leading to university education.

Schooling in Ghana starts at the age of five or six years. The educational system is divided into five levels:

1. Primary education — approximately six years
2. Middle-school education — approximately two to four years, leading to middle-school certificate on completion
3. Secondary-school education — five years, leading to ordinary-level (O-level) certificate
4. Sixth-form education — two years, leading to advanced-level (A-level) certificate
5. University education — three or more years, leading to various degrees

This means that one could spend sixteen or eighteen years going through the whole program of academic education, at a tremendous cost to both the government and the family. It means that education contributes materially to the prolonged dependence on parents which characterizes adolescence. Primary- and middle-school education is virtually free, while secondary and university education are subsidized substantially to make them financially accessible to all. However, there are fewer institutions at the secondary-school level and higher. Many adolescents who want further education, therefore, have to be content with the few kinds of technical, commercial, and vocational institutions available, or with in-service training in employment.

As a result of policies for expansion, a "dual system" has emerged in the pattern of secondary schooling in the country. A distinction is made between the old, established, assisted schools, on the one hand, and the Ghana Educational Trust and Technical schools, on the other. The former are regarded more favorably, as affording high quality academic secondary education. The latter are perceived as representing low quality and nonacademic secondary education (Foster 1965). So far, academic secondary schooling commands entry into all significant positions in public service, in the larger commercial companies, and in the universities. For the average person, and for those who do not have the capital to start their own business or trade concern, it is a vital means of socioeconomic mobility. Many of the young complete middle-school education and then go into a profession or occupation. However, only 55-65 percent of those with a middle-school certificate are successful. In 1961, a Ministry of Labour report stated that out of 31,000 unemployed individuals within the Accra area, almost 10 percent were middle-school graduates (Foster 1965).

The towns and cities in Ghana are also where the compulsory-education law tends to be enforced. These centers, therefore, have higher school-life expectancy than do rural areas. School-life expectancy in Accra is the highest in the country (Kpedekpo 1972).

THE GA

As mentioned earlier, Accra is the heartland of the Ga people. The Ga are a coastal tribe who live in the southeastern part of the Ghanaian coastline. This is mainly a grassland region. The tribe is made up of various divisions and clans concentrated in the Accra region. It is a tribe who used to be mainly fishermen and farmers, and who did a limited amount of trading. The Ga and the Fante fishermen are still noted for their seasonal movement along the West African coastline as far as southwest Africa. Their social organization and religion were built around their occupations. They still have important festivals and ceremonials for the sea gods, Nai and Oyeni, and the *wulomo* is the most revered leader of the Ga, although the economic and political changes in the country are forcing the Ga chief to take a more prominent and active role. Tuesday is still a non-fishing day for the Ga (Field 1940).

The advent of colonialization and academic education has brought additional occupational choices to these people. Some of its population has been drawn into teaching, nursing, and commercial and civil-service fields. Most of the traditional cultural ways of life have remained. Now, living in the capital of Ghana, the Ga find themselves highly urbanized and at the heart of rapid economic, political, and social changes, as well as acculturation. They exert a lot of energy in helping their young people to take advantage of the ever-widening horizons for sociocultural functioning. The Ga market woman is now an archetype of the industrious, resourceful businesswoman who, however illiterate, endeavors to speak some sort of English to sell her wares to foreigners.

The traditional landscapes, of peacefully spread-out clan compounds of cone-shaped buildings and coconut-tree-lined beaches with boats and fishing nets hanging out to dry, are fast being replaced by blocks of modern high-rise buildings and two-way highways with bustling motor and human traffic. However, there is a strong resistance by these people to erasing the original ancestral compounds for the sake of better town planning. Thus, though these ancestral compounds are swallowed up by the expansion of the city and literally compressed into tightly congested populated areas, they still remain important foci for family and clan activities such as weddings, naming ceremonies, and funerals. The symbolic value of the ancestral homes has survived the dispersal of most members of the family into other parts of the city. The modern Ga youth regards these ancestral homes as revered and refreshing places to visit, to renew contact with his kin, to brush up on classic and idiomatic Ga language, and to have a glimpse of the old way of life. Here he can learn the folktales, value systems, superstitions, and religious rites of his tribe. At various stages of the youth's life he is forced into contact with these ancestral places and their functions. The concept of slum and poverty in the Western sense, therefore, does not exist in the mind of the Ga youth in relation to these places, except as congested places with few amenities.

The Ga people have always been familiar with multiple compounds because of the expansion necessitated by the practical problems of their family organization. Thus, the dispersal of the family neither weakens the kinship bond nor does it threaten the traditional way of life or interrelationships within the family. The Ga kinship system is patrilineal. The oldest male member of the lineage governs. He is the guardian of the proper performance of family ceremonies, for example, and the right to use the family and clan names. This set-up alone is of immense importance to the Ga child in terms of his identity. Wherever he may have been born or raised, or have lived, his name will indicate which family and clan he belongs to in Accra and the location of his original ancestral home. He automatically inherits deep roots of ancestral attachment. The Ga youth today is also protected by this system in case he or she has a child out of wedlock. Such a deviation was traditionally punished with banishment. Under the new dispensation, it is mainly frowned upon but accepted. The Ga concept of illegitimacy is in terms of not being given a name or formally admitted into a family nexus. Thus, the outdooring-naming ceremony remains crucial to the legal concept of legitimacy. This duly fits into the right to either monogamous or polygamous marriage. It also makes provision for offspring in the event of separation or termination of the marriage.

The Ga predominantly adhere to a corporate kin-group structure. This ensures vital economic support for the children, as well as social and personal support for individuals. Children are sent out or move out on their own to live with relatives, sometimes temporarily, sometimes permanently. When this happens, the relatives assume a considerable share in the responsibility for their upbringing.

With all the opportunities of the urban milieu surrounding them, the Ga are duly caught up in the fervent drive for education. A higher percentage of Ga adult males between the ages of twenty-four and sixty is likely to have received some schooling than is the case among other tribal groups. In Ghana as a whole, boys are expected to spend about 6.7 years in school, and girls about 3.3 years. The child in the city of Accra, however, spends about 9.8 years in school if a boy, and 6.3 years if a girl. The Ga child is, thus, more likely to attend both elementary and secondary school (since elementary schooling takes approximately seven years). A 1960 census study indicated that the highest percentage of school attendance by children of school age was among the Ga — 69.0 for male children and 39.4 for female children. The next highest percentages in the country were 61.9 for male Akwapim children and 44.8 for female children of the central Togo tribes (Gaisie 1972; Kpedekpo 1972).

GA ADOLESCENT LIFE PATTERNS

Keeping in mind the background features of the cultural milieu, we can now take a look at the life patterns of the Ga adolescent. As I have said earlier, the adolescent period being discussed covers the ages from nine to nineteen. The period is divided into three broad phases, within each of which the aims and goals of socialization are examined. The main institutions of socialization are: (1) the family and kinship group, (2) the school, and (3) the peer group. A somewhat dubious but significant institution is the National Youth Service or Organization. This organization grew up with the development of political idealism in the country after Independence. It has served many functions, both in Ghana and overseas. However, its momentum has ebbed with the political disillusionment of the youth. Its periods of functioning have therefore alternated with periods when various organized voluntary services on the local level gained more prominence. The National Youth Service has been reestablishing itself among youth in Ghana since 1972. This resurgence is mainly a result of the favorable and responsible appeals and approaches to youth by the new military government. The importance of the Service as an institution may lie in the fact that it fits well into the pattern of idealism expressed in the middle and late phases of adolescence. This idealism is not quite unreal, and if nurtured, it could be an important start toward integration of the economic, social, and political facts of the society in the life of the youth (Table 1).

Early Adolescence

This is a period in which the Ga youth is either finishing elementary school, is in the middle school, or is starting his secondary education. This depends on whether he started school early, and whether he went to the private- or preparatory-school system for his elementary education. The latter, by concentrating on academic subjects and on education in English as the medium of instruction, prepares him to take the common entrance examination within six years.

This early period is generally a period during which the adolescent is living at home and is under the daily jurisdiction of his parents and the other elders living in his household. The home is usually patrilocal, although it may be matrilocal in the case of separation. (Couples often resort to separation to lessen marital friction.) The household is generally one which includes other relatives, or roomers who are not members of the family and who come from different cultural backgrounds. The house may be owned by the adolescent's parents, his kin, or by others. Some adolescents live in unilocal settings, especially the children of highly educated parents. The neighbors around are bound to include other Ghanaian, African, Asian, or European groups. The peers of the Ga adolescent are multicultural, and he may be speaking a number of languages besides his mother tongue. He shares a room with at least some of his siblings, and this may continue for the rest of his adolescent period.

Table 1.   Schematic presentation of the life patterns of the Ga adolescent

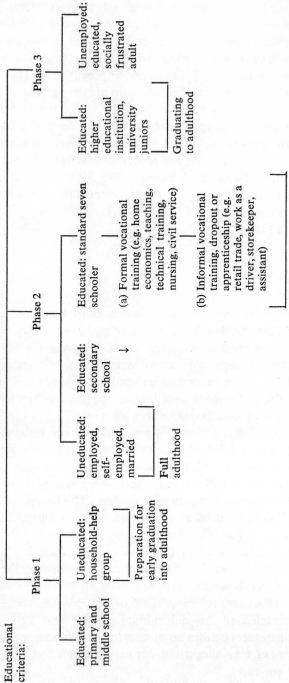

Sociocultural criteria:		
Late childhood: intensive social, moral, and role training; household responsibilities; GIRL — domestic orientation; BOY — domestic and play-group orientation; neighborhood peer group	Early adulthood: two-piece cloth, head tier, limited role in gatherings of kinship group and elders, and in ceremonials; economic responsibility (household); GIRL — controlled extra-familial activities; BOY — more freedom in social activities; peer group of school and neighborhood membership	Adulthood: full role in kinship group; participation in ceremonials and discussions; economic responsibility (household and kin); pressure toward a married status

Adolescent view:		
World of rigid behavior control; adult-child and sibling frictions; play very important	World of freedom; ambivalent oscillation between childhood and adult characteristics; better rapport with parents; social life very important	World of economic and social responsibilities; fear and frustration, but determination in the face of an uncertain future within the structure of the country

Adults in the household tend to be united on the aims of socialization during this phase — mainly character building, with particular attention to proper behavior, including obedience, respect for elders in all aspects of interrelationship, helpfulness, honesty, and a pervasive sense of cooperation and sensitivity toward the needs of the larger community. This last quality is essential for the proper functioning of the kinship system. The adolescent is also taught the cultural norms regarding appropriate sex roles and is helped to achieve emotional maturity and independence from his parents by assuming responsibilities. Respect for elders and submissiveness are considered cardinal characteristics for sociocultural functioning. This includes the concept of reverence for old age and pride in it, and the tradition of ancestor worship manifested in the pouring of libations on many occasions. Children at this age are not allowed to appear or to participate in adult discussion meetings. To the adult this fulfills an important pledge made to the tribe, ancestors, nature, and God at the outdooring-naming ceremony of the child. The pledge says:

Ga born, the wind blows before you talk;
See nothing, hear nothing.

Years ago, the Ga adolescent boy at this phase would have been learning sea fishing, battling successfully with rough waves, and taking care of nets. The girl would have been learning the intricacies of selling wares by hawking. Some Ga adolescents today still pursue this training and enjoy these occupations. But the emphasis is being shifted to prolonged or formal education and to preparation for gainful employment. Today the old traditional activities with the parents are perceived as helpful chores and are delegated to children.

School is considered very important by the parents. Truancy, which is a major problem during this phase, is frowned upon. Both the parents and other adults tend to be strict with the adolescents at home. The schoolteachers may use unstimulating and unpleasant methods of teaching, and childish playfulness is still pervasive at this stage. These factors combine to make truancy a readily welcomed way out. Some children may move to another home if they cannot cope with the restrictions imposed by their parents, or with sibling rivalries or responsibilities for siblings. The adolescent at this stage may also find consolation in activities and relationships with favorite uncles and aunts, or with grandparents. A prestigious role is accorded to old age as the age for taking a break in the pace of life. This makes it possible for grandparents, freed from child-disciplining roles, to indulge their grandchildren and enjoy their pranks of childhood innocence.

During this phase, the school is supposed to reinforce sociocultural training, as well as to take complete responsibiliy for the child's academic training. Homework is, therefore, a very minor concern at home, and few parents take consistent interest in it. The school day begins with a half-hour session of chores such as the cleaning of the classrooms and compounds by the schoolchildren. Prayers and the national pledge are said in an assembly. Schoolchildren help maintain fauna on the school premises. They have class gardening-plot competitions. Sewing, weaving, pottery, and carpentry are also offered in the schools (Wilson 1966).

Other difficulties that develop for the Ga adolescent during this phase center on recreational activities, which tend to clash with urban living. The girls are supposed to be available at home for help. The adolescent may live in family compounds that have become crowded due to the growth of the city. There is only limited open space for the boisterous games and sports of the boys. The house may also be near busy roads. Parents may not want their children to go too far away to play.

Some children join the Boy Scouts or similar formally organized groups, which tend to operate on a sporadic basis. Traditional peer-group activities persist. There are evening sings, folktales, Ananse stories, and riddles. Girls' recreational activities center around quiet indoor games, while boys tend to venture outdoors. Some boys hang around car and taxi parks, serve as porters in stores, and get easily drawn into all sorts of festival crowds passing by. They play *zu-zu,* which is racing floating objects or miniature boats in some of the huge, open gutters that have fast-flowing water. They may hang around bars and night clubs to listen and dance to new pop records, both indigenous and Western. For toys, they may build themselves a variety of things including go-carts, catapults, and kites. Those who have a school truancy problem may find themselves drifting out of the school system with peer-group support. Children in quieter residential areas may wander back and forth to friends' houses, ride bicycles, engage in any of a number of other activities, or do some reading.

The preoccupations of adolescents during this phase are of concern to parents because these may constitute a direct challenge to parental authority and supervision. Sometimes parents take time off from their busy work schedule to do something about the mounting problems of handling young adolescents.[1] Parents may try to enforce stricter disci-

---

[1] Ga mothers have traditionally worked, both to gain some economic independence and, although in a subsidiary role to the husband, for the economic support of

plinary measures on difficult adolescents, including curtailment of privileges and spanking; this approach may result in stubborn rebellion by the children. Parents may enlist the help of relatives, or even send the difficult children away to live with such relatives. Or they may send the child to some missionary boarding school in a rural setting, hoping that the harsher style of living may introduce more structure into the child's life and lead him to develop a positive attitude toward his homelife in Accra. These various measures may serve to reinforce the weakening discipline of adolescents.

The school recognizes its responsibility in helping to remedy such difficulties in adolescent behavior. Considerable energy is, therefore, being put into teacher-training programs for staffing elementary schools. During the years of vast expansion of the schools, staffing was a problem. Often teachers for this early phase of schooling were recruited from among the "failures," those whose own academic performance could not ensure them any other type of employment (Foster 1965; Wilson 1966).

Middle Adolescence

This is usually the period when the Ga adolescent enters the mainstream of the secondary school. Most Ghanaian secondary schools are boarding schools. They are subsidized in substantial degree by the government, so that most families pay fees of no more than about $ 250.00 a year. There are few secondary day-schools. The secondary schools tend to be located in rural or semirural areas. Certain towns (for example, Cape Coast) have evolved into educational centers. The schools tend to be mainly for one sex. Parents prefer the old, established missionary schools, feeling that they offer better quality education and have a better staff. The Ga adolescent eagerly welcomes the opportunity to leave home to further his education and to seek new experiences. He is also glad to take a break from the disciplinary structure at home. Clothing lists are important. For most children it is the first chance of having personal items that are completely their own and under their sole supervision.

At school, the Ga adolescent gets an added chance to learn other

---

the family. Ga market women are among the wealthiest individuals in the country. They organize and control the wholesale distribution of a number of products, both of local origin and imported. Their work may involve long working hours and travel.

Ghanaian languages, and may become fluent in four or more. He starts using English as the sole medium of instruction, and possibly as a second language. In the elementary-school system, he was taught in Ga or in the language of the area; English was then taught as a foreign language. English is an official language of Ghana, and the secondary-school system makes it the required language of instruction.

Whatever difficulties the adolescent may experience in the secondary school initially, he overcomes in the hope of getting the education on which his whole future depends. He takes subjects in the general arts, general sciences, fine arts, technical fields, and probably commercial fields. He is preparing for the all-important O-level exams. He joins a variety of clubs, including the United Nations Student Association, Student Christian Movement, Cercle Français, youth musical groups, drama and cultural-dancing groups, anti-illiteracy groups, voluntary work camps, and the Red Cross. These provide him with a variety of life experiences. The last three groups are especially instrumental in shaping his awareness of the immediate world around him. He engages in community work programs such as building schools, roads, and clinics, and teaching without pay in the rural areas. Rural areas constitute about two-thirds of the country, and make the greatest tax contribution to free education, free medical services, and other tax-paid facilities enjoyed in the country, especially in urban settings. The adolescent may continue with such involvement even during the holidays.

In addition, these clubs or the schools themselves afford a chance for the adolescent to mix and work together with members of the opposite sex, whereby he builds further knowledge of the opposite sex. It is unlikely that he will be able to discuss problems of sex with his parents in any meaningful way. Parental information tends to dwell on things he should not do. Peers are highly instumental here, through informal discussions, jokes, and so on. Peers also help him to keep up with the latest in foreign and indigenous fashions. Peers help him to learn new dances and apprise him of new record releases.

It is during this phase that the impact of modernization and urbanization becomes most acute. This is characterized by undue attraction to Western "pop culture" in clothing, movies, music, and fast cars. In this way, the Ga youth strongly identifies with the youth of the world. These foreign influences that pervade the urban milieu, in combination with the traditional pattern of socialization, during this phase create enormous stress that manifests itself in adolescent social behavior. The adolescents evolve their own language, based on nicknames and slang, including such terms as "jot" for cigarette; "freak" for swinging rhythm; "church" for a dance place; "sermon" for music; "bread," "kana," or "dolla" for money. These terms reflect what the youth consider to be the main concerns of life at this stage. Social life and entertainment are especially emphasized on holidays, since holiday jobs are virtually nonexistent.

The Ga adolescent spends four out of twelve months at home. He looks forward to reunions with his family, and also to his return to school. It is not uncommon to see buses full of boisterous, singing adolescents both at the beginning and at the end of vacation periods. The relationship at the home is so positive that the Western phenomenon of teenage-parent friction and the generation-gap syndrome are not manifested. This situation has been made possible by a number of cultural factors that affect the family's relationship with the adolescent: (1) There is the timely break of going away to boarding school. (2) There is the clear, progressive change in parental authority. During this phase the adolescent is seen as more ready to assume adultlike responsibility in family and kinship-group participation. Some of his age mates who are not in the secondary-school system may be married and, thus, already fully initiated into adulthood. Marriage is still regarded as the final initiation into adulthood. There is no required age for getting married. The traditional guidelines of puberty and maturity are used, but marriage in early puberty is discouraged. There is considerable mutual respect displayed in the parent-child relationship during this phase of adolescence. (3) There is the tacit parental attitude that investment in the adolescent's formal education is beneficial both to himself and to the family. (4) There is the adolescent's newly acquired disciplined tolerance. He has undergone the often unnecessary rigors of hollow human relationships in the missionary-school system, where he has sustained himself with good humor. He has grasped the fact that overt criticism is unpopular and ineffective with adults on whom he is so dependent, at least economically. He is beginning to use more subtle ways of expressing his opinions and wishes to adults. When emotional issues are being discussed with elders, he finds it easier to stay, listen, and simply walk away when the discussion is over. (5) There is the cultural norm regarding the separation of the skills, knowledge, and value-norms of formal education from those of tradition, social experience, and age. In a battle of wisdom, by virtue of his formal education, the Ga adolescent cannot relate to parental figures. Talking to adults and arguing with them as if he and they were equals is considered totally disrespectful. One may dare to argue with appropriately selected adults, using a great deal of wit, humor, and diplomacy. Culturally conditioned, patterned, and regulated relationships with elders prevail. (6) The limited degree of formal education among the greater percentage of parents today makes it unnecessary for parents and children to compete in formal intellectual knowledge concerning recent issues and developments. Such competition is reserved for one's peer group, which tends to have its own angles in relating to issues.

The difficulties that Ga parents have with their adolescent children are on another level. The Ga parent worries about the tedious concern of the adolescent with fashion and popular music. Boys at this stage form music bands that play in many night clubs in Accra. A number of night clubs are patronized by adolescents. These nightly activities and the parties that the adolescents attend during holidays are somewhat unnerving to the parents, and they constantly voice their disapproval. They fear that children who have a weak character and lack self-direction may run into social and moral difficulties. Going to the movies is an important weekend activity for the adolescent. Dating is openly frowned upon at this stage by most parents. Group events, therefore, tend to become meeting places for the sexes and a way of solving the dating problem. Adolescents leave and return to their homes with peers of their own sex. Parents worry especially about their sons, since boys spend a substantial part of the day outside with friends. The Ga adolescent respects his parents for their concern but prefers the less authoritarian parental structure. He tries to participate in family and kinship-group activities, helping to organize family gatherings, cultural ceremonies, and festivals.

Progressive changes in parent-child and authority relationships contribute to a great margin of tolerance in the matter of serious deviations. Premarital sex and pregnancy used to be punished with banishment. Today these bring reprimands in conferences hosted by a number of family friends and kin — the same method is used to handle most parent-child problems at this stage. The pregnancy is then accepted, and energy is concentrated upon preparation for the child and for the future roles of the two families. Traditional marriage rites may be required, including the formal presentation of a gold ring, money, drinks, and a Bible. If it is decided that the new parents should continue with their academic or vocational training, the in-laws may share the childcare duties. It is when the parents cannot afford to absorb the additional economic responsibilities that the adolescent girl faces the full consequences of her behavior by becoming an adult overnight.

Although she may continue to live in the parental household, she starts to assume a role that involves considerable economic independence.

If the adolescent has dropped out of school because of financial or personal reasons, he continues to live with his parents and to be dependent on them. In view of his unfinished schooling, his prospects of employment or vocational apprenticeship are not good enough to cover his overall living expenses.

On the whole, the traditional kinship system not only serves to socialize the adolescent at this phase but also cushions the impact of modern cultural stresses that may result from such behavioral deviations as unwanted pregnancy. The children are not left to bear the consequent pressures alone, relying only on their moral and economic resources.

Late Adolescence

During this phase the Ga adolescent is slowly weaning himself from the drive to pursue social activities to some serious consideration of his future. He is beginning to face economic responsibilities for family and kin. Relatives may begin dropping hints about this as a reminder. The adolescent may now begin to take interest in the economic and political developments of the country. In the traditional past, adolescents could have been given in marriage before reaching what we now term late adolescence. Modernization has changed this, however, except in some rural areas. Economic independence and education are now crucial criteria for adulthood. The main traditional relic of the cultural past is that late adolescents are allowed to participate in gatherings of their elders. The girls are allowed to dress as adults, wearing an additional cloth and headgear.

In the different facets of his life, the average Ga adolescent at this stage is mainly preparing himself for marriage. Economic responsibility serves to defer a hasty trip to the altar. More likely he will be pondering about a future career. Farming, fishing, or living in rural areas do not constitute enticing possibilities. He is likely to be attracted to an urban setting and perhaps to think in terms of work in a technical, commercial, teaching, civil-service, sports, or administrative field.

New political consciousness, which is typical of this stage of adolescence, keeps many young people in voluntary community-development projects during the holidays. The National Youth Service is currently working on the Dawhenya Canal Construction Project. The aim is to irrigate the Accra plains for agricultural purposes. Another instance of this tendency to engage in community service is the project for replanning and rehabilitation of a highly congested and disorganized area in Accra called Nima, a project pioneered by a group of Scripture Union students. The government has continued to support this program. Such activities fit well into the adolescent's mood of idealism regarding educational, social, political, and economic changes in the country. He may join others in voicing criticism verbally, constructively, and nonviolently. He gets an opportunity to test his ideals concerning freedom of speech and thought in the larger society, without inverting the traditional cultural patterns of relationships between generations. In the traditional Ga gathering, he would respectfully ask for permission to express his ideas, and would use the appropriate channels of selected elders to convey these ideas to the chief of the clan or tribe.

The Ga adolescent in the academic mainstream may be preparing for his O- or A-level examinations or may be entering the university. The latter often brings him once more to Accra. If no longer in school, he may be looking for gainful employment, or entering into professional training. Some young people may even be entertaining ideas of going overseas to avail themselves of wider choices in further education. In this they may be sponsored by their parents, or they may receive government scholarships. Educated or well-to-do relatives may be important; any possibility of help they can offer the adolescent toward realizing this goal is explored.

Within the school system, the Ga adolescent at this stage is receiving final training in the assumption of important responsibilities. He may serve as prefect, president, secretary, treasurer, or chairman of various organizations and functions. He receives tangible rewards for interest and participation in school athletics. There are some scholarships available for good sportsmen, and opportunities for training and trips abroad to represent his nation. Adolescents have a chance to visit Europe during the summer through the Students' Charter Flights. This can be of value in broadening their experience and dispelling their misconceptions about life in Europe. On the opposite side of the coin, such trips result in greater attraction to European consumption habits and greater erosion of traditional culture under the influence of newfangled Western modes.

At home, the late adolescent is virtually an adult, with definite responsibility for the character training of younger children. It is unlikely that he will move away from the parental home unless he is transferred from the city, or is given employment with housing attached. Parents resent such an eventuality, for various reasons: (1) Parents at this stage enjoy and value their relationship with their maturing children. The relationship of the parent is more that of a confidant and companion. (2) Some parents are not overly concerned whether their children contribute economically. Rather, they take pride in having raised a child to this level in life. They encourage the youth to accompany them to kinship and traditional ceremonies such as durbars, funerals, engagements, outdooring, and so on. They continue to explain the propriety of such attendance. The youth may feel that the parents take on too many such engagements. (3) Parents believe that having a child of that age at hand is for them an assurance of help in case of future emergencies. The "savior" they have raised may not be made of gold, but he is still their "savior."

The adolescent is likely to hear admonitions from his kinfolk encouraging continued patience and proper conduct with a view to making a good selection of a marriage partner. He is familiar with the important roles played by aunts and uncles, both in the rites to establish the union, and in the maintenance of it. To these relatives the marriage will provide an additional opportunity to display the proud handiwork of their kinship system. Occupational status, sound character, family history, health, and beauty are considered important. Intertribal or intercultural marriages are allowed so long as the traditional marriage rites are performed. Love is felt to be a matter that concerns the two persons involved and not necessarily the relatives.

CONCLUSION

Thus, the modern Ga adolescent is brought up in a multicultural milieu with an early exposure to widening horizons for sociocultural functioning. He is a child of new cultural patterns created by industrialization and urbanization. Yet he is socialized through traditional institutions, albeit operating today with a great degree of flexibility and many pragmatic adaptations. The product is an adolescent increasingly receptive to a broad range of cultures, curious about other ways of life, and less inclined to be critical of them until he reaches the late adolescent phase, when national consciousness and political idealism gain strength.

Equally crucial in developing this greater awareness of modernization are changing school curricula, the mass media (television, newspapers, journals, and so on), and the general tone of politics and urban life. Thus, the modern Ga adolescent is likely to be quite knowledge-able about issues in such faraway places as Canada, Europe, the United States, India, and other parts of Africa.

The relatively easy adjustment to the impact of industrialization and urbanization on traditional Ga life can be explained in part by the fact that much of the bedrock of Ga character has survived. For instance, the main strengths of Ga culture — cooperation and ancestor worship — manage to be passed on to new generations even without the traditional milieu of socialization. This is mainly achieved through the structuring of parent-child and authority relationships. New institutions of socialization are fashioned so as to give continuity in the cultural conditioning of the adolescent regarding the essential aspects of life.

The characteristics of tolerance and flexibility in accommodating to deviations and foreign cultural intrusions probably have deeper historical roots. Traditionally, the Ga have used less harsh measures than their Ashanti counterparts in their sanctions against sociocultural deviations. Thus, in the midst of rapid changes in the sociocultural milieu, they operate with a margin of tolerance for cultural deviations. There is a comfortable blend of the traditional and the colonial heritage in marriage rites and in the judiciary system, without cultural disorganization. There continues to be a strong pride in what is Ga, Ghanaian, and African, and these elements predominate in the culture.

However, certain traditional rites and ceremonies are being slowly eroded, transformed, or discarded. There is a perceptible decline in the use of proverbs, riddles, and idiomatic speech. At the moment, the Ga culture is not unduly jeopardized, because vernacular instruction is a requirement in the primary education. Courses on the various lin-guistic cultures of Ghana are offered in the preparation for the O-level examination in the secondary-school system. At a higher level, similar courses are limited in depth and variety because of a lack of available written materials. With continuing historical, archaeological, anthro-pological, and sociological research, there is hope that this will be remedied. In recent times, there have been indications of strong attrac-tion among the youth to their native dances and drama. This cultural nationalism will ensure the survival of the traditional agencies of socialization amid the adaptations to new modes of life that result from modernization and urbanization.

REFERENCES

Works Cited

ADDO, N. O.
  1971   Some demographic aspects of urbanization in Ghana, 1931–1960. *Ghana Social Science Journal* 1(1).
  1972   "Urbanization, population and employment in Ghana," in *Population growth and economic development in Africa*. Edited by S. H. Ominde and C. N. Ejiogu. New York: Heinemann and Population Council.
ENGMANN, E. V. T.
  1972a   "Food production and population growth," in *Population growth and economic development in Africa*. Edited by S. H. Ominde and C. N. Ejiogu. New York: Heinemann and Population Council.
  1972b   "Some consequences of population movements," in *Population growth and economic development in Africa*. Edited by S. H. Ominde and C. N. Ejiogu. New York: Heinemann and Population Council.
FIELD, M. J.
  1940   *Social organization of the Ga people*. London: Crown Agent.
FOSTER, PHILIP
  1965   *Education and social change in Ghana*. London: Routledge and Kegan Paul.
GAISIE, S. K.
  1972   "Fertility level among the Ghanaian tribes," in *Population growth and economic development in Africa*. Edited by S. H. Ominde and C. N. Ejiogu. New York: Heinemann and Population Council.
KPEDEKPO, G. M. K.
  1972   "Tables of school life for Ghana, 1960," in *Population growth and economic development in Africa*. Edited by S. H. Ominde and C. N. Ejiogu. New York: Heinemann and Population Council.
WILSON, JOHN
  1966   *Education and changing West African culture*. London: London University Press.

Further References

ADAMS, DON, R. M. BJORK
  1969   *Education in developing areas*. New York: David McKay.
AMMAH, E. A.
  1962   Festivals of Gas and Jews. *The Ghanaian* 5:(10).
ANUN, NICHOLAS O.
  1966   "Ghana," in *Church, state and education in Africa*. Edited by David G. Scanton. New York: Teachers College Press, Columbia University.
BERNARD, HAROLD W.
  1969   *Readings in adolescent development*. Scranton, Pennsylvania: International Textbook.

BOATENG, E. A.
1959 The growth and functions of Accra. *Ghana Geographical Association Bulletin* 4:(2).

BROWN, R., D. FORDE, *editors*
1950 *African systems of kinship and marriage.* London: Oxford University Press.

COMMONWEALTH SECRETARIAT
1970 *Education in rural areas.* London: Commonwealth Secretariat.
n.d. *Vocational and social training of primary-school learners in the African countries of the Commonwealth.* London: Commonwealth Secretariat.

DICKSON, K. B.
1971 Nucleation and dispersion of rural settlements in Ghana. *Ghana Social Science Journal* 1.

DORM-ADZOBU, C.
1971 The state and industrial development in Ghana. *Ghana Social Science Journal* 1(1).

GHANA
1968 *Ministry of Education Report 1963–1967.* Accra: Government Printer.

Ghanaian
1960 Ga concept of the universe. *The Ghanaian* 24.

GHANSAH, D. K.
1972 "Family planning and economic developments in Africa," in *Population growth and economic development in Africa.* Edited by S. H. Ominde and C. N. Ejiogu. New York: Heinemann and Population Council.

GRIFFIN, G. W.
1927–1928 The Origin of the Gas. *Journal of African Society* 27.
1930 Specimen of folklore of the Ga people. *Africa* 3.
1937 *Religion and medicine of the Ga people.* London: Oxford University Press.
1962–1963 *Transactions of the Historical Society of Ghana* volume 6.
1970 *Youth and development in Africa.* London: Commonwealth Secretariat.

HANSON, JOHN W.
1965 *Imagination and hallucination in African education.* East Lansing, Michigan: Michigan State University, Institute for International Studies in Education.

JEFFRIES, C.
1967 *Illiteracy: a world problem.* New York: Praeger.

LEWIS, L. J.
1960 The social and cultural problems of urbanization for the individual and family. *Rural Life* 5:(2).

MEDINNUS, GENE R.
1967 *Readings in the psychology of parent-child relations.* New York: John Wiley and Sons.

MINTURN, L., W. W. LAMBERT
1964 *Mothers of six cultures, antecedents of child rearing*. New York: John Wiley and Sons.

PARRINDER, E. G.
1958 *Witchcraft*. London: Pelican Books.

SEIDMAN, JEROME M.
1960 *The adolescent, a book of readings*. New York: Holt, Rinehart and Winston.

UNESCO
n.d. *International Journal of Adult and Youth Education*. Paris.

UNICEF
1968 *Assignment Children*. Paris.

WILLIAMS, T. D.
1971 The economics of educational priorities. *Ghana Social Science Journal* 1(1).

Mississippi Choctaw Youth

JOHN PETERSON

Among the Mississippi Choctaw we find an example of the development of a socially defined grouping of adolescents of very recent origin. That there is no established tradition for dealing with a prolonged adolescence is particularly significant in view of the fact that the population is very young — 50 percent are under the age of twenty-one.

Before 1964, most of the Choctaw were engaged in the cotton sharecropping economy typical of the rural southeastern United States. There were no high school facilities in the local area. Most of the Choctaw lived all of their lives in one of the seven Choctaw-speaking communities. Even before completing the local elementary school, Choctaw children became increasingly involved in the sharecropping economy. At an early age they began to take part in work during the planting and harvesting seasons. Gradually, as they grew older, they became full-fledged members of the production unit. From this point to actual marriage was a short step. There was very little courtship.

After marriage, the young couple lived with whichever production-unit household was convenient — the family of the bride, or that of the groom. There seems to have been little emphasis on either matrilocal or patrilocal residence. It was in the household of the group with which they worked that the couple had their children, and it was here that the children came of age. When the male had established a good reputation as a solid farmer, the couple might move out and become a separate production unit on their own, or they might remain and become the center of the family as their parents grew older. Transition from their childhood to adulthood was at that time a matter of becoming increasingly involved in the economic cycle, a fairly sudden decision to get married, then marriage and parenthood.

Since 1964, four major factors have contributed to an almost total change in this pattern of Choctaw life: the decline in farming and the mechanization of agriculture; the completion of the Choctaw high school; the increase in consumer items; and access to the mass media.

First, there was a decline in farming and a rise in the mechanization of agriculture. This had an uneven effect. Many of the older people, especially the older men, were thrown onto the unemployment or welfare rolls, whereas a certain number of the younger people were able to move into factory employment. But factory employment in the local area has been much more readily available to women than to men. As a result, there has been a heavy out-migration of young men to industrial areas in the North, while many of the men who remained behind have been unable to be productive.

A second major development was the completion of the Choctaw high school. As a result, young Choctaw from the different communities were brought together for the first time, in essence creating an adolescent grouping. Many of the young people attending the high school were separated from their homes. There was a boarding dormitory for about half the students. The teachers were predominantly white and were accustomed to middle-class, white, adolescent groupings. As a result, the usual pattern of school dances and other social events began to develop.

The third factor that changed conditions in the Choctaw community was the great increase in consumer items, especially television sets and automobiles. Despite the fact that an increasingly large number of older people were thrown out of work, at least one-third of the population was able to move into factory employment, bringing a great deal of economic improvement. Television and radio added a fourth dimension of change — exposure to the events and styles of the larger society through access to the mass media.

Initially, these developments brought little change in the pattern of courtship. As recently as five years ago, one never saw individual couples, never saw a boy and a girl walking around together, even on the high school campus. Instead, young people would attend activities such as baseball games in groups with their families.

Dating has just begun to develop. However, young people in the Choctaw community still cannot follow the dating and courtship pattern as it is practiced by the mass society and portrayed in the mass media. Aside from the absence of a dating tradition, because of the very rural nature of the Choctaw area, there are few situations in which normal dating can take place. Due to discrimination, the young Choctaw cannot go into town and sit down to chat together over a soda. They cannot go to a motion picture. They do not have cars. As a result, whatever dating does follow the pattern takes place primarily on the school grounds, in coordination with school activities. Some people, recently married, have said, "We really don't know how to date."

Within the last ten years, because of the establishment of the high school, there has been a delay in the time of marriage, while at the same time there has been a lack of opportunity to engage in or learn to act out the courtship patterns of the surrounding society. Furthermore, the generation of parents does not understand this period in the lives of their children. They ask, "Why aren't they married? Why aren't they productive?" The parent generation has tremendous difficulty dealing with this. In this connection, it is important to keep in mind that over one-third of the people who graduate from the Choctaw high school are twenty years old or older, because of educational retardation as they pass through the school system. Among the Choctaw at present there is not the neat boundary between the young eighteen-year-old high school student and older people that is found in middle-class white communities in the United States. The Choctaw students are old enough to marry when they are still in high school.

Furthermore, in the total population there is a very limited knowledge of the use of contraceptives on any level, either among the children or among the adults, and the result of this is obvious. There is probably a continuation of the earlier behavior, but at the same time the social circumstances have totally changed. This is particularly dysfunctional in the present situation because of the heavy out-migration of young males; the end result is that there are about four women to every three men in the critical child-producing years.

This situation is affecting the total economic and educational development of the human resources of the tribe, because some of the brightest young men find themselves suddenly married when they had no intention of getting married. They are simply married and at once have children. This may occur during high school, or it may occur when they come back home in summer from college — all of a sudden they are married, and they cannot go back to their schooling. Obviously, once they have a wife and child, it becomes very difficult for them to continue in college.

As a result, there has recently been an increasing number of young people of high potential who are trapped because of their family situation. And the unfortunate thing is that this is occurring just at the critical time when professional jobs on the reservation are expanding rapidly.

In addition to the above, young people are growing up at a time when the traditional stabilizing influences of the family are beginning to be affected by disintegrating forces. The factor of rising unemployment particularly affects the older, stable families of the Choctaw communities. These are the older people who cannot find productive work. In addition, there has been a rise in alcoholism and a decline in the traditional social-control mechanism. If nothing else has changed, all of a sudden most households have a car, where before everyone had to walk from one house to another. They can get around; things can happen. As a result of this, there has definitely been a deterioration in the traditional family life. In the past, children could move to a relative's home, depending on the economic situation in terms of what was best for the young. It would appear to me that this movement of children from family to family — which is described in this volume by Eckenfels for Holmes County, Miss. — has been very functional. However, to be useful, such movement requires some points of familial permanence or stability.

A measure of permanence or stability as well as a consistent economic level is necessary so that the children can move about without being a burden at the points to which they are moving. If this generalization is correct, it would seem that what is happening in the present Choctaw case is an overloading of a system that once functioned very well. This is due to the increased movement of children, the decline in the economic level, and a weakening of the stable family points between which the children can move. There is, therefore, an overburdening of those points that remain.

How does this tie in with the question of the identity of the people involved? Who is an adolescent? Or, for that matter, who is a Choctaw? The traditional identity of the Choctaw was vested in a group of related families, located in a single Choctaw community, who all shared a particular subdialect. I have spoken of this as being Choctaw identity because it is rooted in the language, in the very word "Choctaw" — their name for themselves. Now, because of the mass media, radio and television, and contact with outsiders, there is emerging among some Choctaw people the concept of an Indian identity which is not based on being Choctaw, or even on Choctaw culture, but is based on the Indian ethnic group versus "those other guys," "those whites," and so forth. The problem is that that Indian identity exists only in terms of contact with outsiders. It has little adaptive capacity to get people to work together within the Choctaw population. It is mainly an oppositional identity.

A major difficulty is developing a Choctaw identity that would embrace all the Choctaw population, as opposed to an identity rooted in one specific dialect subcommunity. There is some indication that it is the adolescents and the young adults, in spite of the problems they are facing, who may be moving in this direction. The very fact that they have been uprooted to a certain degree, and have had to move around or to live in school dormitories, has made them less deeply rooted in the minute details of the culture of their locality. Now they are learning a shared tribal culture instead. Some of this is actually taking place in the high school. For example, a choral group has been formed in the school to sing the traditional music, because most of the young people have not been getting this experience in their own individual communities. The formation of Choctaw dance clubs is another example. Five years ago, it was mainly older people who did the traditional dances. Now, in many of the communities young adults are saying, "Let's learn our Choctaw dances that our parents didn't teach us." And this, again, is shared by the adolescents.

Thus, several developments are taking place in Choctaw society, influencing youth towards creating a new Choctaw identity. It is probably still true that there is neither a firm concept of adolescence, nor a group identified as adolescents, in the Choctaw population. Right now, it is really the high school students, particularly the senior high school students, and the young adults who share a common experience, whether they are married or not, and whether they have children or not. This vague grouping of the eighteen-year-olds with young adults on up to twenty-five and twenty-seven comprises a youth group that appears to be developing a Choctaw identity.

Future Time Perspectives and Attitudes of New Zealand Maori and Pakeha Adolescents

ROBERT J. HAVIGHURST

For obvious reasons, attitudes toward the future are important in the lives of adolescents. The adolescent is selecting or creating an identity for himself — determining the kind of person he wants to be and the kind of lifestyle he wants to have. Even if he is unaware of these matters, he is making choices and doing things that will affect his future.

Study of attitudes and actions with respect to the future is especially useful to educators who are concerned with educational policy and practices for Maori youth. There is a general notion extant that Maoris are people concerned more with the present than the future. It is often said that they prefer something good in the present to something much better in the future. They are said to be less willing to make sacrifices now for rewards in the future than are Pakehas. It is important to find out how much truth there is in these broad statements.

This is a time when Maori people are getting more education and moving up the ladder of socioeconomic status in New Zealand. But this movement is too slow to satisfy many people. The key to Maori betterment, some people say, is better jobs and more earning power; this requires more of the right kinds of education. For success in an occupation that requires skill and training, there must be a period of training and learning, without much immediate reward. This means a sacrifice in the present for a future reward. A teenager can earn more money by taking a job as an unskilled laborer than he can by serving

The research reported in this paper is part of a larger study of the education of Maori youth in which the author has been engaged with the help of the New Zealand Council for Educational Research.

an apprenticeship for skilled work. If the adolescent chooses to prolong his formal education or to secure an apprenticeship, he is likely to do this (and to sacrifice present earnings) either because his parents or his older brothers and sisters urge him to do so or because he perceives a number of possible desirable jobs ahead of him, and he makes a choice among several options. If the occupational horizon is clouded for him, he cannot see ahead and is not likely to undertake a course of action that may produce rewards later.

This research was aimed at finding out more about the nature of time perspective and awareness of the future on the part of Maori and Pakeha youth in New Zealand.

PREVIOUS RESEARCH IN THIS AREA

The recent research of D. H. Bray of Massey University on temporal values of Maori and Pakeha adolescents (Bray 1971, 1973) has the most direct bearing on this research, and the procedures and results of his research and ours will be compared systematically.

Other related research goes back before 1960 and is less explicitly concerned with the issue of present versus future orientation. The studies of Maori personality development by the Beagleholes and by the Ritchies suggest that Maori culture tends to make Maoris more "happy-go-lucky" with time and money, less driven by ambition, more in search of present gratification, than Europeans. Ausubel had read and accepted the work of the Beagleholes and Ritchie. His empirical study, made in 1957–1958 (Ausubel 1961), was intended to compare Maori-Pakeha differences with rural-urban differences within the Maori and the Pakeha groups. He hypothesized that the DIRECTION of the difference between Maori and Pakeha would be the same as the direction of the differences between rural and urban youth; but that Maori-Pakeha differences would be GREATER THAN RURAL-URBAN differences. It turned out that, although the directions were indeed the same, the size of the differences did not support the hypothesis. The differences were about the same between Maori and Pakeha and between rural and urban students. Ausubel's research instruments dealt mainly with aspirations for education and for occupation. They covered some of the same ground as was covered by the "clarity of image of the future" in this research.

Ausubel's book draws more on his reading of previous psychological and anthropological studies of Maoris than upon his own empirical research. With respect to the Maori attitudes toward work, he says that unlike the Pakeha, the Maori does not value work as an end in itself, as a badge of respectability or as means of getting on in the world. He works primarily to supply the necessities of life; and hence when his immediately foreseeable needs are satisfied and a small surplus is accumulated, he sees nothing immoral in taking a prolonged respite from his labors. In the light of this attitude, monetary reward is a much more important reason than occupational prestige for choosing a career, and possible loss of job is fraught with less threatening ego, moral, and social implications for him than it is for the Pakeha. Thus it is not unusual for him to stay away from work because he is bored or put out with his employer; and if he is fired he feels that he can always "revert to a subsistence economy or fall back on Social Security benefits and the hospitality of relatives" (Ausubel 1961: 71).

The Bray studies, made in 1969 and partially replicated in 1971 (Bray 1971, 1973), are closer in conception to the problems treated by the author in this research. Both researchers were testing the proposition that Maori youth are more present-oriented than Pakeha youth, while the latter have a greater future-time orientation.

The present study and the studies of Bray are fairly comparable in that they attempt to test the same hypothesis, though with different social-psychological instruments.

AIMS AND METHODS OF THE PRESENT RESEARCH

The research reported in this paper was aimed to study Maori-Pakeha differences in future-time orientation and also to study patterns of interest and satisfaction obtained from achievement-oriented activities, compared with friendship and other expressive activities. Consideration was given to sex differences in those matters, and also to differences related to socioeconomic status. This latter point was especially important, because it may be true that a part of the observed difference between Maoris and Pakehas is due to the fact that most Maoris in the past fifty years have been living on the edge of poverty and have had a lower-class occupational status. Only recently have a considerable minority of Maoris achieved middle-class status, and the children of these families may show less difference from Pakehas than do the children of Maoris of the working class.

CONSTRUCTS USED IN THIS STUDY

Three constructs or conceptualized qualities were explored among

Maori and Pakeha youth in this study, each one measured with an appropriate instrument.

Clarity of Image of the Future

This was measured with a rating scale, and the ratings were based on an interview with the respondent. The interview took eight to ten minutes and was conducted by the writer and his wife. With few exceptions, young women were interviewed by Mrs. Havighurst, and young men by the author. After securing information about the age, residence, number of children in the family, ethnicity, and occupation of father and mother, the respondent was asked to talk about his future, as he visioned it. The following questions were asked, with variations suggested by the responses:

Thinking about the future: What will you be doing a year from now?
If your wishes would come true, what would you like to be doing five years from now? If this did not work out, what would your second choice be?
Thinking about your abilities and interests: What occupation would be the very best for you?
As you think ahead twenty years from now, how will your life be different from what it is now?

The respondent's replies were written down on the interview schedule, together with impressions gained by the interviewer. The respondent was then rated on the following scale of "clarity of image of the future":

1. Has no perspective on the future. Does not "see" a future for himself.
2. Sees some change in the next five years in terms of his own behavior and development.
3. Is rather clear about his progress during the next five years but not much beyond.
4. Has rather clear view of his probable development through the next twenty years.

The two interviewers made the ratings. They worked together on the first few interviews, discussing their reasons for the scores they gave. Then they rated independently about thirty interviews and compared their ratings. There were no disagreements of more than one step on the four-point scale. The majority of cases were rated the same by the two judges. Thereafter, the author rated all of the interviews, with occasional checks by Mrs. Havighurst. The boy's ratings were somewhat more reliable than the girls', due to the fact that many girls gave marriage as a major goal during the first five years and were rather vague about occupational development after that time. If a girl was clear and sure of herself in what she said about marriage and having children, she was rated 3 or 4, but the mixture of plans for work and for marriage often blurred the picture and made the rating more difficult than it was for most boys.

Ratings were also made on the following scales: Aspiration for socioeconomic mobility, relative to father's status; Self-confidence; Concern with personal career rather than family, and/or social relationships.

Socioeconomic Status (SES) of the Family

The socioeconomic level of the home was used as a major variable for the study. This was based on the Congalton-Havighurst scale of occupational status for New Zealand, modified by the recent work of Elley and Irving (Congalton and Havighurst 1954; Ballard 1972; Elley and Irving 1972). The following five-step scale proved satisfactory for the occupations reported by the Maori students:

1. Father a laborer; mother doing unskilled work such as cleaning, or not employed outside the home;
2. Father a skilled worker with a ticket, or working as a factory operative or truck driver; mother may be a factory operative;
3. Father a foreman, or overseer, or farm owner;
4. Father in business — sales, or clerical, or small retail shop;
5. Father a professional, or owner of a business with employees outside of the family.

Tables 1 and 2 show the distribution of socioeconomic ratings, with I equal to 2; and III standing for 3, 4, or 5. There were too few Maori fathers with status 4 or 5 to make it possible to set up a separate category for those levels. Thus, the average Pakeha of status III was slightly above the average Maori of status III.

Time Perspective

To measure the relative importance of the future compared with the present, it is useful to ask a respondent WHAT his major goals or wants are, and WHEN he thinks he can satisfy or achieve these wants or goals. Bray asked this kind of question in several ways. For example, he asked students to respond to the following question: Now think of something, that you, yourself, want to happen more than anything else. How SOON do you think of this as happening? In less than one week ——; in 1 to 4 weeks ——; 1 to 6 months ——; 6 months to

Table 1.   Clarity of image of the future, related to ethnicity

		No perspective 1	Short-term view 2	Partly clear 3	Clear view 4	Total
SES	Ethnicity					
I	Maori	22	26	22	6	76
	Pakeha	0	7	4	7	18
	Total number	22	33	26	13	94
		Probability of occurrence by chance: less than 0.01				
II	Maori	12	22	17	8	59
	Pakeha	0	5	14	7	26
	Total number	12	27	31	15	85
		Probability less than 0.02				
III	Maori	5	14	22	10	51
	Pakeha	5	28	33	33	99
	Total number	10	42	55	43	150
		$p = 0.02$				

Note: Probabilities computed by chi-square method.

Table 2.   Clarity of image of the future, related to socioeconomic status (SES)

	No perspective 1	Short-term view 2	Partly clear 3	Clear view 4	Total
SES					
I (low)	22	33	26	13	94
II	12	27	31	15	85
III (high)	10	42	55	43	150
Total number	44	102	112	71	329
	Probability of occurrence by chance: much less than 0.01				

Note: Probabilities computed by chi-square method.

one year ——; 1 to 5 years ——; 5 to 10 years ——; longer than 10 years ——.

Bray asked a number of questions of this general type. He also asked the respondent whether he would prefer a gift of money; and if so, whether he would prefer a small amount now, or greater amounts at various times in the future. Bray's instrument seems to be ingenious, and workable with boys and girls who can read as well as an average eleven-year-old. Actually, he read the questions aloud to his respondents in groups, and adjusted the time to what seemed a comfortable speed.

The method used in the present research is similar to that of Bray in stressing the wants and goals of the respondent. Thereby it avoids the danger of arbitrarily setting goals (money, achievement, friendly social relations, school qualifications, travel, sports) which would have different degrees of attractiveness for different persons. Each person is free to state his own wants and goals, or to think of them in relation to the present and future.

The method used in this research was described by Joseph Nuttin, a Belgian psychologist (Nuttin 1964). It consists of a sentence-completion instrument, in which the respondent completes eleven stems that start with statements expressing a hope, wish, goal, or fear. Nuttin wrote, "Future time perspective is to be studied in the framework of the plans, interests, wishes, strivings, and tasks in which behavioural needs develop in man" (Nuttin 1964: a. 67). He thought that there was an advantage in concealing the interest of the researcher in time perspective, so that the respondent might not be made self-conscious about the time dimension. Yet each response could be placed by the researcher on a time scale, from the past through the present to the distant future. Using his instrument with persons ranging in age from adolescence to old age, he found very few references to the past, and he was able to place the responses on a scale starting from the immediate present to points in the fairly distant future. Thus, he could obtain a time-perspective score for each respondent. He used a sentence-completion instrument with about forty stems to be completed. The present research used eleven stems, on the following form:

Anonymous

What I hope, and want, or dislike
Please fill out the blank spaces on this page by making a sentence to complete the idea that starts each line. Please answer with whatever seems the right thing to say. Of course different people will give different answers.

1. I hope
2. I am working toward
3. I would like
4. I want to
5. I expect to
6. I am trying to
7. I would like it very much if
8. I enjoy
9. I am afraid that
10. What bothers me is
11. I would feel badly if

Your age: ——— years. Male ——— Female ———
Are you Pakeha? ——— Maori? ——— Full ——— ¾ ——— ½ ———
What school grade? Form ———
Your father's occupation ———

SCORING THE SENTENCE-COMPLETION INSTRUMENT FOR TIME PERSPECTIVE

Every response can be located on a time-line, from the immediate present to the far distant future. The question to be answered by the scorer is: WHEN can the action be accomplished, or WHEN is it being accomplished? The scale which the author developed is as follows:

Score	Symbol	Time when the principal part of the action takes place
1	A1	Today
1	A2	This week
1	A3	This month
2	A4	This year
3	A5	During the next five years
2	A	In the general undefined present
3	B	In the general undefined future
3	B1	During the coming educational period — secondary school or university
4	B2	In early adulthood
5	B3	In middle adulthood
5	B4	In old age
5	B5	During adult life as a whole

General Rules for Scoring

If the action can be placed in a definite time period, there is no problem in scoring. Thus I WOULD LIKE: "to have a birthday party next week," is clearly rated A3 (this month), but "to get school certificate" is rated A4 (this year) if the response is made early in the school year, while "to become a carpenter and to have my own business" is located in early or middle adulthood and is scored B2 or B3.

Some responses refer to actions or outcomes that cannot be placed very accurately in time. These are rated A (general undefined present) or B (general undefined future). For example, the following should be rated A:

I ENJOY: "sports"
WHAT BOTHERS ME IS: "the Maori social problem"

But, the following should be rated B:

I HOPE: "We will conserve our natural resources"
I WANT: "to be independent"
I AM TRYING: "to save money"

The reason for rating these B is that they all have a strong future implication, even though some of the action is in the present.

The Appendix contains a number of examples of responses from Maori pupils, with their time-perspective scores. It is clear that many of the responses are personal and probably quite genuine. The content categories are interesting, but not relevant to this research. They tend to indicate the prevalent interests and concerns of the young respondents. The score for an individual respondent is the sum of the scores for his responses divided by the number of responses. The range was 1.9 to 3.6, with all but a few scores ranging from 2.2 to 3.3. The standard deviation of those scores ranged from 0.26 to 0.29 for the several subgroups whose scores are reported in Table 3.

Table 3. Time perspective in relation to Maori-Pakeha, socioeconomic status, and sex differences: mean time-perspective scores*

	I	II	III
SES			
Maori	2.68	2.68	2.74
Pakeha	2.85	2.87	2.82
Significance of difference	p 0.02	0.01	0.12
	Male	Female	Significance
SES			
III	2.86	2.74	01
II	2.74	2.70	n.s.
I	2.71	2.66	n.s.

* Significance of differences between means computed with a t test. Standard deviation in these samples ranges from 0.26 to 0.29.

THE ACTIVITY-SATISFACTION INVENTORY

Though not a measure of time perspective or image of the future, the activity-satisfaction inventory was included in this research to test the generally held notion that Maoris are more interested in socially gratifying activities than they are in activities that require a drive for achievement or are bookish. The instrument was as follows:

Satisfaction with activities
Please place a check on each line below, to show how much you like the following activities:

	Much —— Some —— Not Much ——		
1. Being with friends	——	——	——
2. Doing well in sports or athletics	——	——	——
3. Getting good marks in school	——	——	——
4. Having many friends	——	——	——
5. Reading a good book	——	——	——

6. Earning money ———   ———   ———
7. Doing something important,
    but hard to do ———   ———   ———
8. Helping other people ———   ———   ———
9. Doing new things — having new
    experiences ———   ———   ———
10. Doing things with friends ———   ———   ———
11. Working with my hands ———   ———   ———

Items 1, 4, 8 and 10 are placed in the FRIENDSHIP category; items 3, 6, 7 are categorized as ACHIEVEMENT; the other items are treated separately.

THE SAMPLE OF YOUNG PEOPLE

The young men and women who were studied in this research were either attending the fifth form of secondary schools or were working as apprentices or young learners in business and industry in Whangarei, Auckland, and Wellington. The actual numbers interviewed are reported in Table 4. Three secondary schools in the Northland area were chosen because they drew students heavily (by bus) from rural communities and because the influence of Maori culture would presumably be at a maximum in those areas. (A similar argument could be made for schools in the eastern part of the North Island, but a choice had to be made.)

Table 4.   Interviews with fifth-form students

	Maori students percent	Male		Female	
		Maori	Pakeha	Maori	Pakeha
Northland					
School A	10	7	18	11	13
School B	30	16	6	20	8
School C	50	17	3	18	3
Whangarei*		15	4	12	13
		55	31	61	37
Urban Wellington					
School D	20	9	16	13	14
School E	40	9	10	14	5
School F	10	8	7	10	8
School G	30	6	5	5	5
		32	38	42	32
Total		87	69	103	69

* These were not in school. They were out-of-school youth aged sixteen to twenty-one, in Wangarei. As a group, they were not notably different from the other groups in their responses.

The other set of four schools are all located in the urbanized areas of Wellington or Auckland, with substantial numbers of Maori pupils. The parents of the respondents are employed in the urban economy, and the vocational horizons of adolescents are presumably wider and clearer than in the rural Northland.

Compared with the samples studied by Bray or by Ausubel, this sample is more representative in some ways and less in other ways. Bray's sample consisted of third-form students in seven secondary schools. He excluded students who describe themselves as "partly Pakeha and partly Maori." Thus, Bray's sample is more representative of Maoris who describe themselves as of "full Maori" ancestry. Also, his sample does not suffer from the differential dropping out of Maori and Pakeha pupils when they reach the age of fifteen, which tends to decimate the Maori enrollment, especially at the fifth form.

Ausubel's sample consisted of pupils in the third, fourth, and fifth forms in secondary schools in two areas: a rural east North Island area, and an urban-rural west North Island area. What he called his urban sample attended a technical high school in Wanganui. But, of forty-eight Maori pupils, only nineteen lived in the city proper, while twenty-nine lived in rural neighborhoods and came by bus to school. This was in 1957–1958, when there were relatively few Maori pupils in the schools of Wellington, Auckland, and the other larger cities.

Neither Bray nor Ausubel treated socioeconomic status as a variable to be studied by breaking the sample into socioeconomic subgroups. Ausubel matched Pakeha and Maori on the basis of fathers' occupations, and thus was able to keep SES (socioeconomic status) constant in his study. Bray's urban school drew heavily from a low-income area, and he concluded that his city-school sample was rather similar in socioeconomic status to his rural-school sample.

The sample in the present research has the advantage of being divisible into three socioeconomic groups for the purpose of studying socioeconomic differences. It also has a fuller contrast of rural- versus urban-background pupils.

One possible disadvantage of the present sample is that the Maori sample of pupils suffers from the differential loss of Maori pupils at the age of fifteen, when more Maoris than Pakehas drop out of school; this may be partially compensated by the presence of out-of-school youth from Whangarei, many of whom dropped out before reaching the fifth form. A second possible disadvantage is that the present sample included a number of pupils who described themselves as Maoris of three-quarters or half Maori ancestry, while Bray excluded this group. The New Zealand census includes as Maoris all who claim half or more Maori ancestry, plus any others who claim to be Maoris, even though they have less than half Maori ancestry. Thus, the present sample represents Maoris as they are reported in the New Zealand census.

There is also a question as to whether the samples in this research are truly representative of the school groups from which they were drawn. The school authorities were asked to provide a "range" of academic ability and adjustment, but were not asked to make a truly random selection. The Maori sample is certainly fairly representative of the Maori fifth-form pupils. In schools A, D, E, F, ALL fifth-form Maori boys were interviewed if they were present at school on the days when the interviews were conducted. Nearly all fifth-form Maori girls were interviewed in those schools, but a few were not seen due to the fact that girls were more numerous than boys. As for the Pakeha samples, they were drawn from a larger number of pupils, and there is a chance that they are not as truly representative of their groups as are the Maori pupils. However, the author saw nothing to indicate that the Pakehas might have been selected with a bias. For example, the classes were streamed according to academic performance in several of the schools; and in such situations, equal numbers of Pakeha and Maori pupils from a given stream were provided.

VALIDITY OF THE INSTRUMENTS

Since we are dealing with time perspective and with values in relation to present versus future orientation, we recognize that these are complex constructs and are not likely to be measured with the kind of accuracy with which height and weight can be measured. The debate about the validity of various intelligence tests will help us to understand the complexity and the difficulty of the validity concept applied to social-psychological instruments.

There are three kinds of validity that may be considered for a given measuring instrument.

1.   CRITERION VALIDITY: Close correlation of the scores on the instrument with a behavior criterion that is recognized as valid. But we have no agreed-upon criterion of time-perspective behavior. A good approach to this might be a set of ratings by judges who know a person well, concerning his actions with respect to present and future goals.

Does he actually sacrifice present gratification in the pursuit of a long-term goal? Or does he concern himself mainly with the achievement of goals that can be achieved within the next few hours, days, or weeks? These ratings would then be examined for the degree of their correlation with the instrument for which we wish to establish a degree of validity. But this procedure is so expensive and time-consuming that we are not likely to carry it through adequately. Hence, we are not likely to establish the criterion validity of this kind of instrument.

2.   FACE VALIDITY: Do various people who examine the instrument agree that it SEEMS to be getting at the entity which it purports to measure? But this is a weak form of validity.

3.   CONSTRUCT VALIDITY: Does the instrument give results that correlate substantially with other instruments which purport to measure the entity that is being studied? If two different instruments give exactly the same results, so that their correlation coefficient is close to 1, we may assume that they measure the same entity. Even if they correlate only as 0.8, they are likely to be measuring almost the same entity, since each instrument has less than perfect reliability on a test-retest trial. In general, if two instruments that we believe do measure the entity x have a coefficient of correlation as high as 0.5, we can say that they each measure a part of the entity which they purport to measure. The correlation coefficient indicates the extent of the overlap of the two instruments. But each instrument may also measure a part of the complex entity which the other does not measure, and thus both instruments may have some validity. An average of scores from the two instruments should have greater validity than either score alone.

When attempting to measure a complex social-psychological entity, it is desirable, therefore, to use two or more instruments that possess face validity. If their intercorrelation is of the order of 0.4 to 0.6, the average of the scores has a rather high construct validity.

In the case of this research, the instrument used by Bray and our time-perspective instrument might well be used with a given group of students to get greater assurance of their mutual construct validity. This was not possible, but something approaching it has been done by comparing Maori versus Pakeha performance on the two instruments. If the results of this comparison are generally in agreement, we may suppose that the combined evidence is stronger than the evidence from either instrument alone.

RESULTS OF THE RESEARCH

Clarity of Image of the Future

Tables 1 and 2 report the data on the ratings of "clarity of image of the future," related to ethnicity and to socioeconomic status. There is no reliable difference between the sexes. There is a strong relation between clarity of image of the future and SES, students of lower SES showing much less clarity. Fifty percent of the ratings of 1 (no perspective on the future) came from respondents with SES 1, or 28 percent of the total sample.

When SES is held constant, there is also a superiority of Pakehas over Maoris; but this superiority is greater at the lowest SES level than at the highest SES level. Compared with children of unskilled workers, Maori children whose parents have achieved the status of foreman or independent farmer or proprietor of a small business have a clearer view of their vocational options, as well as models of greater vocational competence in their own family.

Ausubel's comments concerning the situation in the late 1950's are still true, but not as broadly true. He wrote:

Maori parents are less capable than their pakeha counterparts of helping their children with appropriate vocational advice, information and guidance. They are generally less sophisticated than pakeha parents about the prevailing range of occupational choices, about the current availability of various kinds of jobs, and about the requirements and procedures for entering a given field of employment. The larger size and lower per capita income of Maori families also make Maori parents more reluctant about committing themselves to plans involving long-term vocational preparation (i.e., prolonged schooling or apprenticeship) for their children. It is true that Government bursaries and tribal trust funds are often available for these purposes, but most Maori parents are hopelessly confused about the procedures involved in applying for such assistance.

A related problem is found in the tendency for Maori parents to start too late in placing their children in suitable jobs. They typically wait until the end of the school year, by which time all of the vacancies are filled by pakeha youths (Ausubel 1961: 63).

Time Perspective

Data on time perspective are shown in Table 3, in relation to Maori-Pakeha, socioeconomic status, and sex differences. The Pakeha groups have reliably higher TP (time-perspective) scores than the Maori, for the two lower SES groups, but SES group III does not show a statistically reliable difference. Males are higher than females, but the difference is reliable only at the SES III level. The SES differences are not statistically reliable. In general, these findings parallel those of Bray.

Results From the Activity-Satisfaction Questionnaire

Table 5 gives the results for all ethnic-sex groups from the activity-tatisfaction questionnaire. The full hypothesis was tested by means of chi-square for the differences that seemed to merit this kind of inquiry. The results are as follows:

FRIENDSHIP ACTIVITY: Girls reported more satisfaction than boys in both ethnic groups ($P = 0.001$). Pakehas reported slightly more satisfaction than Maoris ($P = 0.200$).

ACHIEVEMENT ACTIVITY: Pakehas reported more satisfaction than Maoris with achievement activity ($P = 0.01$). This was due almost entirely to differences between the two groups of young men. Young women did not show a reliable Pakeha-Maori difference, though their difference was in the same direction as that for the boys. The difference between the Pakehas and Maoris was entirely due to the Pakehas expressing more satisfaction than the Maoris with the category DOING SOMETHING IMPORTANT, BUT HARD TO DO.

READING A GOOD BOOK: There was no reliable ethnic difference, but girls gave somewhat more favorable responses than boys ($P = 0.15$).

SPORTS: There was no reliable difference between ethnic groups, or between boys and girls, but boys tended to be more favorable to "sports and athletics" than girls ($P = 0.2$).

With one exception, these findings agree with the general notions about Maori-Pakeha differences. The Pakehas reported slightly more satisfaction with FRIENDSHIP ACTIVITIES than did the Maoris, although the general notion is that Maoris take more pleasure in associating with friends and meeting friendship obligations. The Maori-Pakeha differences on READING and on WORKING WITH HANDS are in the "expected" direction, but not large enough to be statistically reliable.

DISCUSSION OF THE FINDINGS

This research agrees in a general way with that of Bray on temporal values. The earlier discussion and recommendations of Ausubel still

Table 5.   Satisfaction with various kinds of activities: scores of Maori and Pakeha youth

Activity	Number of items	Degree of satisfaction											
		Much				Some				Not much			
		Maori		Pakeha		Maori		Pakeha		Maori		Pakeha	
		M	F	M	F	M	F	M	F	M	F	M	F
Friendship	4	1.93	2.48	2.22	2.60	1.78	1.45	1.55	1.21	0.31	0.09	0.24	0.07
Achievement	3	1.45	1.46	1.80	1.66	1.10	1.23	1.11	1.10	0.35	0.30	0.11	0.18
New experience	1	0.51	0.58	0.62	0.62	0.33	0.37	0.34	0.31	0.14	0.04	0.05	0.04
Reading	1	0.30	0.52	0.34	0.38	0.53	0.42	0.49	0.47	0.17	0.08	0.13	0.15
Manual activity	1	0.55	0.42	0.51	0.32	0.36	0.41	0.33	0.45	0.09	0.15	0.12	0.24
Sports	1	0.45	0.37	0.40	0.26	0.48	0.48	0.42	0.60	0.07	0.18	0.15	0.13
Number of persons		57	65	55	53	57	65	55	53	57	65	55	53

The scores report the average number of items checked for degree of satisfaction by the members of each subgroup. Totaling across a row for a particular group gives the number of items, with slight variation due to rounding of fractions.

have some validity; but the rapid urbanization of the Maoris, as predicted by Ausubel, both improves the opportunity of Maori youth for earning a living in New Zealand and increases the problem of Maori youth in coping with the contemporary situation.

The differences between Pakeha and Maori youth may be decreasing in some important respects. The contrasting patterns of values and attitudes that were written about by students of Maori culture twenty or thirty years ago do not seem to be such great contrasts today. As Maori people move up the socioeconomic ladder into white-collar occupations and skilled trades, it appears that this subgroup differs less from the Pakeha than do the Maoris in rural and in lower working-class occupations.

The educational and employment policies of the New Zealand government are opening opportunities for socioeconomic advancement to Maori youth. But the vision of the future is still very cloudy for most Maori youth, especially those who have been reared in rural areas and those who have grown up in lower working-class families. For all of its desirable characteristics, the typical Maori family of the lower working class needs substantial assistance from educational and welfare agencies to do the following things for Maori youth:

1. Improve the school achievement of Maori youth.
2. Increase the proportions of Maori youth who continue in school to the ages of sixteen and seventeen.
3. Provide more vocational information, work experience, and apprenticeship opportunity for Maori boys and girls.

APPENDIX

Examples of sentence-completion responses on time perspective from Maori fifth-form students

Score	Rating	Response
3	A5	*I hope:* to get picked for the Wellington Rugby Team
3	A5	to become an air hostess
4	B2	to be a highly qualified cabinetmaker
2	A4	that I get my S.C. this year
3	A5	*I am working toward:* an office job to save and travel
5	B3	a stable position in this society
4	B2	getting a good home for a family if I have one
3	B	*I would like:* to see more Maoris taking advantage of things given them

3	A5	to go back on the farm and help my father
5	B3	very much to have fifteen children
4	B2	to be an A-grade welder

4	B2	*I want to:* be able to work and still have time for my children
4	B2	help teenage delinquents to understand life
3	B	be able to show others how proud I am to be a Maori

4	B2	*I expect to:* raise children to be better than me
5	B3	die a natural death after fulfilling a competent and full life
4	B2	stay single if I can

3	A5	*I am trying to:* get S.C. and then move back to the country
2	A	get my parents to trust me going out
3	B	gather enough money so that I can buy a car
2	A	lead a better life than my sisters led

2	A	*I would like it very much if:* people were allowed to smoke in school
2	A	I was allowed more freedom
1	A3	I had a job during school holidays

2	A	*I enjoy:* marching, netball, and my boyfriend's company
2	A	playing rugby, indoor basketball, water polo, the piano
2	A	being a Maori because I think black is like white — they are both beautiful

3	A5	*I am afraid that:* my parents might die before my marriage
4	B2	I won't be able to cope with life
4	B2	When I grow up I will be unsuccessful

2	A	*What bothers me is:* I don't know how to do some of my subjects
2	A	bullies, no money, no job
2	A	that teachers are prejudiced against me
3	A5	the amount of time it takes to get a welder's ticket

3	B	*I would feel badly if:* I hit my brother too hard
3	B	nobody took any pride in me
3	B	I do not pass my exams, and if I had to fall in love with someone
2	A4	I had no horse or guitar

REFERENCES

AUSUBEL, DAVID P.
1961 *Maori youth: a psychoethnological study of cultural deprivation.* Wellington: Price Milburn.

BALLARD, K. D.
1972 A comparison of two measures of socio-economic status. *New Zealand Journal of Educational Studies* 7:167–172.

BEAGLEHOLE, E., P. BEAGLEHOLE
1946 *Some modern Maoris.* Wellington: New Zealand Council for Educational Research.

BRAY, D. H.
1971 Maori adolescent temporal values: distance of goals perceived as important and delayed gratification, as compared with Pakehas. *New Zealand Journal of Educational Studies* 6:62–77.
1973 "Attitudes and values of Polynesian and Pakeha: social and educational implications of research findings," in *Contemporary New Zealand.* Edited by K. W. Thomson and A. D. Trlin, 174–185. Wellington: Hicks Smith and Sons.

CONGALTON, ATHOL A., ROBERT J. HAVIGHURST
1954 Status rankings of occupations in New Zealand. *Australian Journal of Psychology* 4:10–16.

ELLEY, M. B., J. C. IRVING
1972 A socio-economic index for New Zealand based on levels of education and income from the 1966 census. *New Zealand Journal of Educational Studies* 7:153–167.

NUTTIN, JOSEPH R.
1964 The future time perspective in human motivation and learning. *Acta Psychologica* 23:60–82.

RITCHIE, J. E.
1956 "Basic personality in Rakau." Department of Psychology, Victoria University of Wellington.

RITCHIE, JANE
1957 "Childhood in Rakau: the first five years of life." Department of Psychology, Victoria University of Wellington.

The Economic Importance of Children in a Javanese Village

BENJAMIN WHITE

While there has been comparatively little research in Java on fertility attitudes and practices, there are several quantitative and qualitative studies which indicate the prevalence among both rural and urban couples of the desire for large numbers of children, matched in practice by a high level of marital fertility (see, for example, Gille and Pardoko 1965; IPPA 1969a, 1969b; Geertz 1961; Koentjaraningrat n.d.). These studies on the whole confirm Jay's impression that "The value that Javanese society places upon a family full of children can scarcely be exaggerated.... Across the entire social spectrum... children are desired in abundance" (Jay 1969: 97).

In view of the acuteness of the population problem in Java, one's first impulse perhaps is to regard the desire for children "in abundance" as totally out of step with the reality of Javanese economic life, as a prime example of the "irrationality" that social scientists so frequently describe in peasant life. In the aggregate or statistical sense — that is, from the point of view of the Javanese economy as a whole — there is ample justification for the view that high fertility will in the foreseeable

Field research (beginning in August 1972 and still in progress at the time of writing) was carried out in a village in Kabupaten Kulon Progo, special district of Jogjakarta, as part of a project on "The economic cost and value of children in four agricultural societies" under the general direction of Dr. Moni Nag, Columbia University. The project was funded by the National Institutes of Health — National Institute of Child Health and Development, under Contract Number NIH — NICHD–71–2209. I am very grateful to Moni Nag and Anne Stoler for advice and encouragement at all stages of the research; also to Drs. Masri Singarimbun, Hanna Papanek and Mely G. Tan for the opportunity to present earlier versions of this paper in seminars at Gadjah Mada University, Jogjakarta and University of Indonesia, Jakarta.

future mean only more mouths to feed in that crowded island and more children to educate, who when they reach potentially productive age, will add themselves to an already overcrowded and underproductive labor-force. Population growth certainly implies, for the large majority of the children born each year, increasingly bleak economic prospects. However, because the basic unit of demographic behavior (and likewise, in Java, of economic behavior) is the family, if we wish to examine the economic rationality or otherwise of demographic behavior, we must transfer our attention from large-scale statistics to individual couples in their individual economic environments. In doing so, we should not assume that the Javanese family economy merely replicates in miniature the Javanese economy as a whole. In this paper, I hope to question the view that rural overpopulation implies that prospective Javanese parents have no economic justification for producing large families of potential child laborers.

Such a view, I think, is based on dubious assumptions concerning the implications of overpopulation in terms of labor opportunities and the value of children's labor within the family. Overpopulation and the existence of a labor surplus in the Javanese rural context do not mean that large numbers of people are reduced to complete idleness for long periods of time ("idleness" in the sense of having no opportunity to work at all, is perhaps a peculiar characteristic of the unemployed in industrial economies, as depicted in the cry of America's depression years, "How can I work when there's no work to do?"). On the contrary, people are forced by population pressure into increasingly marginal and UNDERproductive activities, (that is, activities with increasingly low returns to labor) and must therefore work increasingly LONGER hours to achieve the required minimal returns. Labor is abundant, and cheap in the market, but since it is the only resource available to so many Javanese families, it is still for them a valuable resource. Under these conditions, rather than assuming *a priori* that the economic costs of children to their parents outweigh the economic benefits, we should consider carefully the extent to which Javanese parents may derive benefit (although their children, and the economy as a whole, do not) from the production of large numbers of children as a potential source of labor. In what follows, with the aid of preliminary results from field research in a Javanese village, I shall attempt to outline some of the economic benefits arising from high fertility, considered from the parents' point of view.

No systematic research on this topic has yet been done in Java, or in other agricultural societies so far as I know; but there are some studies which, though not specifically concerned with the cost and value of children, give us some general information about the ages at which Javanese children begin participating in production, and the kinds of tasks they engage in. Slamet, for instance, estimates (1965: 173) that by the age of eight children in Java have begun to join in all the sub- sistence activities and daily work of their parents. Koentjaraningrat (n.d.: 146ff.) notes that in Tjelapar (South Central Java) regular school attendance is rare; instead, girls are engaged in household tasks, cook- ing, pounding paddy, or caring for younger sibs, while boys are sent by their parents to collect branches and leaves from the woods (for use as wrappers or for weaving), to help in garden cultivation, etc. A majority of boys and girls also earn wages herding water-buffalo, cows, goats, or ducks. The conflict between children's education and the need for their labor is mentioned also by Budi Prasadja (1972: 46), who notes that in Gegesik (West Java) economic pressures often force small farmers and landless laborers to neglect their children's educa- tion, because they need their labor, especially in the case of male children. Gille and Pardoko note that "As soon as he reaches school age [six or seven years] every child born into a farmer's family is put to work on the land during the peak periods of planting and harvesting, when all available labour is used" (Gille and Pardoko 1965: 503–504). In rural Modjokuto (East Java) Jay wrote that he:

... observed children to be industrious, even at an early age, in picking up small piecework jobs such as hulling peanuts or sorting and bundling onions. ... As the children move into adolescence, their labour of course becomes more valuable. A daughter in particular is able to carry much of the load of housework and also to work with the mother in the fields for cash wages when there are opportunities. Sons are helpful not so much for the work they may do with the father, which in my observation was mini- mal, but for the exchange labour they can perform as a young male of the household (1969: 69).

In small-town Modjokuto, "little girls [i.e. pre-adolescent] ... soon learn to do the whole family shopping alone, and — if the mother sells in the market — may take over the mother's stand for short periods." During adolescence, boys may start to earn money ...

... by occasional farm-work, as a labourer in a shop making cigarettes, as a ticket-collector on one of the many jitneys [or] as apprentice to a tailor or carpenter. Girls rarely work except in the mother's business ... they usually remain at home, occupied with a continual round of domestic duties (Geertz 1961: 116, 118ff).

While these observations are of interest, much more quantitative research is necessary if we wish, for instance, to compare the Javanese case with Clark's estimate that children in Asian peasant societies may become "net producers" (i.e. produce more than they consume) at ages as low as seven years (Clark 1970: 226). Indeed, the question turns out to be a very complex one on closer examination.[1] In order to compare the "economic cost" with the "economic value" of children, we require a substantial amount of data from families of various sizes and economic levels on at least the following points. With regard to the COSTS of children, we would need to know as a minimum: (1) the economic costs of pregnancy and childbirth; (2) the cost of feeding, clothing, educating, and otherwise caring for a child at various ages; (3) the cost of all the social and ritual obligations incurred from the time of the mother's pregnancy until the child reaches adulthood (in Java these costs are considerable); and (4) the opportunity costs involved in the production and rearing of an extra child, e.g. the time lost by the mother in pregnancy, childbirth, and nursing when she might otherwise be productively employed. In addition, we should determine from current mortality levels (5) the probability that a child will survive to a given age, and thus the costs "lost" on children who fail to reach productive age. Turning to the economic VALUE of children, two kinds of values should be considered: (6) the value of children as sources of security for parents in old age (a factor whose resistance to quantification does not negate its importance in the shaping of reproductive decisions); and (7) the value of children as a source of productive or useful labor in the household economy. Since it is clearly impossible to deal with all of these questions here, I shall confine myself almost entirely to the last one. This question itself requires data on the following points: (1) At what ages do children of either sex become CAPABLE of performing various productive or useful activities? (2) How does their output at various ages compare with that of an adult? (3) Granted a given level of POTENTIAL of children in productive or useful activities, what is the ACTUAL extent of their involvement in the household economy? — in other words, to what extent does the over-populated, "labor-surplus" economy still allow room for the participation of children.

It is important to remember that while the POTENTIAL of children for various kinds of economic activity depends largely on physiological factors (levels of health and nutrition, etc.), the extent of their actual

---

[1] Various approaches to the study of the economic value of children in agricultural societies, and some relevant ethnographic data, are discussed in Nag (1972).

participation in the economy depends upon a number of additional factors specific to the particular economy and society in question. Thus, before providing any data on children's economic activities, I shall attempt to put the material in an economic framework with a brief description of the economy of the village sample studied, and the available opportunities for productive activity.

Economic Characteristics of the Population Studied

The population studied consists of several hamlets in a village complex approximately twenty-five kilometers northwest of the city of Jogjakarta. Basic demographic and economic data were obtained from about 500 households, but I shall deal here with only forty households which were selected for detailed research on the participation of children in the household economy. This small sample (which at a later stage of research was increased to 100 households) consisted of small farmers and landless laborers and the households selected contained at least one child of potentially working age (over six years) so that the average household size (6.3) was considerably larger than the average for the village as a whole (4.5). Average land-holdings per household and per capita are shown in Table 1.

Table 1. Average land-holdings in the forty household sample (in hectares)

	Per capita	Per household
Sawah [irrigated rice-fields]	0.0170 hectares	0.1066 hectares
Pekarangan and *tegalan* [house-compounds and dry fields]	0.0289 hectares	0.1811 hectares
Total:	0.0459 hectares	0.2877 hectares

In the region in question, the varying quality of *sawah* (mostly rather low) and an uncertain water supply make for equally uncertain yields, so that it is not easy to estimate how much *sawah* is necessary to supply the average household's rice needs. However, taking 125 kilograms of hulled rice as the average per capita requirement per year (see Penny and Singarimbun 1972: 83) and thus almost eight quintals as the annual requirement of a household of average size in our sample, we can be certain that at the very least, all households with less than one-tenth hectare (that is, almost three-quarters of the forty-household sample) fall in the category of those unable to meet their rice requirement from their own land in normal years. Garden crops are also sold for cash or in exchange for rice, but there are no households in our

sample whose primary source of income or subsistence is garden cultivation. The large majority of our sample, then, are compelled to rely
on activities outside the "family farm" for a major part of their basic
subsistence. I shall briefly describe the most important of these other
subsistence activities.

Sharecropping   With this system, the land-owner usually provides none
of the inputs (cost of seeds, fertilizer, cultivation, etc.) although he
usually pays the land tax, and receives as rent one-half of the total
yield. It can thus be said that from the sharecropper's point of view,
the returns to his inputs of cash and labor are approximately one-half
what they would be were he cultivating his own land. There are nine
sharecroppers in our forty-household sample.

Agricultural wage-labor   Irrigated rice, besides requiring almost continual attention, demands large amounts of labor over short periods of
time at three stages in the cycle (hoeing, planting, and harvesting); even
small holders can rarely provide this labor from their own families, and
must therefore seek outside labor. Some small farmers enter reciprocal
(*gotong-royong*) labor exchange arrangements for this purpose, but the
large majority engage hired labor. At the time of my research, wages
for these tasks were as follows:
Male labor (ground preparation): thirty to forty rupiah for three to
    four hours
Female labor (planting): fifteen to twenty-five rupiah for three to four
    hours; (harvesting): one-sixth to one-tenth of the total rice she
    harvests.
A day's harvesting yields more in rice than other kinds of wage labor
(Anne Stoler's research in the same village showed the average share
or *bawon* received by harvesters to be 3.5 kilograms of unhulled rice),
and this partly explains why planting wages are so low; those who have
participated in the planting expect later to be invited, or at least allowed, to join in the harvest. Some do not even ask for planting wages,
in the hopes that their *bawon* at harvesting will be increased. Wages
are quoted for half-day periods of three to four hours because labor
is normally engaged by the half-day, and only at peak periods can
laborers obtain an occasional full day's paid labor.

Handicrafts for cash sale   The main handicrafts for cash sale are
tikar [pandanus sleeping-mats], woven by women, and *kepang* [split-
bamboo mats], used often for drying rice, and usually woven by men.
Almost all the households studied engage in mat weaving as a part-

time occupation. Some also gather, cut, boil, and soften pandanus-leaves for sale to *tikar*-weavers. Most of the *tikar*-weavers produce on an average one *tikar* each five days, weaving for about four hours each day; the cost of materials is thirty-five rupiah, while the finished product sells for sixty to 120 rupiah depending on size, quality and on the season. Thus the weaver makes only one to four rupiah per hour; returns to labor for a *kepang*-weaver are only slightly higher.

Small trading   In the forty households, a large number of women and a few men are engaged in small-scale trade as a permanent or seasonal source of income; carrying loads of goods or produce, usually on foot and occasionally by bicycle, from home to market, from market to town, or from market to market over a range of up to thirty kilometers, for very small profits. Given the distances covered, this is a very time-consuming occupation (a minimum of four hours daily, and a maximum of twenty-four hours in the case of the distant markets). Most of these small traders or *bakuls*, with a working capital of 500-1000 rupiah, earn perhaps fifty to a hundred rupiah on their selling days.

Animal husbandry   The forty households own and care for a large number of animals: altogether 298 chickens, 61 ducks, 46 goats or sheep, 32 cows, and 4 water-buffalos. Chickens generally find their own food, apart from being fed kitchen scraps, but all other animals require a considerable amount of labor to care for and feed. Ducks must be fed and taken to water for extended periods each day; goats, sheep, cows, and water-buffalos all require fodder which is generally cut and brought to them from gardens, roadsides, river banks, irrigation channels and the edges of rice fields. In addition, cows and water-buffalos must be taken to water. For those households with enough labor to care for them, these animals provide an important means of storing wealth, besides a regular source of income in the case of laying chickens and ducks, and a seasonal source of income in the case of working cows and water-buffalos. An idea of the value of the larger beasts is given by two common practices. First, a household with enough labor to care for a beast but not enough capital to purchase one will often undertake to care for animals belonging to a richer household. The animals remain the property of the original owner, but half of their offspring become the property of the "sharecropping" household. Second, a cow or water-buffalo requires at least one large basket of green fodder each day, mixed with another of paddy-stalks; an owner who cannot provide the labor from his own household will pay from thirty to fifty rupiah per day (compare this with the wages quoted above) for that amount of fodder. It should be noted that here, as elsewhere in rural Java, animal husbandry does not provide a significant source of meat or eggs for home consumption; 95 percent of the eggs, and virtually all the animals, are sold. The major source of protein is the much cheaper *tempe* [fermented soy-bean cakes].

Production of food for sale   Twelve of the forty households are engaged in the production of various food items for cash sale, mostly in the collection of coconut-palm sap and the process of boiling it down to produce *gula Djawa* [palm sugar]. A man will climb the trees twice daily (about two hours in all) to collect the sap (*nderes*), while his wife will boil the sugar (*nites*) for about four hours. Also, up to two hours daily will be necessary to provide sufficient firewood. These labor-inputs (figures are for a household tapping four trees) produce a daily yield of sixty to eighty rupiah. Other items produced for sale are *tempe* (the fermented soy-bean cakes mentioned above) and *dawet* [boiled drink made from rice or arrowroot flour, coconut milk, and *gula Djawa*]. Both of these require comparable amounts of labor in preparation, as well as firewood. To these labor-inputs should be added the hours spent in selling the finished product — a whole morning at the market, unless the product is bought in the house, at a lower price, by neighbors or small traders.

The above summary indicates some important characteristics of household economy in rural Java. If we compare wages or returns to labor from the activities described above with an individual's rice needs (about 1/3 kilogram daily) and with the local price of rice (which rose gradually throughout the research period, from forty to seventy-five rupiah per kilogram), it is clear that though the returns from those activities may meet or even sometimes surpass the rice-requirement of one adult, they definitely fail even to nearly meet the requirements of a whole household of four to six people; even more so if we include a household's other daily expenditures on kerosene for lamps, tobacco, tea, etc. In such conditions, ALL family members in addition to the household head must take whatever labor opportunities there are in order to meet the household's needs. For those households with insufficient land resources and without enough capital to engage in large-scale trade, the most profitable activity in terms of returns per hour is agricultural wage-labor, particularly harvesting with the *bawon*-system. This is confirmed by the common practice of stopping or reducing all other activities during the busy agricultural seasons in order to avail oneself of the more profitable opportunity. But because of the strictly limited nature of such opportunities, all family members must usually spend a large majority of their time in the less productive sectors mentioned above, however low the returns may be, or in other words, WHATEVER THEIR COST IN LABOR TIME to produce the necessary minimal return. The question we now turn to is to what extent under such conditions a married couple may expect to derive economic benefit from the accumulation of large numbers of children as sources of labor.

The Value of Children in the Household Economy

Age of beginning various economic activities   First we need some idea of the ages at which children are capable of performing various economic activities, and the ages at which they begin regularly performing them. A total of 146 household heads were asked at what age their children had begun performing ten types of activity; fetching water, care of chickens or ducks, care of goats or cattle, cutting green fodder, hoeing irrigated rice fields, hoeing dry fields, transplanting rice, harvesting rice, care of younger siblings, and wage-labor of any kind. I have included such activities as fetching water and child care under the heading of "economic activity" (and later shall include others, such as cooking and other housework) because, while not strictly productive, these tasks are necessary for the maintenance of the household, and may frequently be indirectly productive when performed by young children through the freeing of an older household member for more productive labor. The results are summarized in Table 2. From the table it can be seen that while there are isolated cases of children beginning various tasks at five or six years of age, most children begin them at a somewhat later age. This is confirmed by more detailed observations described below. Thus for the sake of simplification I have omitted children below the age of seven years from further consideration in this paper, because the majority of them cannot be considered significantly productive or useful to their parents before that age. But from ages seven to nine, it appears, children of both ages will have begun regular performance of such tasks as water-carrying, animal care, fodder-collection and (in the case of the girls) rice-planting and harvesting; while the heavier tasks of hoeing a wet or dry field (boys) and all kinds of wage labor (both sexes) are not generally begun until thirteen years. An exception to this last is harvesting for a *bawon*-wage, which as we shall see is often performed by very young girls.

Table 2.   Numbers of children engaged regularly in various productive or useful tasks, age of beginning (youngest case) and average age of beginning (from a sample of 146 households)

Activity	Number of children Boys	Girls	Age of beginning (youngest case)	Average age of beginning
Fetch water	29	66	5 years	8.8 years
Care of chickens/ducks	38	18	5	7.9
Care of goats/cattle	58	9	6	9.3
Cut fodder	80	4	6	9.5
Hoe *sawah*	41	—	8	13.0
Hoe dry field	39	—	10	13.1
Transplant rice	—	50	5	9.9
Harvest rice	8	61	7	9.7
Care of younger sibs	36	35	5	8.0
Wage labor	12	8	8	12.9

Productivity of children's labor   With this information as a beginning, we next need to know how the productivity per hour of children at various ages compares with that of adults in various tasks. Relative productivity, in all kinds of manual occupations, depends on a combination of skill and strength (in the forty households there was only one man, a teacher, engaged in non-manual work). So far as skill is concerned, very few of the tasks commonly performed by members of our sample can be classed as skills which take great lengths of time to acquire (the exceptions are tasks performed almost exclusively by adults, such as plowing and perhaps certain kinds of trading). In agriculture, for example, a boy can do all the tasks involved in preparing a rice field (apart from plowing) with as much skill as an adult after about one season's experience. This does not mean, of course, that farming is not a highly skilled occupation, demanding years of experience of differing weather conditions, crop varieties, pests, market conditions, and many other variables. The point is that these skills lie largely in deciding what is to be done and when to do it, rather than in the actual performance of the tasks once the crucial decisions have been made.

From detailed observation of daily activities in the forty-household sample (the methods used are described below), some interesting facts emerged with regard to the productivity of children's labor, if the level of wages received can be taken as an indication of productivity. In the case of wage-labor by boys aged thirteen to fifteen years (hoeing *sawah* or *pekarangan*, and weeding), the wage was in every case the same as

that received by adults; for girls of thirteen to fifteen, from a much
larger number of observed cases, the wages for planting were in all
cases the same as the adult wage. There were also two cases where a
girl of eight years received the same wage as her mother, for the same
hours of work, in the same field. In the case of harvesting with *bawon*-
payment, Anne Stoler's research shows that the *bawon* received by
girls below ten years and in the eleven to fifteen age group averaged
3.0 kilograms of unhulled rice, while that of the over-fifteen age group
was 3.5 kilograms. These data indicate that the productivity per hour
of children's agricultural labor of the most common kinds, at least from
the early teens, is not much lower than that of adults. The same appears
to be true of non-agricultural wage labor, from the few cases that we
observed. Boys of fourteen years regularly received an adult wage for a
full day's labor in construction projects, and girls of fifteen weaving on
handlooms in a small local factory, though paid at piece-work rates,
took home the same wages as their adult counterparts.

For other tasks, particularly those in which younger children are
engaged, it is much more difficult and in some cases impossible to
estimate absolute or relative productivity per hour. In the case of cutting fodder (the most common of all male children's tasks), it frequently
occurred that an adult male would one day cut grass for two hours to
feed the household's animals, while a few days later a boy in the ten
to twelve or thirteen to fifteen age group would spend the same amount
of time to feed the same number of animals. For those below the age
of ten, productivity in this task may be somewhat lower, because the
basket in which they carry the cut grass is usually smaller than that
which adults and older children use. Girls of thirteen and above seem
to be able to weave *tikar* with the same speed as their mothers, although the quality may be somewhat lower if they have only recently
begun weaving, and may thus fetch a lower price. But what of the
productivity of young children in such tasks as taking cattle to bathe,
herding goats or ducks, scaring birds from a field of ripe paddy await-
ing harvest, or staying at home cooking, caring for younger children
and keeping chickens from a *kepang* full of rice drying in the sun, while
the mother is working in the fields or trading at the market? The most
that can be said is that these tasks are very frequently performed by
extremely young children; that they involve long periods of time but
little physical effort; that although these tasks in themselves may not be
productive, they are all NECESSARY in the sense that they must be done
if the household in question wishes to keep animals, to save its rice
from depredation, or to free an older household member for more

productive labor. Furthermore, there is nothing in my observations to suggest that an adult could perform these tasks any better or faster than a small child, although on the other hand, there are many OTHER tasks in which an adult can be more productive than a small child, if he or she is freed from these "necessary but unproductive" tasks. The same would be true of many other tasks such as fishing in streams and irrigation channels to supplement the family's diet, collecting firewood, fetching water (an extremely time-consuming task in the dry season, when water must be scooped in coconut shells from a seep-hole by the water's edge, the river water not being clean enough for household use without this filtering). It is thus interesting, though not surprising, to see that small children spend large amounts of time every day in these "adult-freeing" tasks (Table 3).

Many other cases concerning other tasks could be mentioned if space allowed, each of them suggesting the same conclusions. First, there are a large number of economically useful, sometimes necessary, but not very productive tasks — both in household maintenance and in the productive effort itself — in which small boys and girls from ages as low as six in some cases, and generally by the age of nine, can be virtually as productive or efficient as their adult counterparts could be. However, they remain largely children's tasks because adults and older children can be more productively occupied in other ways. Second, most of the more productive tasks (such as mat weaving, cutting fodder, planting, harvesting, hoeing) can be performed by children thirteen to fifteen years old with a productivity virtually equal to that of adults.

Extent of children's participation in household economy   Given this POTENTIAL for the participation of children in household economy and production, we turn to the question of their ACTUAL contribution to the total production of the household. In other words, having estimated their relative productivity per hour in various kinds of work, we must discover how many hours per day they actually spend in these tasks compared with adults, because a given potential of children, however great, is of no practical significance unless the household economy, and the larger framework of the "labor-surplus" village economy surrounding it still leaves room for the actual exercise of that potential. In order to ascertain the average number of hours spent daily by children and adults of various ages in various kinds of activity, a regular series of visits was made to each of the forty selected households in order to ask each family member how he or she had spent the twenty-four hour period immediately preceding the interview, and the time of beginning and ending each activity. The households were each visited every six days over a period of several months (although I am using here only the data from the first two months, because the remainder were not yet processed at the time of writing). The six-day interval was chosen so that visits should not coincide either with the Javanese five-day market week or with the seven-day week which might have affected the pattern of daily activities, for instance, in trading and school attendance respectively.

Because the writer could not attend each interview, a majority of the interviews was delegated to a team of local secondary-school children or secondary-school graduates, who came from the same hamlets as the small group of households they interviewed and thus were already well acquainted with their subjects.

A number of questions may be raised concerning the accuracy of data collected in this way, particularly in regard to the extent to which the household members, possessing no clocks or watches, will have known with any accuracy the duration of each of their activities. So far as it has been possible to check independently the accuracy of the information recorded, it seems that while there have undoubtedly been omissions and inaccuracies, the general level of accuracy is much higher than I had expected. Omissions that could be easily checked (involving activities that must be done every day, such as cooking, cutting fodder, etc.) were very rare, while irregular or unusual activities (such as *gotong-royong* labor) are of course much more easily recalled. With regard to the accuracy of the times recorded, I found to my surprise that the majority of people whom I asked could correctly estimate the time of day to within a quarter of an hour. It is interesting to note that several features of everyday Javanese village life combine to give both old and young a considerable awareness of the time of day. One might mention the relatively invariable time of sunrise and sunset in a region close to the equator; the practice of gong-beating by hamlet heads at various relatively fixed times of day and night to announce that all is well; the close attention to how many hours are spent in agricultural labor, since the pay varies in accordance with the time spent; the presence in the middle of crowded hamlets of primary schools whose classes begin and end at specific times; and finally the five obligatory daily Moslem prayers, which although performed by only a few of our sample, at least were performed by some of their neighbors. What inaccuracies there are will probably have occurred throughout the whole sample, so that the material, whatever its absolute errors, can be used with some confidence for internal comparisons.

It should be noted that the two months of data used here (from mid-October to mid-December 1972), covering the end of the dry-season harvest and the beginning of the rainy season, are from a relatively peak period of labor-inputs in agriculture. Subsequent data will determine how much the levels of productive activity are decreased, or channeled into different types of activity, at other times of year.

In order to present the results simply, all economic activities have been grouped into eight broad categories as follows:

A1 *Care of small children*

A2 *Household* (includes fetching water, house cleaning, washing clothes and kitchen implements, drying paddy and other crops, all kinds of food preparation)

A3 *Collecting firewood*

B *Production outside agriculture* (weaving and all other handicrafts, food preparation for sale, trading, fishing)

C *Animal care and feeding* (cutting fodder, collecting other food for chickens, ducks, cattle etc., herding and bathing of animals)

D *Non-agricultural wage-labor* (weaving in a small factory, carpentry, construction, carrying goods for a wealthy trader, etc.)

E *Exchange or communal labor* (unpaid labor building or repairing a neighbor's house etc.; does NOT include reciprocal agricultural labor — see category F — and does NOT include non-productive labor such as serving guests at a neighbor's ceremonial)

F *Agriculture* (all agricultural labor, on one's own or another's land, whether unpaid, paid in cash or with *bawon*, etc.)

Taking the data from a series of eight days and ordering them in the above eight categories, I have divided the totals by eight to give a picture of the average number of hours spent *daily* by individuals according to age group, sex, and type of activity. The results are presented in Table 3. From this table it can be seen that the average time spent by adults in "work" each day is nine hours (men) and twelve hours (women), or if we exclude care of small children, nine hours (men) and eleven hours (women).[2] Girls of age thirteen to fifteen and sixteen to eighteen almost equal the adult contribution, while children in the other groups contribute about one-half as much, with the exception of boys of seven to nine who contribute only one-fourth of the adult working hours. Looking more closely, we see that children exceed the adult contribution in some important tasks both in the "useful" (A1 -

---

[2] These figures confirm the view of Koentjaraningrat (n.d.: 355) that Javanese villagers "need no enticement or encouragement to work hard." Rather, they need help that can increase the productivity of their work.

Table 3. Average hours per day per person devoted to various tasks, according to age, sex and type of activity (N = forty households, eight days of observation per household)*

Age group, sex, and number in the sample:	7–9		10–12		13–15		16–18		19–29		30+	
Activity:	M (N = 18)	F (10)	M (14)	F (10)	M (18)	F (11)	M (9)	F (12)	M (6)	F (12)	M (39)	F (42)
A1 Care of small children	0.2	1.2	0.5	1.7	0.5	1.5	0.3	0.1	—	0.6	0.4	1.2
A2 Household	0.1	1.2	0.3	1.1	0.2	2.3	0.2	2.8	0.1	3.1	0.3	4.3
A3 Collecting firewood	0.7	0.2	0.6	0.3	0.7	0.5	0.2	0.1	0.1	0.1	0.3	0.1
B Production outside agriculture	0.2	1.3	0.4	0.2	0.8	1.9	0.2	4.9	3.2	4.8	1.8	4.9
C Animal care and feeding	1.2	1.0	2.7	0.5	2.2	0.1	1.6	0.1	0.8	—	0.8	0.1
D Non-agricultural wage labor	—	0.1	—	—	0.1	0.4	1.7	0.3	2.1	1.3	1.1	—
E Exchange or communal labor	—	—	0.2	—	0.2	0.1	0.7	0.2	0.4	0.3	0.6	0.1
F Agriculture	0.1	0.8	0.7	0.7	1.1	2.1	3.2	2.3	2.6	2.3	3.7	1.6
Total hours of "work" per day	2.5	5.8	5.4	4.5	5.8	8.9	8.1	10.6	9.3	12.5	9.0	12.3

* Because these per-person, per-day averages are derived from a sample of at least nine individuals in each group, and from a total of eight days of observations, they do NOT give a realistic picture of one day in the life of one individual. In reality, each member of the sample spends a greater amount of time in a smaller number of activities each day.

A3) and "productive" (B - F) categories. Children of ALL age-groups spend more time on the average than adults in child care, with the result that only a little of the adults' time is spent in this way; an example of the function of children in freeing adults for more productive labor. The collection of firewood and animal care are clearly in large part the responsibility of children rather than adults. In all kinds of "productive" activity (categories B, C, D, and F) boys and girls of sixteen to eighteen years almost equal, and in some cases exceed, the contribution of adults, so that if all these activities are counted together, we find that the totals of productive activity almost equal those of adults in the case of girls, and exceed them in the case of boys. Recalling the observation of Jay (1969) that male children frequently replace the adult in fulfilling *gotong-royong* [communal or reciprocal labor] obligations, it appears that boys in the ten to twelve and thirteen to fifteen age groups regularly engage in *gotong-royong* labor, but that their contribution is small compared to that of the sixteen to eighteen age group, who slightly surpass the adult contribution in this activity. The table also shows that during the two months covered, girls of thirteen and over spend as much time as adult women in agriculture, but that girls of seven to nine and ten to twelve spend only one-third of that time; there is, however, a possibility that when the period is extended to cover the whole of a harvest season, the contribution of small girls will be much greater. Anne Stoler's research during the 1973 wet season harvest, with the same forty households, found that the number of days spent harvesting according to age group was as follows: up to ten years of age, 12.6 days on the average per person (N = 12); eleven to fifteen years, 21.1 days (N = 11); sixteen years and over, 14.5 days (N = 56).

Having compared the contributions of the various age groups and sexes, it is interesting to see if there are any significant differences to be found WITHIN those groups; for example, it is important to know whether children from large families do more or less work, and what kinds of work, compared with children from small families. This question is very closely related to that of the "cost and value" of high versus low fertility. In the economic environment of "labor-surplus," it might easily be supposed that the larger the family size, the smaller the productive contribution of each child in the family must be, because the household can only provide strictly limited labor opportunities for them. Or possibly we might find that although children in large families work for long periods, the greater the family size, the greater the likelihood that children's work will be less productive. In this case even the elder children would be engaged in the less productive activities in large families, simply because the household cannot provide them with the chance to be more productive, although they are potentially capable of being so. If this were the case (i.e. if the number of children in the family varied inversely with their productivity), we would have to conclude that increasing the number of one's children results in economic "loss" to the parents, because of the effect hypothesized above. In order to examine the validity of such an argument, the sample was divided into two further groups of children: (1) children with only one, or no sibs in the potentially productive age group seven to eighteen years, i.e. "children from small families" and (2) children with two or more sibs in that age group (i.e. "children from large families"). Dividing these new categories into only two age groups (so as to retain a sufficiently large sample in each group), and calculating per-person averages in the same manner as previously, some interesting results emerge which are presented in Table 4.

Table 4. Average hours per day devoted to various tasks by children according to age, type of activity, and number of siblings ($N = 102$ children in forty households, eight days of observation per household)*

Age, number of sibs in that age group, and number in the sample: Activity:	7–12 years		13–18 years	
	0–1 sibs $N = 15$	2 or more sibs $N = 37$	0–1 sibs $N = 15$	2 or more sibs $N = 35$
A1 Care of small children	0.5	0.9	0.8	0.5
A2 Household	0.4	0.6	1.3	1.2
A3 Collecting firewood	0.5	0.5	0.3	0.5
B Production outside agriculture	1.9	1.1	1.9	2.4
C Animal care and feeding	0.7	1.2	1.4	1.0
D Non-agricultural wage-labor	—	0.1	0.5	0.5
E Exchange or communal labor	—	0.1	—	0.4
F Agriculture	0.3	0.6	1.3	2.2
Total hours of "work' per day	4.3	5.1	7.5	8.7

* Those in the left-hand column of each age-group have one or no sibs in the potentially productive seven to eighteen age-group, and are referred to in the text as "children from small families"; those in the right-hand columns, with two or more sibs in that age-group, are referred to as "children from large families."

Taking the children of seven to twelve years first, it can be seen that children from the larger families (those with many sibs) do MORE work in ALL types of activity (excepting "non-agricultural production") than do their counterparts from the smaller families. In the case of the older children of thirteen to eighteen years, the children from large families also do more work (comparing the total work-hours daily), and that difference is due to the fact that children from large families work more in the directly productive categories of B - F, while those from small families work more in the useful but nonproductive categories of A1 - A3 (with the exception of animal care and feeding). If these differences can be taken to indicate a significant trend (which can be subsequently tested by the calculation of similar totals from a total of a hundred households over a period of several months), then they clearly tend to refute the argument examined above, leading us instead to the conclusion that CHILDREN FROM LARGE FAMILIES TEND TO BE NOT LESS, BUT MORE PRODUCTIVE THAN THOSE IN SMALL FAMILIES. Perhaps the reasons for this might be as follows: first, that children with many sibs are encouraged by the presence of elder sibs to participate in all kinds of work, and using their elder sibs as examples, begin performing each task at an earlier age than usual; and second, that children with many sibs, precisely because of their younger sibs' earlier participation in the useful but unproductive chores, are themselves liberated from those chores and free to engage in more productive activity.

In any case, there seems to be a strong possibility that in the village studied, high fertility does not reduce the productivity of children in the family economy, but rather tends to raise it. For the majority of households whose land and capital resources are severely limited — for whom the large part of their income must be sought in the application of their labor in whatever opportunities are available outside the household's own resources — the productivity of labor is determined by the population-resources ratio of the larger economic environment, over which they themselves have no significant control. In other words, productivity depends on the general demographic and economic conditions obtaining OUTSIDE the individual family, not on the size of that particular family. Certainly, the situation might improve if EVERY family were to limit the number of its children, but in the absence of this it is possible that individual parents may derive relative economic benefit from producing large numbers of children, in direct conflict with the needs of the economy as a whole, whose difficulties stem in large part precisely from a century and a half of steady and continuing population growth.[3]

A great deal more research is necessary before the question of costs and benefits of high versus low fertility to Javanese parents can be resolved, particularly in the area of costs of children, which I have not attempted to cover here. However, I hope at least to have suggested the value of further research along these lines, both in rural and urban communities. For example, one imagines that urban children in Java are considerably less productive than their rural counterparts, but there are certainly no data to prove this. The streets of Jakarta and other cities teem with small boys, collecting bags full of cigarette ends for "recycling," selling old magazines, shining shoes, or simply begging; how does their "productivity" compare with the cost of their keep, and with that of their rural cousins, cutting grass and bird-watching in the *sawah*? Finally, we should consider whether there are any practical conclusions to be drawn from the data and preliminary conclusions presented above, from the point of view of the effort to reduce fertility in Java through the Indonesian National Family Planning Program. Suppose it were confirmed in further research that high fertility does tend to result in net economic gain from the parents' point of view. Such a conclusion does not necessarily imply bleak prospects of success for the family planning program; for, although I have been narrowly considering the economic consequences of high fertility from the parents' point of view in this article, it is not at all the case that these are the only factors entering into reproductive decisions. Even casual research shows that Javanese parents are extremely anxious for their children's future economic welfare as well as for their own, and that they are acutely aware that whatever the consequences of high fertility for themselves, the consequences for the welfare of their children are disastrous. In this case, perhaps the argument for family planning most likely to succeed is not so much "limiting the number of your children will benefit YOU" (an argument which may not be valid), but rather "limiting the number of your children will benefit your children" — an argument which is known to be true, and therefore might be easily received by the generation of prospective Javanese parents who must make the crucial reproductive decisions.

[3] For those readers interested in population history, I have suggested a basically similar hypothesis to account for Java's demographic growth under colonial rule in White (1973).

REFERENCES

BUDI PRASADJA, A.
1972 "Pembangunan desa dan masalah kepemimpinannja." Unpublished thesis, University of Indonesia.

CLARK, COLIN
1970 "Economic and social implications of population control," in *Population control*. Edited by A. Allison, 222–237. London: Penguin.

GEERTZ, HILDRED
1961 *The Javanese family*. Glencoe: Free Press.

GILLE, H., R. H. PARDOKO
1965 "A family life study in East Java: preliminary findings," in *Family planning and population programs*. Edited by Bernard Berelson et al., 503–523. Chicago: University of Chicago Press.

IPPA
1969a "KAP survey, knowledge, attitude and practice of family planning, Djakarta, Indonesia, 1968." Draft Report of the Preliminary Findings. Indonesian Planned Parenthood Association, Jakarta.
1969b "Hasi 12 Penelitian Pengetahuan-Sikap-Praktek Keluarga Berentjana, Kabupaten Bekasi 1967." Indonesian Planned Parenthood Association, Jakarta.

JAY, ROBERT
1969 *Javanese villagers*. Cambridge: MIT Press.

KOENTJARANINGRAT
n.d. "Tjelapar: sebuah desa di Djawa Tengah Bagian Selatan," in *Masjarakat Desa di Indonesia Masa Ini*. Edited by Koentjaraningrat, chapter eight. Jakarta, Yayasan Penerbit Fakultas Ekonomi, University of Indonesia.

NAG, MONI
1972 "Economic value of children in agricultural societies: evaluation of existing knowledge and an anthropological approach," in *The satisfactions and costs of children: theories, concepts, methods*. Edited by James T. Fawcett. Honolulu: East-West Center.

PENNY, D. H., MASRI SINGARIMBUN
1972 *A case study in rural poverty*. Bulletin of Indonesian Economic Studies 8(2):79–88.

SLAMET, INA A.,
1965 *Pokok² Pembangunan Masjarakat Desa*. Jakarta: Bhratara.

WHITE, BENJAMIN
1973 Demand for labour and population growth in colonial Java. *Human Ecology* 1(3):217–236.

The Community of Young People in a Transylvanian Village

MÁRIA KRESZ

The village of Nearsova-Nyárszó lies in Transylvania, in the district called Kalotaszeg, which consists of thirty-nine Hungarian villages between Oradea Mare and Cluj. Kalotaszeg was the first region to be "discovered" in the 1880's because of its folk art. Its elaborate costumes, embroidery, and woodwork became well known through early encouragement of home industry (a large volume illustrating these arts appeared in 1909) and through frequent visits by artists, architects, and musicians — including Walter Crane, who spent "a few enchanted hours" there, and Béla Bartók, who wanted to buy a house in one of the villages. The center of the region is Huedin-Bánffyhunyad, on the main road. Nearsova-Nyárszó lies in the valley of a brook, hidden from the road by a little hillock. The inhabitants number about 400, consisting of Romanians (one-third) who are Greek-Catholics, and Hungarians (two-thirds) who are Presbyterians. In the center of the village the Hungarian and the Romanian churches stand opposite each other. The Romanians live among the Hungarians, influenced in their culture by the association, and there is much intermingling between the two groups but no intermarrying.

Research on this area was initially done by the author in the early 1940's, but the present paper is based on detailed ethnographic fieldwork done in 1967–1968. At that time I returned to the family who were my former informants, a family with two "big girls," taking my own two daughters to observe Christmas customs, tape-record the songs and recitations, and make photographs of the proceedings. These Christmas customs have not yet been discovered by tourists as the village is hidden from the main road nor are foreigners present in the village. Few ethnographers have ever photographed these customs, which are known through oral description rather than through field observation. Other villages of Kalotaszeg are, however, better known, and these are frequented by visitors.

When I revisited the village in 1967–1968, it was apparent that although little outward change had taken place in this agricultural region in twenty-five years, great internal changes had occurred. The size of the population was almost the same; the houses differed little, although quite a few new ones had been built; on Sundays a majority of the people still went to church in their traditional costumes, and at Christmas the traditional ceremonies of the young people were performed. The three children of my former hosts were now married, with children of their own. In one family two adolescent daughters did all the housework suitable for their age, worked in the fields when necessary, and embroidered as their mother did (although they did not spin); but these daughters also studied in high school and college, were well-read, spoke two languages, listened to the radio, and watched televistion. They kept their Kalotaszeg costumes for holidays, but they usually dressed according to the current fashion, although their mother still wore her traditional clothing. The young men had jobs (either in the agricultural cooperative or in industry), or were studying in college. The agricultural cooperative of this area no longer required the labor of children, nor did schooling leave much time for agricultural work; children worked far less in the fields than their parents had. It was neither possible nor desirable to buy land; the endeavor of families was to secure further education for their children. As one peasant said, "Our aim is not [to own] the land, but to learn!"

THE TRADITIONAL CHRISTMAS IN KALOTASZEG

The organization of the community of young people has special significance in Kalotaszeg even today, and participation in the special customs and celebrations, especially at Christmas, marks a formal division between the age-groups of childhood and youth. The traditional customs are still being practiced. The general community of young people is closely united by these customs: for example, my elder daughter, being a guest, was to be honored by being escorted home by one of the "inviters," a young student who was considered suitable for this role by the community. But another boy, lower in the social scale, had the presumption to accompany her home. As a result, he was caught and beaten by the other boys for acting against the will of the community.

A few weeks before the holidays a "trial dance" was held at which the

Plate 1 (a, b).   Carol singing on Christmas eve
a.   Young girl listens to the carol singers behind the door
b.   Party for carol singers given by the young girl while her parents lie in bed

Plate 1 (c, d). Carol singing on Christmas eve
c. The carol singers are invited to have drinks and food
d. The young girl drinks with the carol singers

Plate 2. The "inviters"
with their staffs,
carried during the
Christmas church service

Plate 3. The Christmas
service: the place of the
young men in church is
the choir; note the
ribbons, given by the
girls, hanging down
from the staffs of the
"inviters"

Plate 4. The Christmas service: one of the girls is wearing her "pearly wreath"

Plate 5. The Christmas dance in the snow in front of the church on Christmas morning

young men chose those who were to play various roles during the festi-
vities. In the celebration I observed, two "judges" were selected, a
Hungarian boy, representing the majority of the population of the village,
and a Romanian boy, so that the Romanians were represented as well.
Two Hungarian boys were voted to be "inviters"[1] and were each given
a decorated staff presented by the girls. All the young men were sons of
village peasant families, but many of them worked in nearby towns as
factory laborers, coming home to their family only for Sundays and holidays, while others were students. Some of the girls were also studying in
the nearby town.

On Christmas Eve the group of young men go carol singing. They start
from the Presbyterian church and visit the clergyman and his family first.
The carol singing and the recitation of Christmas good wishes takes place
at the door of the house, and then they are invited to enter and are offered
brandy and cakes. Leaving the clergyman's house, they continue on their
way, singing loudly as they walk through the dark village street. They
stop only at the homes of "big girls,"[2] and they are always invited to have
drinks and sweetmeats which are arranged for them on a table. Sitting
around the table, they sing merry songs — no longer carols, but worldly
folk songs, love songs, etc. The length of time they spend at each house
varies; if there are two sisters in the family, or if the girl in the family
holds a more esteemed social position (being more wealthy or more
beautiful, or being a student), they stay longer. The parents may have
already gone to bed, and inasmuch as the bed is in the same room, they
sit up in bed, enjoying the sight of the young people enjoying themselves.
This situation is most typical, for in the Kalotaszeg villages the accepted
way of courting a girl is always to visit her AFTER the family has gone to
bed. It is considered improper for a young man to make a visit to a young
girl during the daytime, when everyone can see where he is going. So it
is not unusual for the parents to be in bed while the young girl receives
her visitors. Courtship is, however, restricted to certain days of the week,
and the young girl is expected to keep her maidenhood, for only then is
she allowed to wear the "pearly wreath" on her head — a symbol of
maidenhood worn on the most important church holidays and later on
her wedding day. Or, at least, it used to be so. The "pearly wreath" was
once known all over Hungary, but at present only the Kalotaszeg villages
have kept this part of the traditional Hungarian costume. To be a "young

---

[1]   The role of the "inviters" is to visit the house of each "big girl" every day of the
Christmas holidays, inviting her formally to the Christmas dance.
[2]   "Big girls" are girls over sixteen who have been confirmed.

girl wearing the pearly wreath" means to belong to the organization of "big girls" of the village.

The carol-singing boys go from house to house visiting each "big girl," and it is well after midnight by the time they have completed the round. At every house they receive a present of cakes, which they collect in a bag.

Early in the morning on Christmas Day the two "inviters" set off on a similar round to invite the "big girls," in formal verse, to the dance to be held that evening in the village "dance house," and they are again offered a drink at every house. Gypsy musicians also go from house to house playing a Christmas tune as a holiday good wish; they, too, receive a drink, and also some money.

On Christmas Day only those who are able to take communion go to church, i.e. those who have been confirmed. The spirit is solemn, and people wear their most festive clothes. Formerly the girls wore the "pearly wreath"; in 1968, however, only one girl wore it — Kata Hadházi, engaged to be married, who knew it was her last opportunity to wear it at Christmas. Communion is taken strictly by order of age and sex: first the men, in a row with the senior of the village at the head, receive communion; then it is the women's turn, followed by the girls, with the youngest girl being last. Thus throughout their lives, every time these people take communion, each is reminded of his or her station by age; each person stands beside his or her own contemporaries, with whom they were confirmed, all together in the same year; and everyone knows who the oldest man in the village is, who the oldest woman is, and who the youngest is. The place where people sit in church also follows a strict convention according to sex and age: women and girls sit in family stalls with the men opposite; the young men sit in the choir above the men, and small boys sit in the choir above the women. At Christmas the two "inviters" carry their festive staffs into church and hang them on the panels of the choir, with the ribbons given them by the girls dangling down the front. The "inviters" are first to leave the church when the service is ended. Outside, the gypsy musicians wait, ready to begin playing their instruments as the crowd leaves the church.

On Christmas morning, after the church service, a unique custom takes place, practiced only by the Hungarians of Kalotaszeg: the young people dance in front of the church in honor of Christmas. The "pearly wreath" is never worn for dancing except on this occasion, for it and the clothes worn with it are considered too festive for a dance and are only worn to church on a very great holiday. In 1968 some of the young girls were still wearing the traditional costume, their hair in a pigtail with a ribbon tied at the end (again a symbol of maidenhood — even older, unmarried women wear their hair in a pigtail in these villages), and wide, pleated skirts with embroidered aprons; some girls, however, wore modern coats and boots. But even those girls who have changed to modern clothing usually keep their traditional costumes to wear on rare occasions. In 1968 none of the young men wore traditional costumes. The older women were all dressed traditionally, wearing black boots, pleated skirts, smocked aprons, jackets decorated with beads, and colored scarves. As they stood in two long rows on either side of the church watching the young people of the village dancing in the snow, the scene was one of an open-air performance.

After the Christmas meal, in the afternoon, dancing commences in the village "dance house." The dancing continues for a full five days and is exhausting. It is done mostly to the tune of a gypsy band, but sometimes a phonograph is also used to help out. The gypsies are provided for by the organization of girls, who take turns giving them meals. The gypsies come to the house of the girl whose turn it is, accompanied by the two "inviters" and some of the young men. Thus, throughout the holiday, the fiddlers and the happily singing young men parade through the village, all of them drinking more and getting merrier as the days go by.

Although the dancing in the "dance house" is mainly the entertainment of the youth, all generations participate. Married women take their children or grandchildren along, and sit on a bench against the wall. They hurry to the "dance house" early to get a good seat so that they will have a fine view of the dancers. Married men also go to the dance, and in the intervals between the dancing they have a round of singing together. Small children dance at the farthest end of the hall, sometimes a boy and a girl in a pair, but more often little girls dancing together. The "dance house" is unheated; it gets its heat from the warmth of human bodies dancing merrily in the overcrowded space, sometimes to the tune of a modern "hit," but usually to traditional folk music. The dancing goes on continually from early afternoon till after midnight, although the adults take a recess to go home to feed the animals. Even small children are present late into the night. Young mothers who have been dancing themselves carry their slumbering children home in the dark.

In this way, the celebration of Christmas goes on for days, intensified at intervals by the celebration of name days — Saint Stephen's on December 26th, for example, or, Saint John's on December 27th — when good wishes and drinks go around again. The fifth day of Christmas is, however, the one young people enjoy most of all, for on that day no adults are present in the "dance house," and after distributing to the musicians their pay in kind (beans, potatoes, hemp), the young people are free to play all sorts of kissing games without being observed by their elders.

When the Christmas holidays are scarcely over, it is the New Year, which is celebrated in a similar fashion. At midnight, while the bells are knelled for a full hour, the young men lay a fire to be leaped over — a winter, midnight fire, similar to the Midsummernight's fire known all over Europe. The fire is laid near a fountain from which water, known as "golden water," is taken. Again the group of boys goes from house to house to visit each girl in turn, singing an ecclesiastical song at the door, reciting a poem of good wishes, and offering her and her family a drink of "golden water," the first drink of the new year, for which the young men are thanked by an offer of brandy.

There is no sign that the traditional Christmas customs will decline. It is true that certain changes may be observed; it is likewise true that the customs become less picturesque as the traditional costumes go out of fashion. But even now, when many young people work or study in town, at Christmastime everyone comes home for the holidays, and Christmas would not be Christmas if it were not celebrated in the traditional manner. New customs are sometimes included, partly deriving from the urban influence: Christmas trees are erected, gifts are given, and small children recite Bible texts in church, where the children have a celebration of their own.[3] Although in 1968 our host family watched their newly purchased television set showing the Budapest Christmas program, their main entertainment was still the enjoyment of their own customs. For, as my daughters remarked, these peasant parents show no resentment of the high spirits and enjoyment of their children. It seems the most natural thing in the world to these parents, knowing as they do the hardships that lie ahead in life, that young people should enjoy their youth, should have fun in the holiday season, and should be happy in the prime of their life.

---

[3]   Small children have a number of customs of their own age-group: e.g. little boys go to the houses in the village reciting verses of good wishes on Christmas eve and New Year's morning, and they go carol singing in a group of their own.

Community Interrelations with the Government: A Study of Adolescent Group Movements in a Japanese Fishing Community

TSUNEO AYABE

SCOPE OF THE STUDY

The purpose here is to explore the relationships between the "traditional" and self-motivated activity of a community, and the outside society's intentional directions and interference that are questioned in any community development. This exploration is done through studies of various adolescent groups in Katsumoto-ura, Iki Island, on the one hand, while making more or less clear one phase of relationships between the central government and the local community through these studies. In the process of analysis, we may also be able to refer to the correlations of a small community's formal educational organizations — kindergarten, elementary school, middle school, commercial high school — and informal, adolescent educational organizations — Seinenkai [traditional youth group], Seinenbu [youth section of fishing cooperative], Seinendan [government-made youth association], etc., and their respective roles.

The concept of the so-called "folk society" in social anthropology, in which a traditional local community is considered as a self-sufficient and independent unit, had been posited only as a kind of an "ideal type," even at the time when this theory appeared. Moreover, the social anthropological interest over the past twenty-odd years has been directed toward the interrelations between the local community and the outside society surrounding it. In analyzing the interrelations of a certain local community with the surrounding sociocultural milieu, the following relationships between the community and the outside world can be considered: (1) intellectual awareness; (2) human mobility; (3)

material diffusion; and (4) organizational affiliation. The first, intellectual awareness, implies the community inhabitants' intellectual interest in and understanding of the outside world which they gradually accumulate through various means and experiences. The second, human mobility, means the relationship with the outer society that the inhabitants acquire through jobs outside their community, homecoming of the former inhabitants, traveling, etc., as well as through visitors from the outside, including sightseers. The third, material diffusion, is the relationship of the inhabitants with the outer society through things that come in from the outside (such as clothing, food, machines, etc.). The fourth, organizational affiliation, implies the relationships that are created through the process of being woven into the super organizations of the outer society; the local community's groups, such as a youth or women's club, or a pig or citrus fruit cooperative; or associations such as fishing or farmers' cooperatives, or administrative organizations, etc. We shall discuss the fourth type of interrelations through problems of youth groups in relation to the social structure of the fishing village Katsumoto-ura. As mentioned previously, the discussion is focussed on the "tradition" of Katsumoto-ura and the outside society's intentional directions. Before going into the main theme, beginning in the third section, I shall give a brief outline of the geographical, sociocultural background, and the formal educational institutions of this area in the form of an ethnography.

Setting of the Community

GEOGRAPHY AND POPULATION Iki is a small island in the Genkai sea, 138.5 square kilometers in area, fifteen kilometers east-west by seventeen kilometers north-south. It belongs to Nagasaki Prefecture administratively, but since it is only three hours by sea and thirty minutes by air from Fukuoka City, it is culturally and economically more closely tied to Fukuoka City than to Nagasaki. The whole island forms an gentle hill, and the complicated coastline has good natural inlets which now consist of three harbors and seventeen fishing ports. The climate is warm and mild due to the Tsushima warm current, but there is little rainfall in summer, often leaving the inhabitants with a water shortage between July and September. According to the census of October 1965, the population is 45,654 (male population: 21,878) and households number 9,610; the population has been declining for the past ten years. There are four administrative districts in the island: Gono-ura, Katsumoto-machi, Ashibe-machi and Ishida-mura. Katsumoto-machi is further divided into three wards, geographically and historically: Urabu, Zaibu and Yunomoto. This study deals only with Urabu.

Geographically, Katsumoto-machi is divided into two parts, the area developed in the lowland along the coast, and the hilly area behind it. Houses are densely built in the coastal area since fishing and commerce are the main professions, and the area is called either *Urabu or Machi* [town]. The hilly area is called *Zaibu* or *Inaka* [country], where a few farm houses are scattered. Urabu has a population of 3,284 (778 households), which is subdivided into seventeen *buraku* [hamlets], each of which is called *cho*, a local community of spontaneous generation, and at the same time a terminal organ of administration. Head of each *cho* is called *Kominkan-cho* [head of civil house] and has the function of a village chief.

ECONOMIC AND SOCIOCULTURAL BACKGROUND   The industry of Katsumoto-ura consists mainly of fishing, accompanied by marine product manufacturing and shipbuilding. The people are engaged mainly in coastal fishing for yellowfish, sea bream, and squid, the annual catch being sold for more than 700 million yen. There are 504 motor ships (sixty-three ships less than five tons) and seventy-nine ships without engines; most of them are ten-ton motor ships with three-, four-, or five-man crews. The nuclear organization of fishing in Katsumoto-ura is the Fishing Cooperative, which has 921 regular members and 249 associate members, totaling 1,170 members. Acquisition of membership is on an individual basis. As the biggest business organization of the Ura district, the Cooperative has influence over all phases of industry in Ura. For example:

1. *Okidome* is a regulation prohibiting going out for fish in bad weather, to prevent shipwreck; the prohibition is decided on by the Cooperative's committee *Oki-sewanin*. Whoever violates it is deprived of all the catch. However, now that there are more boats over ten tons, in keeping with the trend to build larger fishing boats, there are voices against this regulation since big boats can go out fishing even under *Okidome*. But in any case, all the members entrust the decision to the *Oki-sewanin* committee of the Cooperative.

2. *Shinyo-bu* (Treasury Section) is the most important part of the Cooperative, where all money matters are dealt with, such as savings, loans for shipbuilding, etc.

3. Joint forwarding provides that each member of the Cooperative brings his daily catch to the Cooperative store, which sells the entire catch in bulk.

4.   Purchasing section: All the fuel, bait, fishing tools, and ship's fittings are bought through the Cooperative for the benefit of the members.

Significantly, 60 to 80 percent of the fishermen's sons on Katsumoto-ura remain on the island each year after graduation from middle school to take over the fathers' jobs. Prosperity of the Cooperative and of the entire Ura district has much to do with the abundant young labor which brings about an increase in fishing boats and the catch.

Formal Educational Institutions in Katsumoto-machi

There are three kindergartens, three primary schools, two middle schools and one high school in Katsumoto-machi; all except the high school are town schools. Ura district alone has a kindergarten, a primary school, and a middle school.

KATSUMOTO KINDERGARTEN   In present-day Japan, going to kindergarten before primary school is viewed as the normal procedure. The town kindergarten in Katsumoto-ura was established in 1927, when kindergartens were still rare in Japan, and has maintained an almost 100 percent attendance rate of all qualified children ever since its establishment. Because of the strong tie between the kindergarten and the primary school, they appear to have a seven-year primary-school system.

The Katsumoto kindergarten was established with the strong support of the inhabitants, and parents' interest in kindergarten education is keen. The facilities, most of which are the result of the parents' contributions and volunteer service, are excellent. An important reason for the kindergarten's having such strong support from the inhabitants, over and above the inhabitants' enthusiasm for education, is the parents' strong desire to have the small children in the safest possible place.

Mothers of Ura are busy. Katsumoto-ura traditionally suffered from a water shortage, until the introduction of the waterway, housewives were so busy carrying water that they could not take care of children. Even with the waterway, the women are busy preparing dried squid at home, as the women's labor is a big factor in sustaining the household economy where fishing is greatly dependent upon weather. It is evident that such time-consuming labor made the kindergarten indispensable, just as the needs of working mothers in modern apartments stimulated the creation of day nurseries. Since its establishment, it has been customary for the head of the primary school to be the head of the kindergarten concurrently. The kindergarten schedule is made to accord with that of the primary school. Such strong ties with the primary school seem to have made the Ura inhabitants consider their kindergarten as part of compulsory education.

KATSUMOTO PRIMARY SCHOOL There are three primary schools in Katsumoto-machi — Katsumoti, Isabushi, and Kasui — and the enrollment structures in the respective schools are different, reflecting the parents' occupations. For instance, all of the pupils of Katsumoto Primary School are from Urabu, and farmers' children go not to Katsumoto Primary School but to Kasui Primary School, even if their homes are in the vicinity of Katsumoto Primary School. Children from Yunomoto usually go to Isabushi Primary School. Needless to say, it is not that schools are chosen according to the parents' occupation, but the school district system operates on the *buraku* basis. But this division seems to arouse strong classmate affiliations among Urabu youth, the center of cohesion being the alumni association. Generally speaking, it does not matter whether classmates come from the primary school or middle school, both being compulsory but it is to the primary-school graduates of a certain year that people relate, with whom they get together on *Bon* festivals, and with whom they drink. This affiliation seems to be lifelong, or at least it persists as long as they remain in Ura. That they come from the same hamlet and share the same occupation seems to serve as a strong base for this lasting relationship, as opposed to the case of the middle school, where an approximately equal number of students come from Urabu and Zaibu.

In Katsumoto-ura, the PTA (parent-teacher association) has been called *Ikuyukai* since before the war. This association is said to have been mainly a money-collecting organ for enlarging and improving school facilities. The chairmanship was formerly taken over by a person of high status in Ura, even if he had no child attending the school, and it was a typical pressure group collecting almost obligatory donations and interfering in personnel matters concerning teachers. Although it has now become a more democratic association, one cannot deny the fact that this characteristic of *Ikuyukai* connected the local influential people to the school and compensated for the poor education fund. In many cases, the relationships between school and community are warped because the state has not fulfilled its responsibility after imposing compulsory education, the case of the Katsumoto-ura *Ikuyukai* being an example.

KATSUMOTO MIDDLE SCHOOL   There are two middle schools in Katsumoto-machi: Katsumoto Middle School and Isabushi Middle School. Graduates of Katsumoto and Kasui Primary School go to Katsumoto Middle School, and those of Isabushi Primary School go to Isabushi Middle School. The community inhabitants who contributed money but did not speak up for education itself now have opinions with respect to the content of education in the middle school, a terminal organ of compulsory education. For instance, once voices were heard for establishment of a fisheries course, since more graduates began to remain on the island to take over fishing, around the years 1961–1967. The principal of the school decided to spare two hours per week for a selective fisheries course out of the five-hour English course. This was backed by 40,000 yen in annual assistance from the prefecture, as part of the policy to encourage the fishermen's successors, and further assistance came from the Fishing Cooperative, which lent boats and engines. This course served well for the study of cultured *wakame* [sea weed] but it lasted only until 1968 and has now become part of the extracurricular activities. The Fishing Cooperative still wants to have it reestablished. The reasons for the termination of this course were: (1) lack of a licensed teacher; (2) too high cost; (3) not enough members to organize a course (about seven a year); and (4) that this course had the image of an elite class and was unpopular among parents who were fishermen. Sons of fishermen go aboard the fishing boats from childhood to help parents, and, because what they can learn at school they can learn from their parents, the fathers do not expect too much from the fisheries course. This poses the problem of how to compose the education curriculum in local communities.

IKI COMMERCIAL HIGH SCHOOL   There are two high schools on Iki Island. One is the ordinary Iki High School in Gono-ura, and the other, a commercial high school in Katsumoto-ura. This used to be a branch school of the Iki High School, to which was added a commercial course in 1950 and which became an independent commercial high school in 1959. The occupational distribution of the parents of Katsumoto Middle School are: fishing, 40 percent; agriculture, 40 percent; and commerce, 20 percent. The graduates show the following distribution:
1.   Boys: Fishing — Most of them remain as fishermen, whether they are first-born, or second or third sons. Agriculture — The first-born stay, whereas the second and the third sons leave home to become carpenters or plasterers in and around Kasuya County, Fukuoka Pre-

fecture. Commerce — They usually get good marks and proceed to higher schools; otherwise they find employment in companies in technical fields.

2. Girls: Regardless of the parents' occupation, a good many girls enter Iki Commercial High School, and the rest go out to work for textile factories in middle and middle-western Japan.

The characteristic feature of the middle-school graduates may be that boys take up fishing and girls go to high school. According to the prefectural survey of middle-school students' future plans in 1968, 80 percent of the first, second, and third grade boys hoped to go into fishing. Prefectural policy here is concerned not with how to secure successors, but how to avoid arriving at the saturation point of fishermen, or even how to let some of them leave the island. The popularity of fishing is due to the tremendous amount of income that a fisherman earns when the catch is good, although there are fluctuations.

Table 1. Courses taken by middle-school graduates: the past five years' trend of the fishermen's sons graduated from Katsumoto Middle School

	Year of graduation	1965	1966	1967	1968	1969
Boys	Main courses					
	Total	33	31	27	29	22
	Fishing	19	26	20	19	17
	Higher education	9	5	6	8	5
Girls	Total	24	24	28	38	32
	Textile industries	11	8	9	7	9
	Higher education	9	14	12	23	20

As can be seen in Table 1, girl's high-school attendance increased rapidly in the past few years, with the result that a dressmaking school run by the town, called *Katsumoto Koto Jogakuin*, had to be given up due to student shortage over the previous three years. In spite of the predominant number of graduates who remain on the island as fishermen, there is no movement toward establishment of a fisheries high school, as mentioned before. Even if the middle school suggests that the graduates go to fisheries high school elsewhere, only one or two go each year. This would offer a point of discussion in considering local education, together with the case of the above-mentioned middle school.

As outlined so far, the formal educational organizations in Katsumoto-ura had an important role in enlightening the inhabitants and educating them as Japanese citizens, but one cannot say that they have been playing direct and positive roles toward innovation in the Ura community. Compulsory education organs exist in any Japanese local community, and an increase in students getting higher education is now a general trend. However, even if they are government-made organs imposed by the outer society, would the inhabitants not expect them to serve as organs for diffusion and betterment of their culture in some way? If such an expectation is not directed toward school education, it must be either because there is absolutely no need for an education adjusted to the needs of the local community, or because there is some other organ taking its place. We shall now go into the discussion of adolescent groups in Ura with the above points in mind.

Socioeducational Institutions

HISTORICAL SKETCH OF THE JAPANESE YOUTH MOVEMENT   The custom of youth forming groups for various activities is seen in many parts of the world. In Japan, also, the origin of the youth groups, called *wakamono-gumi or wakashugumi*, goes way back in history. It is said that in an old record handed down to the Sesegushi *Seinendan* of Kiire Mura, Ibusuki County, Kagoshima Prefecture, there are letters indicating the year *Bunei Gannen* (1264), demonstrating that the Japanese *wakamono* system had existed in some localities as early as the Kamakura Era (1192–1338). Moreover, if one considers the *wakamono* system from the viewpoint of initiation, men's association, and age group, he may have to go back to the stage of "tribal" culture. Needless to say, it is not difficult to imagine that there were vast differences in the content of Japanese *wakamonogumi* at a time when local differences were outstanding. For instance, agricultural and fishing communities in southwestern Japan are known to have had, since quite early times, such youth groups as *wakashugumi* and *wakarenju* in charge of guarding the village and other volunteer services. Again, it is difficult to ascertain the exact date of appearance of *wakashugumi*; but remaining records suggest with some certainty that it goes back to the Tokugawa era (1603–1867).

It was customary for these youth groups to have their own code, called *Gojomoku*, the oldest known of which was written in 1677 in Gamo County in Omi-no-kuni (presently Shiga Prefecture). Young men of that time were recognized as adults only by joining these groups; then they were allowed to marry and help guard the community. *Waka-shugumi* usually had its own clubhouse where members came to stay together at night and submit themselves to the strict rules and orders of the elders.

The ascription of status in terms of age seems to be universal in youth groups the world over. The Japanese *wakashugumi* also follow this principle, and members go up through grades as they grow older. They usually leave when they marry, but there are some localities where they follow other rules. Even at present, some local agricultural and fishing communities maintain such institutions, where middle-school graduates are asked without exception to join the group and are given practical education closely connected to the life in that area. It is not rare to see temporary revivals of similar organizations at festivals and rituals, in villages where such an institution no longer exists. Thus, Japanese traditional youth groups were natural and spontaneous folk products, unlike the YMCA, YWCA, Boy Scout, and Girl Scout organizations, which were intentionally established on a nationwide scale.

Wakashugumi, after the Meiji restoration (1868), had a tendency to grow weaker as Japan began to reorganize as a modern nation. *Wakashugumi* was now behind the times, and its outmoded system could no longer be accepted in the new society; its negative features alone, such as degenerate morality, became conspicuous. In the meantime, educators and innovators in some localities were trying sporadic reform of youth in the form of high schools and supplementary schools. This became suddenly popular after the Sino-Japanese (1894–1895) and Russo-Japanese (1904–1905) Wars. Particularly after the latter, the Japanese government began to supervise local youth groups as part of its "enrich and strengthen the nation" policy. In 1906, these youth groups were put under the supervision of the Ministry of Education and the Ministry of Interior.

In 1920, the government decided that the *Seinendan* should include male youths up to twenty-five years of age instead of the previous limit of twenty. During 1926–1927, the All Japan Youth Association and All Japan Female Youth Association were established. Thus, the Japanese government, which had become more militaristic after the outbreak of the Sino-Japanese War, established in 1939 a compulsory youth school (*Seinen Gakko*) and began training reserve forces. The student body of the *Seinen Gakko* was identical to that of the *Seinendan*. In 1940, enrollment of the *Seinen Gakko* comprised about three million students, more than 50 percent of the entire youth population of the time. In 1941, the *Seinendan* was consolidated on the national level with the All Japan Boys' Association. The nature and purpose of this organization were extremely militaristic and formed the basis for military recruitment and training.

In 1945, at the end of World War II, the youths' and boys' groups were dissolved, and *Seinen Gakko* was abolished in 1948. However, as the postwar turmoil began to subside, the nationwide League of Japanese Youth Associations was established. This organization made efforts to free youth groups from political affairs, in accordance with the new idea of democracy, and tried to encourage self-motivated management by the youth. As the result, many small voluntary groups for singing, improvement of daily life, creative writing, improvement of agricultural techniques, reading, and such were formed. But this movement did not advance as far as establishing nationwide organizations. Moreover, the recent change in Japanese industrial structure tended to force the youth to urban areas and out of fishing and agricultural communities, and the rural youth group movement is now facing the new obstacle of youth population drain.

So far we have been discussing the historical outline of Japanese youths' activities, but such a general tendency does not necessarily apply in individual communities. There have been many cases in which government-sponsored youth association movements could never penetrate into rural communities. The following description of Katsumoto-ura will introduce a case of the government's continuous failure to encourage youth association movements because of their indifference to village structure and to the needs of the community. Through this case, one can observe the conflict between the traditional youth group sprouting out of a fishing village of Katsumoto-ura and the purposeful administrative directions on the part of the government, which tried to integrate it into the nationwide youth association organization in accordance with national policy. With the history of the Japanese youth groups in mind, let us now turn to the changing phases of a Katsumoto-ura youth group, including its rise and fall.

YOUTH GROUPS IN KATSUMOTO-URA   In Katsumoto-ura, in pre-Meiji times, there existed a traditional organization called *Wakamonoyado* in each *cho* or *buraku* [hamlet]. All the boys were initiated into one of the *Wakamonoyado* at the age of thirteen and began to stay there at night to receive training from the elders. Each youth house in turn had its youth club (*wakate-gumi*), and these small groups in the entire *cho* gathered together to form one big youth group, *Wakamonoju*. The *Wakamonoju* seems to have shared the following tasks: (1) enculturation of youths into adulthood; (2) securing and maintenance of the area's property, sharing of cooperative labor for community projects; (3) guarding; and (4) preparing for and carrying out festivals.

Thus *Wakamonoju* was tightly woven into the structure and function of the community on the *cho* basis and had an important function as an educational organization in relation to the maintenance and development of the local community's social sanctions and value system. Generally, there are two types of age groups in Japan:

1.   People who have reached a certain age or ages form an age group (set) annually or at a certain interval, in which case there are many strata of such sets within the community, and members never change their affiliation throughout their lives.

2.   People who have reached a certain age join an age group in the community, which is subdivided into several age grades, in which case a member goes up the grades one by one as he grows older. The age serves as a reference point for establishing statuses.

In either of the two cases a community member is forced to join his community's group, and his public and private behavior is checked by the age group to which he belongs. The *Wakamonoju* in Katsumoto-ura exemplifies the latter case.

In Katsumoto-ura, members of the *Wakamonoju* were divided into age grades of *kowakate* (15–25), *chuwakate* (25–30), and *owakate* (30–35), and had officers such as chairman, vice-chairman, treasurer, and secretary. They had subgroups for cooperative works, sports, volunteer services, recreation, and cultural activities. As mentioned above the *Wakamonoju* was formed on the *cho* basis of residential area, the status within each group being determined solely on the basis of age. There was, however, no superorganization of *Wakamonoju* which would include the entire community of Katsumoto-ura. Toward the end of the Meiji era the name of the youth group was changed from *Wakamonoju* to *Seinenkai*.

Government control over various local adolescent groups was enforced after the Sino-Japanese and Russo-Japanese Wars, and by the end of the Meiji era and toward the beginning of the Taisho years, government-sponsored youth associations could be seen in any hamlet. In the case of Katsumoto-ura, the government-sponsored *Seinendan* was first established by a government order in 1918, right after World War I. However, the *Seinendan* never grew strong enough to absorb the traditional *Seinenkai*, so that the two coexisted. Because the government-sponsored youth association included youths between the ages of thirteen and twenty-five, the youth in Katsumoto-ura up to twenty-five years of age had double membership. The coexistence, however, was nominal, and the only activity that the *Seinendan* organized was an athletic meeting. This *Seinendan* once became quite active around 1933, but when many of the members were drafted during the Sino-Japanese War beginning in 1937, the group gradually diminished and then disappeared.

After World War II, another attempt was made by a few people, mainly from the agricultural area, to reestablish the *Seinendan*, supported by the local authorities. These innovators were inclined to impose their ideas upon the younger people without realizing the discrepancy between the older and the younger. The effort was short lived and the *Seinendan* dissolved after a little more than a year. Again in 1953 another attempt was made to reorganize the *Seinendan* but it had dissolved again within two years. Again in 1961 the *Seinendan* was reorganized with the guidance of a social education advisor from the local authorities, in accordance with the policy of the national government. The youth between fifteen and twenty-five joined it, but it could exist for little more than two years.

Here mention must be made of another youth group in Katsumoto-ura, the *Seinenbu* of the Fishing Cooperative. In 1949, a Fishing Cooperative was reestablished, but it had little support as the people lacked confidence in it and each fisherman feared he would be hurt if he shared his secret fishing spot with others. However, an extremely poor catch forced the fishermen to turn toward the Cooperative. This was done mainly by several chairmen of the *Seinenkai* in *cho*. The chairmen established a *Seinenbu* [youth section] in the not-so-popular Fishing Cooperative and encouraged the members of the *Seinenkai* to join the new youth section, visiting them from door to door. They were successful in recruiting members, and they made themselves executives. Thus in 1953 the *Seinenbu* absorbed the traditional *Seinenkai* as a kind of subsidiary organ and became the first functioning association of youth for the entire community.

Seinenbu declared its goals to be: (1) orientation of youth toward the Fishing Cooperative; (2) overcoming feudalism; and (3) acquisition of practical knowledge about the society.

Activities of the *Seinenbu* included study of fishing methods, search for new fishing grounds, publication of a bulletin, education of new members, volunteer work projects, and several other activities entrusted to them by the Fishing Cooperative. Soon the results of improved fishing methods and equipment introduced by the *Seinenbu* became apparent, and they gained the confidence of the executives of the Fishing Cooperative. In 1964 the *Seinenbu* received a grant of money from their adult counterpart. Comparison with the aforementioned school curriculum incident tells us that direct technical innovation is realized through such an active youth group as the Youth Section of the Fishing Cooperative, and not through formal educational institutions. This should give an important suggestion in making a middle-school curriculum in a small community like Katsumoto-ura. The *Seinenbu* keeps close structural contact with Katsumoto-ura through the traditional *Seinenkai* which became its subsidiary. The executives are very closely knit, and status among them is decided according to the principle of age, as is the case in most fishing villages. In other words, the executives are composed of those who graduated from Katsumoto Primary School in the same year, so that they know each other as they know themselves. On the other hand, in the case of the *Seinendan* organized in 1961, the executives are elected, which did not appeal to the members who traditionally respected the principle of age.

Thus, we have seen that there have been three kinds of youth groups in Katsumoto-ura, namely, *Seinenkai, Seinenbu* of the Fishing Cooperative, and *Seinendan.* Because the fortunes of these groups are directly connected to the changes that took place in Ura community, it would be better to consider them from a broader point of view, taking social structural problems into account. In the following section, before going into the newly organized Urabu *Seinendan,* we shall discuss changes in the life, ritual organization, administrative units, etc., seen through the integration process of small *kumi-* and *ku-*level organizations into that of Ura level.

Changes in Social Structure in Terms of the Integration Process at the Community [Ura] Level

CHANGES IN THE PRODUCTION SYSTEM   At present there are four wholesale fish dealers in Katsumoto-ura, but during the most prosperous time for the dealers, before the Meiji era, there were thirteen. Up to the end of the Tokugawa era, Katsumoto-ura was also known as a whaling port, and at the end of the Meiji era angling for bonitos became common and the discovery of a great fishing spot called *shichiri-gasone* spurred bonito fishing. Most of the fishermen in Katsumoto-ura of that time did not own boats and were hired by certain shipowners under the name of *wakkashi* [the young set]. The shipowners in turn were connected with a wholesale dealer in patron-client form; he lent the owners the money for buying boats and fishing tools. The borrower, in return, had to sell all of his catch through the particular dealer, and this relation was called *shikifune.* The dealers had a system of price agreement called *netate,* which yielded great profit for them. The dealers had a council called *tonyayori* for liaison and adjustment among themselves; the main purpose was specification of price, and their commission was 5 percent. Even if the fishermen were dissatisfied with the *netate*, they had no means to counter it. Generally, the fishermen were too poor to transport their catch directly to the market, so that the dealers' profit from the fluctuation of price was immense, and the poor fishermen were at the mercy of the dealers in every aspect of their lives.

At the beginning of the present Showa era (1925–), the fishermen's growing dissatisfaction with the unfairness of the dealers developed into a movement to establish their own fishing cooperative. The first thing they did was to cut the *shikifune* bond between the dealers and themselves, for which repayment of the loan from the dealers was the first condition. This was achieved with the aid of a fishing cooperative already established in the neighboring village of Kashii Mura. As a result, the dealers who lost their client-fishermen fell rapidly.

In 1932, the first fishermen's own cooperative was organized; then in 1936 they began making ice. This enterprise was followed by joint sales in 1937, and then by joint purchase of fishing tools and ship fitting in 1938. Their activities stopped temporarily during World War II, but revived in 1949 and rapidly gained financial power in accordance with the government's National Planning for Structural Modernization which began in 1957. Thus, Katsumoto-ura Fishing Cooperative succeeded in unifying the entire Ura community. The Youth Section of the Cooperative was also successful in making a Ura-based organization, with the Fishing Cooperative as its strong backer.

The Cooperative elects sixty representatives, or one out of twenty members, to serve on a fishing committee, festival committee, or as liaison man, etc. The festival committee to which we shall refer later takes care of Ura-based festivals. That the Cooperative embraces the festival committee indicates a strong tie between the credulous fishermen and rituals, as seen at festivals when they perform a service praying for a big catch.

CHANGES IN RITUALS   Here we shall discuss ritual organization, or the social unit in connection with rituals. In Katsumoto-ura, traditional folk beliefs concerning fishing are relatively unchanged in spite of the rapid increase of fishing motorboats and technical improvement in fishing. But the change of social units for rituals and festivals in the past decade is striking. The process of change differs according to each ritual, but it may be characterized as segmentation and integration of ritual organization. Katsumoto-ura is divided into two districts, Hon-ura district and Shomura district, each of which is further subdivided into several sections. For instance, the Inyaku Shrine, traditionally worshipped in the four sections of Hon-ura, is now worshipped, or maintained, by just one of the sections, due to the unsolved problem of maintenance cost. The Shomo Shrine encompasses the entire Katsumoto, including agricultural communities, and a boat race called *Funagoro* used to be held between the fishing community and the agricultural community. After the agricultural community dropped out, it became a race between Shomura District and Hon-ura District, and now each section takes turns to manage the race. These two cases are examples of segmentation of a *ku*-level organization into a *kumi*-level organization.

On the other hand, Wakamiya Shrine, which had a form of *miyaza* consisting of Ura pioneers, gradually became a shrine of entirely Ura-level. Gion-sama and Kompira Shrine, which had traditionally been worshipped on *kumi*- or *kumi*-compound-level, have now become shrines of the entire Ura-level. The importance here in lieu of such level changes is the relation with the Fishing Cooperative. As the Cooperative of Katsumoto-ura is the only organ integrating the entire Ura, the enlarged shrine organizations are necessarily integrated into the organization of the Cooperative, because the maintenance cost is taken care of by the Cooperative and also because the festival committee and the shrine representative serve concurrently as the Cooperative's representatives. Just as in the case of the Katsumoto-ura Primary School Alumni Association, to which we shall refer later, many of the organizations having to do with the entire Ura, like the ritual organizations and the Cooperative, or like the Alumni Association and the Youth Section of the Cooperative, compose the world of Ura, while being closely interrelated among themselves.

CHANGE IN ADMINISTRATIVE UNIT Integration at the community level is also seen in the change in administrative units. The seventeen *cho* that had once been independent political and social units are practically losing their independence due to administrative reform by their super-organizations. On the other hand, the importance of Ura as an administrative unit is increasing. Relations and associations among fishermen are also being intensified. This has much to do with the great advance of the Cooperative which fostered an increase of motor boats by loan and an increase of wireless communication. Technical innovation brought homogeneity of fishing methods, and communication among the fishermen is incomparabel greater than it used to be, contributing toward the integration of Ura.

Tradition versus Intentional Direction in the Organizing Process of the New Seinendan

It was in November 1968 that the Ura *Seinendan* which disappeared in 1963 was reorganized. As was mentioned above, several trials for organizing a *Seinendan* in Katsumoto-ura ended in failure each time it was tried. However, the organization of the new *Seinendan* in the fall of 1968 is worthy of notice as a case in which the intentional direction of the outer society and the internal needs comfortably coincided. The external direction came from the socioeducational supervisors. Two ardent supervisors in Katsumoto-ura, who had been conscious of deteriorated public morals in the past few years, called for a conference of heads of the civil house, where they discussed how to organize a new youth association. Because success of a youth association depends on leaders, the two supervisors asked the heads of the civil house to recommend a leader in each *cho*. In October 1968 they summoned the leaders to talk about the ideal civil house, the need for a youth association, and the importance of self-reliance. This was in fact the intentional direction on the part of the supervisors who belong to the outside world.

In the meantime there have been voices raised in support of establishing an association besides the *Seinenbu* of the Fishing Cooperative, to include girls. One of the factors that made them want a new association was the system of Juvenile Guidance Committees.

In spite of the recent increase of high-school attendance and increased employment outside the island, twenty to thirty middle-school graduates remain on the island each year to engage in fishing. During *Okidome*, due to bad weather, Ura is crowded with vigorous young men — a scene that can never be seen in mountain and farming villages where the absence of youngsters is a big problem. On the contrary, the problem in this community was increased crime, due to lack of an outlet for youthful energy and also due to lack of an organization systematically integrating the entire community. This was the background for the Juvenile Guidance Committee in each *cho*, initiated by the Prefectural Police and the Katsumoto-machi Board of Education. Members of the Guidance Committee are selected either by the Prefectural Police or by the Katsumoto-machi Board of Education (in Urabu there are five of the former and six of the latter members, from whom three are selected by each). This system seems to have hurt the pride of the Urabu youths, who worried that the sightseers who saw the sign might think that the island was full of juvenile delinquents and felt that the

system dishonored them. It was then that the socioeducational supervisors suggested to the youth that they organize a new association. The
young leaders of Ura decided to start an association with a particular
stress upon sports which the other youth groups could not carry out.
On October 20, 1968, they held a softball tournament which was
also the beginning of a new *Seinendan*. Membership is composed of
young men and women between the ages of fifteen and twenty-five, and
is obligatory for males and optional for females. At the time of establishment, the socioeducational supervisors, the Board of Education, and
the Primary School Alumni Association cooperated, but it was run by
the association on its own. Town officers and the Cooperative's representatives were invited to the first general meeting. During the first
year, sports such as volley ball, softball and ping-pong were their main
theme, but at the beginning of the second year, in March 1963, structural reorganization was called for from within the association, the
main point being the method of election of the executives that takes
place every April.

ORGANIZATION OF THE NEW SEINENDAN   In Urabu of Kasumoto-machi,
well over twenty boys remain on the island after graduation from
middle school, which is different from Zaibu, or the countryside. This
group is very closely knit, as they have known each other since primary-
school days. As mentioned before, the principle of age has traditionally
been strong in Urabu, and one is quite obedient to those who are one
grade above him (whereas in agricultural Zaibu, the more able can
become executives, even if young). There was an opinion from a member that all of the eldest, or those who are twenty-five years old, should
be executives. This means that after their retirement, the next eldest
group takes their place. The socioeducational supervisors found it suitable for Urabu, and suggested that they also set up the office of branch
chiefs to be filled by the second eldest group members. All the executives including the head are mutually elected. This method of choosing
executives in accordance with the principle of age that was proposed
from within the group is said to be quite successful. This also stems
from the traditional social structure of Katsumoto-ura, where age is
considered to be one of the most important principles of human relations. In the next section we shall describe this "human relations according to age" in more detail.

ALUMNI ASSOCIATION OF KATSUMOTO PRIMARY SCHOOL   Katsumoto Primary School *Koyukai* has an important position in running any organ-

Table 2. Executive posts of Urabu *Seinendan* (1969)

President	1	Athletics section	
Supervisor	2	Chairman	1
Vice-president	2	Vice-chairman	3
Treasurer	1	Social section	
Clerk	1	Chairman	1
Culture section		Vice-chairman	3
Chairman	1	Recreation section	
Vice-chairman	3	Chairman	1
		Vice-chairman	3

ized groups in Katsumoto-ura. This association has an age limit, unlike many alumni associations, and is composed of graduates between the ages of fifteen and thirty-five, i.e. exactly the same as the components of the *Seinenbu* of the Fishing Cooperative. Their main event is the Peiron Boat Race, held every August, when the fishing industry is not busy, as an important part of the festival in Ura. This is not participated in by all the members, but only by the thirty-five-year-old classmates, who seek recognition throughout Ura for their solidarity and ability on this occasion. In other words, they are evaluated: "Graduates

Table 3. Branches and members of Urabu *Seinendan*

Name of town	Number	Name of town	Number
Shioya	22	Kachu	9
Tsukidashi	25	Kasai	17
Yuda	17	Tama	18
Sakaguchi	19	Kawajiri	10
Kurose	14	Shomura	16
Kotohira	9	Nakaore	18
Kato	14	Babasaki	16
		Total	224

of 19— are excellent," or "They are dumb," etc., according to how they performed in the Peiron Boat Race. It is in the selection of executives of the *Seinenbu* of the Fishing Cooperative and the Alumni Association that the principle of age, or the elder-younger order of Ura, is particularly clear. At the annual election, all those who are or will be thirty-five in March get together and they elect executives for the *Seinenbu* of the Fishing Cooperative. The remaining members become executives in the Alumni Association. For example, if there are twenty classmates and seventeen of them are on the island, they first choose thirteen executives for the *Seinenbu*, and the remaining four become the executives of the Alumni Association. In other words the only qualification for becoming an executive is that one must be at least

thirty-five years old; it has nothing to do with one's ability. One can easily see that this age principle has much to do with the choice of executives in the Youth Association where twenty-five is the upper age limit.

FUNCTION OF THE NEW YOUTH ASSOCIATION Ura now has three co-existing youth groups: the *cho*-based *Seinenkai*, the Youth Section of the Fishing Cooperative, and the new Youth Association. How are they related to each other? In particular, what *raison d'être* and function does this new association have in the presence of the other two?

Let us first review the *Seinenkai*, the oldest traditional group which has been maintained on a *cho* basis. Since the establishment of the Youth Section of the Fishing Cooperative, the *Seinenkai* was inclined to become almost a subsidiary organ of the former, although it did maintain its solidarity as an independent organization. As the Youth Section is practically based on the *Seinenkai*, and as both groups are composed of men between fifteen and thirty-five, the two groups overlap completely. Gradual loss of independence of each *cho* in the process of integration into Ura level is also seen in various other phases, such as ritual organization, *cho*-administration by the civil house, and the economic activities that tend to cohere in the Fishing Cooperative. Whereas the *Seinenbu* of the Fishing Cooperative has been active in fields closely conected to the inhabitants' enterprise, such as the study of fishing tools and methods and joint purchase of ships' fittings and fishing tools, there have been few independent activities on the part of the *Seinenkai*. It must have been a necessary result of the fact that the *Seinenkai* was too closely tied to the *Seinenbu*, like the back of a shield to the front.

In contrast to the repeated failure of the government-sponsored youth associations, in which the history of youth groups and actual conditions in the area were ignored, the Youth Section of the Fishing Cooperative was said to be successful and structurally stable because it was community-based. What, then, does the favorable evaluation by the inhabitants of Ura of the new association established in 1968 mean? The Urabu *Seinendan* started with a particular stress on recreation (mainly sports) which the former two groups could not fulfill. They tried to cover their structural deficiency by the application of the age principle which was traditionally predominant in Ura. The difference of age limit, thirty-five in *Seinenkai* and twenty-five in the new association, had been considered the weakest point of the government-sponsored associations. In spite of this, the new association seems to have solved this problem by shifting from this detrimental age difference to a difference between the married group (twenty-six to thirty-five) and the single group (fifteen to twenty-five), although twenty-five is not such a clear-cut dividing line between the married and the single. Still, the members up to twenty-five years old have double membership, and as most of the activities of the *Seinenbu* and the new *Seinendan* are performed during bad weather, the problem of overlapping membership remains to be solved in the future. For example, the date of editing the bulletin "*Sunadori*" of the *Seinenbu* and the date of a group activity of the *Seinendan* happened once to coincide. In this case *Seinendan* members helped the others because the bulletin manuscript

Table 4.　Activities of Urabu *Seinendan*

Month	Activity	Section in charge	Month	Activity	Section in charge
4	Curved-mirror cleaning	S	9	Curved-mirror cleaning	S
	Cleaning of mountains	S		Cleaning of Tatsumoto	
	Lecture on navigation	C		Port	S
	Lecture for executives	C		Movie	R
	Softball tournament	A		Dancing lesson	R
	Dancing lesson	R	10	Curved-mirror cleaning	S
5	Cleaning of curved mirrors	S		Making of pedestrian	
	Making of pedestrian			signals	S
	signals	S		Cleaning of Katsumoto	
	Conference with women's			Port	
	club	C		Volley ball tournament	A
	Dancing lesson	R		Dancing lesson	R
6	Curved-mirror cleaning	S	11	Curved-mirror cleaning	S
	Lecture on technical			Lecture on oil	C
	engineering	C		Softball tournament	A
	Training-conference with			Dancing lesson	R
	other youth association	C	12	Curved-mirror cleaning	S
	Dancing lesson	R		Christmas party	R
7	Curved-mirror cleaning	S		Dancing lesson	R
	Cleaning of Nakaore Beach	S	1	Curved-mirror cleaning	S
	Cleaning of Cape Benten	S		Ping-pong tournament	A
	Dancing lesson	R		Dancing lesson	R
8	Curved-mirror cleaning	S	2	Curved-mirror cleaning	S
	Cleaning of Tatsuno			Movie	R
	Shima Beaches	S		Dancing lesson	R
	Recreation on Tatsuno			Volley ball tournament	
	Shima	A		(age group)	A
	Athletic meeting	A	3	Curved-mirror cleaning	S
	Movie	R		Dancing lesson	R
	Dancing lesson	R		General meeting	

S = Social section
C = Cultural section
R = Recreation section
A = Athletic section

Table 5.   Activities of female section

Month	Activity	Month	Activity	Month	Activity
5	Cooking Conference with women's club Dancing lesson	9	Cooking Make-up training Tea with male members	12	Cooking Kimono wearing lesson Christmas party
6	Cooking Conference with other youth group Dancing lesson	10	Cooking Volley ball tournament Dancing	1	Cooking Ping-pong tournament
7	Cooking Kimono wearing Dancing lesson Camping	11	Softball tournament Cooking Dancing lesson Participation in "Cultural Exhibition"	2	Cooking Volley ball tournament
8	Cooking Recreation on Tatsuno Shima Athletic meeting Bon festival			3	Cleaning of Amagahara Dancing lesson General meeting

had to be submitted to a printing shop promptly. Some believe that people between fifteen and twenty-five should belong to the *Seinendan* and those between twenty-six and thirty-five to the Youth Section. In other words, members under twenty-five and over twenty-six have different attitudes toward life, and as most of the younger group are single, they can participate in recreational activities different from those of the older group. In any case, that all of the young men of such a small community as Katsumoto-ura belong to two different groups means that some kind of adjustment of activities is necessary. One cannot deny that the appearance of the new *Seinendan* decreased the *raison d'être* for the traditional *Seinenkai*. Perhaps the greatest problem that the *Seinendan* has to face will be the adjustment among the members of the *Seinenbu* of the Fishing Cooperative under the age of twenty-five. The *Seinenbu* in turn seems to have been dwelling on a routine pattern within the powerful organization, the Fishing Cooperative having more or less lost the passion and urgency of the initial stage. Now that the new *Seinendan* with the traditional age principle can stand on its own and is quite active, there is some question as to whether the two will always have to coexist.

CONCLUSION

Our main purpose was to look at the history of adolescent groups in a fishing community with particular reference to the relationship between the native, traditional groups that are structurally related to the community, and the groups intentionally created by the outside world (the state and prefecture in this case). As we have seen, the government-sponsored youth groups were repeatedly established and dissolved, while the traditional *Seinenkai* and *Seinenbu* have always been quite stable; the contrast is extraordinary.

Three adolescent groups, *Seinenkai*, *Seinenbu*, and *Seinendan* were all established as organizations with more or less similar socioeducational functions. While the former two were created by the socioeconomic needs of the community, the *Seinendan* was imposed on the community as part of government policy and had no bearing upon the community life and its value system. For instance, it is evident that one of the causes of its failure was indifference to the principle of age. Because the members of the traditional *Seinenkai* were composed of young men between fifteen and thirty-five, and because age was the decisive factor for ranking, the *Seinendan*, which was composed of men under twenty-five, was at at disadvantage within the traditional value system of Ura in which the elders are respected. Besides, whereas the *Seinenbu* and *Seinenkai* were inseparably connected to the economic life of the community, the *Seinendan* created after World War II was nothing but a recreation group. Generally speaking, institutions created by the need of the community itself are deeply connected to the customs and social structure of that community. Among the important factors that brought forth the development and organizational stability of the *Seinenkai* and the *Seinenbu* of the Fishing Cooperative, one could probably name dissolution of the patron-client relation between wholesale dealers and fishermen and of the status structure of *ie* in Ura that followed, and also the trend toward each hamlet being integrated into a bigger community.

These conditions have much to do with the changing value system of the inhabitants and development of the Fishing Cooperative run on the principle of equality among all the members. Success of the *Seinenbu* of the Fishing Cooperative is greatly influenced by this integration or centralization in Ura and the dissolution of the status system. One should also take into consideration the fact that the postwar Japanese educational system and the actual education based on the democratic philosophy had much to do with the changing values of the *Seinenbu* members. At the same time, the lively activities of the *Seinenbu* must have had great influence over the inhabitants' attitudes.

Needless to say, not all the government-sponsored educational systems are as unstable as the one in Katsumoto-ura, and compulsory educational organizations must be considered separately from socio-educational ones. For instance, the rate of primary- and middle-school attendance is almost 100 percent, which seems to mean that this kind of educational institution has strong support from the community, although the high attendance rate is partially attributable to its being compulsory. The primary goal on the national level of such general educational institutions is to transmit basic culture, knowledge, and a standardized national language through the primary educational system. Although not strongly connected to the economic life of the area like the Youth Section of the Fishing Cooperative, public schools assume the role of educating young Japanese citizens so that they can adapt themselves to the larger society surrounding them. It is compulsory in Japan to attend the primary and middle schools, and the government schools in each community contribute to the maintenance and development of the community as a part of the Japanese society. On the other hand, government-sponsored youth associations in former times did not have the powerful reason for existence as a socioeducational organ in a community, although they did have the function of relating the community to the larger society. We have already seen that one of the defects of the government-sponsored *Seinendan* was that it failed to absorb the traditional *Seinenkai* which had the above-mentioned function.

However, the relationship between "traditional" and "governmental" instruction in Katsumoto-ura youth groups seems to have shown a subtle change since 1968. Observation of establishment processes in the new *Seinendan* in Urabu in October 1968 reveals that while government organization offered suggestions and instructions in which Ura tradition was fully taken into account, the Urabu youth started the *Seinendan* on their own, with the changing social conditions of Ura well in mind. The new *Seinendan* neither absorbed the traditional *Seinenkai* nor changed the age limit of twenty-five. In this respect they are just the same as the former government-sponsored associations that experienced repeated establishment and dissolution. Why, then, is this new one so popular and successful? Two factors — success in management and changing ways of thought and life throughout Ura — can be considered.

The important managerial factor is that they adopted the old principle of age in the selection of executives. That is to say, they were conscious of the strong solidarity among fisherman of equal age and decided that all the twenty-five-year-olds or those who had reached the upper age limit (classmates from primary school) be automatically placed in some kind of executive post and retired the following year, leaving the posts to the one-year-younger group. By the revival of the traditional age principle, the *Seinendan* was able to make use of the "tradition" and succeed in their stable personnel management.

The second factor, changing values and way of life, having to do with nationwide trends in Japan, can be interpreted here as relating to increased economic stability and leisure. During the postwar years when life was hard for the fishermen, a youth association in which recreation was the sole purpose was of no use. *Seinenkai* or *Seinenbu* could do it just as well. However, as the waves of economic development throughout Japan are extended to the inhabitants of Katsumoto-ura, and stimuli are brought here by television, sightseers, summer visitors for swimming, and by the young men and women who come home occasionally from their places of employment outside the island, all these, together with increased economic capacity, have created a condition where simple recreation undertaken by the *Seinenkai* or *Seinenbu* could not long satisfy the young inhabitants of the island.

The somewhat dull spirit of the *Seinenbu* helped to cause its failure and also may have helped in the establishment of the new *Seinendan*. The ten-year age gap between the *Seinendan*, with an upper age limit of twenty-five, and the *Seinenbu* with an age limit of thirty-five, forced the former to the inferior position in this community where the elders are respected. However, this age gap does not seem to bother the new *Seinendan* because they consider the *Seinendan* as a group for bachelors under twenty-five years of age, and the *Seinenbu* as mainly for the executive class who are over twenty-six and are married (with some exceptions). It has been only a year and a half since the establishment of the *Seinendan* and we need to wait several more years for a real evaluation. Still, one can see at this point, through the analysis of adolescent groups, that the community of Ura is on the point of a great shift, more than two decades after World War II.

Generally speaking, innovative planning for a community does not enchant the inhabitants unless the plan has some bearing upon the traditional society and cultural system. There is little chance of success for a proposed community development if there is no understanding of interrelations with existing customs and institutions and if it cannot function within the existing social structure and social strata. The alienation phenomenon resulting from new factors thrown into the existing society is often caused by the above-mentioned conditions. The cases of the government-sponsored youth associations in Katsumoto-ura before 1968 illustrate cases of failure in adaptation due to indifference toward the tradition and structure of the community. On the other hand, the new *Seinendan* seems to make good use of the tradition of the community, although it did receive some sort of "intentional direction." Besides, the predominant motivation came from under, rather than from above; from within, rather than from outside. The most important factor in community development is to promote the inhabitants' active participation, which seems to be applicable to the case of Katsumoto-ura *Seinendan* also.

REFERENCES

AYABE, TSUNEO
  1965   "Cultural barriers to educational change for youth in a Japanese fishing community." International Development Seminar, The East-West Center, Honolulu.
BEARDSLEY, R. K., *et al.*
  1959   *Village Japan.* Chicago: University of Chicago Press.
DAHRENWEND, BRUCE P., ROBERT J. SMITH
  1962   Toward a theory of acculturation. *Southwestern Journal of Anthropology* 18(1):30–39.
EISENSTADT, S. N.
  1956   *From generation to generation.* Glencoe, Illinois: Free Press.
FOSTER, G. M.
  1962   *Traditional culture and the impact of technological change.* New York: Harper.
FUKUTAKE, TADASHI
  1960   *Nihon noson no shakaikozo* [Social structure of the Japanese farm village]. Tokyo: Tokyo University Press.
GAMO, MASAO
  1952   Nihon shakai no chiikisei [Locality of Japanese society]. *Nihon chiri taikei* [Japanese Geography] 2. Tokyo: Tokyo University Press.
GOODENOUGH, W. H.
  1963   *Cooperation in change.* New York: Russell Sage Foundation.
KOMATA, KINICHI
  1956   Sengo ni okeru seinendan undo no suii [Transition of the youth movement in postwar Japan]. *Bulletin of the Faculty of Education,* Kyushu University (4):1–16.
KUMAGAI, TATSUJIRO
  1942   *Dai nihon seinendan shi* [History of the Japanese youth group]. Tokyo: Nihon Seinenkan.
LINDSTROM, DAVID E.
  1960   *Community development in Seki-Mura.* Urbana, Illinois: University of Illinois College of Agriculture, Agricultural Experiment Station.

MEAD, MARGARET, *editor*
   1955   *Cultural patterns and technical change.* New York: New American Library.
MIYAMOTO, MATAJI
   1957   *Kinki noson no chitsujo to henbo* [Order and change of the farm village in Kinki]. Tokyo: Yuhikaku.
NAKAYAMA, TARO
   1930   *Nihon wakamonoshi* [History of Japanese youth]. Tokyo: Shunyodo.
NORBECK, EDWARD
   1954   *Takashima: a Japanese fishing community.* Salt Lake City: University of Utah Press.
SMITH, ROBERT J., E. P. REYES
   1957   Community interrelations with the outside world: the case of a Japanese agricultural community. *American Anthropologist* 59: 463–472.
SUZUKI, JIRO
   1956   *Toshi to sonraku no shakaigakuteki kenkyu* [A sociological study of urban and rural communities]. Tokyo: Sekaishoin.
TAKAHASHI, TOICHI
   1958   Nihon ni okeru nenreishudan no shoruikei [Several types of age groups in Japan]. *Bulletin of Tokyo University* 12:131–140.
TAKEUCHI, TOSHIMI
   1952   "*Kodomogumi* [Children's group]," in *Nihon Shakai Minzoku Jiten* [Dictionary of Japanese society and folklore], volume one, 428–431. Tokyo: Japanese Society of Ethnology.
YOSHIDA, TEIGO
   1963   Cultural integration and change in a Japanese village. *American Anthropologist* 65:105–116.

Parental Authority and Family Size:
A Chinese Case

M. C. TANG

Virtually all works concerning Chinese family forms accept that there is a very general pattern in Chinese society by which wealth and social standing are associated with family complexity. Their differences lie upon the explanation of causality. I myself have no intention to negate such a widely accepted possibility, but wish to show that different degrees of parental authority, reflecting intergenerational relationships from the dynastic period to the present, do affect family size in addition to the family's wealth and social standing.

THE DYNASTIC PERIOD

In the dynastic period, parental authority was almost unchallenged. It was sanctioned by the state because the family in Imperial China had important administrative functions. Domestic harmony in premodern China was viewed as being in the interest of the state (Freedman 1961–1962). Although the degree of conformity to such a standard varied, it was politically and legally enforced. An ideal standard of kinship was adopted and used for hundreds of years as the foundation of state ideology for controlling people's thought (Ch'ü 1961; Hsiao 1960). It served as a major means for maintaining order at the local level, which was mostly formed by primary groups. The social norm of kinship derived from such ideology, upon which parental authority rested, was influential in domestic behavior in Chinese society in general.

The system of Chinese terminology has its built-in rules applicable to regulating behavior. According to Murdock's classification (1949: 224), Chinese kinship is close to the Sudanese type, and in Lowie's definition (1928: 265–266), it belongs to the bifurcate collateral type. Seven of the nine criteria of the fundamental categories of relationships, which were first proposed by Kroeber (1909: 79) and Lowie (1928: 84–89), are recognized in the system of Chinese kinship terms. (For a general analysis of Chinese kinship, see Feng [1937] and Chen and Shyrock [1932]. But note that both works were based on kinship terms found in dictionaries.) Among the seven criteria, three of them — sex, generation, and age — are of strategic significance in regulating behavior among Chinese kinsmen. The concepts of male superiority, subservience to the ascending generation and respect for seniority are all based upon them.

The generation and age rules of kinship were reinforced by Confucian *Ju-chia* teaching. Of its four advocated virtues — *hsiao, ti, chung,* and *hsin* [filial piety, brotherly subordination, loyalty, and sincerity] — the former two are standards of kinship behavior based upon age and generation criteria, while the latter two are derived from kinship and are standards for nonkin behavior. The logical implication and expectation are that a filial son makes a loyal official; a man who respects his elder brothers is a sincere friend. Proper kinship behavior which results in stable families means a stable society: an axiom of Chinese political thought (Sa 1969: 51, 147–63). It was one of the basic assumptions of Chinese political theory that the good state would automatically result if each individual punctiliously cultivated the garden of his own family duties.

Therefore, the Confucian doctrine of *li*, which the writer prefers to phrase anthropologically as "a set of expected patterns of behavior among kin and nonkin in accordance with the Confucian ideology of status," was formed to regulate behavior by beginning from the very bottom of society. Thus, proper kinship behavior would eventually regulate the state at large. Ideology of kinship, of which parental authority is the focus, is important in this connection; for it is regarded not only as the basic rule of interpersonal relations, but also as the basis for training in general citizenship (C.K. Yang 1959b, 1959c).

Furthermore, kinship norm in China was incorporated in the legal codes. A father's authority over children was stipulated in law (Tai 1963) and has been enforced by the state since the Sui dynasty (A.D. 518–618). The system of five mourning grades, which is clearly defined in all of the premodern law codes since then, gave the father a dominant and definite position over the sons.

From the historical materials, we see that encouragement and restriction by the state did influence the form of the family. The joint family in China was in fact not encouraged until the T'ang dynasty (A.D. 618–906). From the first dynasty Ch'in (221 B.C.) to T'ang, it was the stem form of family instead of the joint form that received government approval. The reason for this was that the unified empire saw its incompatibility with the old lineage system because large and strong familial groups could be potential enemies of the government (Ruey 1961; for the original historical records see SCCSHPC n.d.). Another reason for this, according to T'ao Hsi-sheng, a contemporary social historian, was that in that time people were encouraged to support colonization and intensive agriculture. A small family was more compatible with such practice. Therefore, the law of Ch'in stipulated that no family should have more than one married son living together with the parents, or the tax of the family would be doubled (*Old T'ang Shu*, fu-sui).

From the Han dynasty, the dynasty which followed Ch'in, the circumstances with respect to family were different. Confucian teaching of moral principles and kinship became state ideology in the early period of that dynasty. The T'ang dynasty, succeeding the Han, was the most prosperous dynasty in early Chinese history. State control over the people was very sophisticated. It was in the early T'ang that Confucianization of Chinese law was completed (Ch'ü 1961). Kinship norm was incorporated into law for the benefit of the government, the joint family was idealized, and lineal ascendants were given more authority over the descendants in the family. Along with such practice was the incorporation into Confucianism of many ideas from pre-Ch'in philosophers, which were useful for the unification of the country. Doctrines of frugality from Taoism (LTCK 1968: 16; H. C. Wang 1955), and Mu-chia were the important ones (W. Tai 1956). In T'ang, such an ideology was also adopted by pre-modern Japanese for similar purposes (Dore 1958: 93–94).

The legal power which the state granted to the parents increased from T'ang to the last dynasty. For instance, during the Han dynasty, a parent who killed a child was executed (Ch'ü 1961) in T'ang, killing a child or a grandchild, irrespective of the reason, was punished by imprisonment. Under Yüan (1260–1368), Ming (1368–1644), and Ch'ing (1644–1912), if parents killed a child who had been unfilial to the point of scolding or beating them, they were not found guilty. There are even cases where parents were not found guilty when the child was killed "inhumanely" (Ch'ü 1961: 23–24). In Ch'ing time, besides recognizing the parents' authority to punish a child, the law also gave them the right to ask to have the children punished by the local officials (Ch'ü 1961: 25).

In fact, parental authority over children, as part of the state mechanism for controlling people, increased to a formidable degree during the last thousand years of the Chinese dynastic period. The end-product is that the characteristic of parental authority in the Ch'ing time required the detached minds of foreign scholars to evaluate it. A Japanese scholar, Niida, once commented that the paternal power in premodern China was unified, exclusive, subjective, absolute, and unique (Niida 1952; Freedman 1966).

On the other hand, divison of family, an eventuality which remains in the developmental cycles of the family a crucial variable to family form, was also legally checked. Division of the Chinese family consists of three aspects (TWSH 1910–1911: II, 203): (1) physical separation and constitution of another living group; (2) exclusive economic relations and partitioning of estate; and (3) segregation of the worship of ancestors, i.e. dividing of the ancestral tablets.

From the T'ang dynasty on to the last dynasty, legal codes also prescribed the proper conditions for family division. Division of a family had to be carried out under the consent of the family head — the father or grandfather. In T'ang and Sung times, the penality for breaching such a law was one year's imprisonment; in Ming and Ch'ing times it was eighty strokes. Also, in T'ang times division between brothers during the mourning period of parents was also prohibited; violation of this was a crime bringing a one-year jail sentence.

Parental authority entitled the seniors in a family to be taken care of in their old age by the juniors. Such a norm also affected the form of the family.

The legal enforcement of the duty for taking care of the seniors in the family has been mandatory in all of the legal codes of China from the T'ang dynasty to the present time. It is not only legal support but support ritualized in a religious manner by ancestral worship and Buddhism. One must be filial not only to one's living parents and grandparents, but also to the deceased ancestors. Their blessing is eagerly sought. Prosperity and success in imperial examination were thought to be the result of the accumulated virtue of one's ancestors (Ho 1962). Consequently, filial piety and ancestral worship are concomitant; one reinforces the other (Freedman 1958: 134). As Kulp put it, the two are one, theoretically as well as practically (Kulp 1925).

Buddhist teaching, however, was tolerated in China (Weber 1951): part of its belief is congenial with the kinship ideology. Two Buddhist tenets further reinforced the virtue of filial piety: (1) the Buddhist concept of judgment and reward after death according to one's conduct in life; and (2) the idea of reincarnation as animal or human depending on how many merits one has accumulated in his lifetime; filial piety, manifested through support and obedience to one's parent, has the highest merit (second only to loyalty to the emperor). There are many legends in Chinese folklore of how Buddha helps filial sons, and how an unfilial son was punished both in life and in the other world.

THE MODERN PERIOD

With the birth of the Republic of China in 1912, parental legal auhority has been much reduced, particularly since the promulgation of the first civil code in 1931. But the heirs of tradition, comparatively speaking, Chinese fathers still have considerable legal power over the children. The civil law, in accommodation to the tradition, provided the parents with the authority of "instruction and discipline" over the children — a legal power, although much restricted in comparison with that of the old days. On the other hand, the regulation governing domiciliary registration in Taiwan also grants the parents a legal right of consent over any change of items registered in the domiciliary records. As a result, among other things, an official division of family would be impossible if the parents withheld consent.

As to the matter of the children's duty of supporting the aging parents and grandparents, the current law of the Republic of China also stipulates this both in the civil code and in the criminal code (see F. L. K. Hsu 1959; P. Y. Hsü 1932; Tai 1970).

Even in mainland China, taking care of the seniors in the family is legally enforced. The family there is still a viable institution. It has not been abolished (as some journalistic opinion would have one believe). Filial piety is also still a virtue there, although it is interpreted in socialist terms — parents should be corrected and worthy of respect (Fried 1959). The functions of the family in mainland China, however, have been reduced (Freedman 1961–1962) and many families are now of the stem form; yet in addition to the relationship of spouses and parents-sons, the service of taking care of the old members in the family is also emphasized as one of the important functions of family. The Law of Marriage of the People's Republic of China, promulgated in 1950, stipulates that:

Parents have the duty to rear and educate their children; the children have the duty to look after and assist their parents. Neither the parents nor the children shall mistreat or desert one another. The foregoing provision also applies to stepparents and stepchildren. Infanticide by drowning and similar criminal acts are strictly prohibited (C. K. Yang 1959a:223).

As can be seen, the children's duty of taking care of old parents is stipulated in moderate yet definite terms. There is field information concerning stem family and joint family in mainland China in the 1960's, where aged members of families lived together with married juniors (see Myrdal 1965: 38–44).

It is significant to see that filial piety in taking care of the old in the family has been such an age-old concern in China. The dynastic, the republican, and the communist governments all stress this. Such a state-supported kinship norm certainly affects the form of the family.

TODAY'S FAMILY IN A TAIWAN COMMUNITY

The following field material was collected from a community in Taipei, Taiwan, which I call First Row Yellow Rock. In 1970 there were 1,093 persons living in 196 residential units. Among them, 623 were adults: 70 percent of them were native born, 26 percent were Min-nan Taiwanese from elsewhere in Taiwan, and only 4 percent were main-landers. Educationally speaking, 55 percent of the adults finished 6 years of primary school, 27 percent had 7-12 years of schooling, 7 percent had college education, and 11 percent were illiterate. Of the adults, 343 were employed, of whom 137 were self-employed (most of them owned family stores and stands); 100 were white-collar em-ployees, and 106 were artisans and workers. The jobs people in First Row hold, generally speaking, bring in only a low income.

The term residential unit is used for designating a group of primary kinsmen who live and eat together. Many of them coincide with the family in the Chinese sense. However, many others are only parts of a family. A family in First Row is defined as a group of lineal and close collateral, patrilineal kinsmen and their wives who live together or are dispersed but undivided. They share the inherited estate when there is any. The extent to which there is economic cooperation among them varies.

In order to discover the changing family structure from the point of view of ecological adaptation together with parental authority, the 196 residential units are first classified according to the conventional way. They are typed as follows: single person (15), nuclear (132), patrilineal stem (34), matrilineal stem (7), joint (6), and fraternal joint (2). After being so classified, the residential units are analyzed in terms of family. There are 155 families. The discrepancy between residential units and families, together with other domestic arrangements, indicates that the changing structure of the family in the city is a result of compromise between parental authority and its implied rights and ecological adaptation in an urban milieu. The following facts emerged during our research.

First, there are many families with members living separately, yet still remaining a family unit. As has been noted in many anthropological works on Chinese domestic institutions, dispersion of members is one of the characteristic features of the Chinese family. That is, some of the family members do not live together. However, previous anthropological literature has largely explained the dispersion of Chinese family groups from the economic point of view; dispersion has been regarded as a part of the diversification of the family economy and as a means of achieving success.

In First Row, the dispersion of family members for economic reasons is not uncommon. Generally, every family wishes some of its members to disperse to the outside world to seek more advantageous occupations that carry both material benefit and prestige (Fried 1953). Education and social ties, kin and nonkin, are all so oriented. However, dispersion for economic reasons alone is not sufficient to explain the residential patterns of family members in First Row, because, in fact, there are also many cases of "dispersion" not related to economic purpose. They disperse not only to Taipei or other places, but also inside the community for noneconomic reasons. In some instances the older generation disperses instead of the younger. There are even cases of married brothers and their parental residential units residing separately yet in the same houses. In other words, in First Row, many parts of a family often live on their own in a nuclear type of residential unit in the form of pseudo-smallness (for opinion of pseudo-largeness of family, see Hsu [1948] and Wittfogel [1938]). They live separately, yet remain members of the same families. Relations between parents and married sons and between the married brothers are thus shown as being mediated by the kinship norm centered around parental authority.

There are many cases in which there is a low degree of economic involvement among the members. The ideal type of economic relation between Chinese family members, as often noted in anthropological literature (see Kulp 1925: 148; M. Yang 1945: 76–77), is that in the composite families, whose economy is inclusive. However, in First Row, in the stem and joint families, domestic economy is not inclusive, and only a meager economic relationship exists among the parents and the married sons, and among the married brothers who live separately. Completely inclusive economy between the parents and the married sons in stem families, as well as in the joint families, is not found. In the composite form of family the parents and the married sons diversify in economic activities and maintain strategic resources separately. Sons who work for the fathers in self-employed family businesses are permitted to keep their incomes. The married sons have their own budget, while domestic expenditures are mostly met by the father. There are cases in which the senior and the junior generations in the same family exploit different appropriate economic niches. First Row provides such a social milieu. First of all, many residents are houseowners. In the relatively insecure economic situation that the people of First Row have been facing, economic security for the family depends mostly upon ownership of the house. In the composite families, most of the houses are owned by the senior generation. Houses there are not merely for consuming purposes, but also for production. The house is not only used as a residence, but is also occupied by a business, so as to create opportunities for self-employment; in addition, other members of the family work outside. Part of the house is rented out, in most cases, in order to further augment family revenue. The family stores and the incomes derived from house renting are often in the hands of the senior generation of the family, while the juniors have jobs in the city. First Row is a community in which both locally-oriented people and those who are city-directed can pursue complementary courses. An economic arrangement with separate control of the family economy maintains the family as a unit — although by the kinship norm, father-sons should be inclusive in economy. Such a practice is a result of compromise between them.

Although weakening parental authority in the modern city is one of the factors attributable to the practice of allowing married sons to reside separately and to maintain exclusive economy with other members of family, the delay of division of family in First Row, that is, continuation of holding family property by the senior generation, is a manifestation of parental authority in its positive manner. By the Chinese kinship norm, when the parents are old they should enjoy the support of the sons. Taking care of aging parents is the children's duty (see Kulp 1925: 136; Lang 1946: 26; and C. K. Yang 1959b: 17). A survey of 2,326 married women carried out by the Taiwan Provincial Institute of Family Planning in 1970 (KAP III) revealed that 90 percent of the wives expected their sons to support them in their old age.

In First Row, to be cared for by the junior members in the family is a recognized practice. However, it has been carried out in several modified patterns. Seniors prefer to make sure of old-age comforts by controlling family economic resources as long as possible. They do not wish to retire from being in charge of the family. The division of family is thus delayed and in turn affects family form.

Thus, in First Row, retirement from business of the older generation does not necessarily mean the sons taking over everything in the family from the parents; rather, it often means that the junior generation is now given a turn to run the family with a relatively free hand. In most cases, as evidenced by the field data, the parents have *de facto* control of the real estate. Many of them have the estate legally transmitted to the sons' names so that the inheritance tax can be avoided. However, the sons would not actually possess the property until the death of the father.

Some of the heads of the joint family who are not successful in holding the family together live in residential units of the stem type with one of the married sons, in order to be cared for by them. Seniors are those who have little of their own or have a different status in the family. They do not always live comfortably. Kinship norm alone does not guarantee this. Equal right of consumption among the family members is merely an ideal (TMHTP 1969: 217–218). Daughters-in-law are "less filial" than the sons, as some of the senior people in First Row put it. In fact, in First Row, dependent senior people must conform to the value of thrift, and some of them are being neglected so that they must do odds and ends of housework.

People in First Row regard dependency as undesirable; the senior members of the family who control nothing and are dependent upon the juniors for their living are an object of pity.

In First Row, owning a nonproductive house is not always sufficient to ensure a comfortable life in retirement supported by the sons, for some of the sons take the houses they are going to inherit for granted. This accounts, in part, for the fact that many people of the senior generation wish to continue to control the estate of the family and manage their own resources as long as physically possible. An urban milieu of multiple resources makes this feasible. Multiple opportunities for employment in a city environment have certainly allowed the seniors and the juniors, in most cases, to be engaged in divergent economic pursuits. Furthermore, the holding of the family estate and the income derived from it by the seniors would not jeopardize the juniors' occupational activity as could be the case in a rural situation.

The residential pattern of separate living of family members, the loose economic inclusiveness between parents and the married son and the married brothers within a family, and the delayed occurrence of division of the family, as I view it, are the results of forces in the urban area working in opposite directions in affecting family form and structure. One direction is the general tendency in the evolution of the family, the world over, to break down composite forms of family life into simple forms (Fried: 1961). This is occasioned because of increased opportunity for both spacial and social mobility created by the current technological evolution (Linton 1959). The other direction is parental authority, lingering on from premodern kinship ideology and from legal stipulations.

Elsewhere in Taiwan, Pasternak found that from 1905–1930, families in Taiwan divided at a much slower rate than they did after 1930 (Pasternak 1972). Admittedly, there are other variables at work. But it may also be viewed from the point of parental legal authority. It was certainly stronger in Taiwan before 1945. Ethnographical materials from mainland China before 1949 bear similar information (K. Y. Chen 1970; Fei 1939; Fei and Chang 1945; Naoe 1967; Niida 1952; Shiga 1967; and M. C. Yang 1945). Parental authority does prolong division of the family and keep the composite family together longer.

In conclusion, I believe that although the rich-large, poor-small model is fine, parental authority does provide an additional dimension in the study of Chinese family form and structure. Family resources may help to make the sons stay, yet the power of the parents which is given by the state can restrict the sons' leaving. If both variables are working toward the same direction, the large family would be getting larger and lasting longer, and when parental authority is weakened, we see the compromised arrangement between generations in the family. Therefore, my argument is that the form of Chinese family, whether it is due to adoption of different ecological models or is regarded as a result of an ideal cultural pattern, continues to be affected by parental authority.

REFERENCES

AMYOT, J.
  1960   *The Chinese community of Manila: a study of adaptation of Chinese familism to the Philippine environment.* Chicago: University of Chicago, Philippine Studies Program, Department of Anthropology, Research Series 2. Mimeographed.

BUCK, J. L.
  1930   "The farm family and population," Chapter 9 in *Chinese farm economy: a study of 2,866 farms in seventeen localities and seven provinces in China*. Chicago: Institute of Pacific Relations.
CHEN, KU-YÜAN
  1970   *Chung-kuo fa-chih-shih* [A history of the Chinese legal system]. Taipei: San Min.
CHEN, T. S., SHYROCK, J.
  1932   Chinese relationship terms. *American Anthropologist* 34.
CH'Ü, T'UNG-TSU
  1961   *Law and society in traditional China*. The Hague, Paris: Mouton.
COHEN, M. L.
  1970   "Development process in the Chinese domestic group," in *Family and kinship in Chinese society*. Edited by M. Freedman. Stanford: Stanford University Press.
DORE, R. P.
  1958   *City life in Japan*. Berkeley and Los Angeles: University of California Press.
FEI, HSIAO-TUNG
  1939   *Peasant life in China. A field study of country life in the Yangtze Valley*. London: G. Routledge and Sons.
FEI, H. T., CHANG, C. L.
  1945   *Earthbound China*. Chicago: University of Chicago Press.
FENG, H. Y.
  1937   The Chinese kinship system. *Harvard Journal of Asiatic Studies* 11:2.
FREEDMAN, M.
  1958   *Lineage organization in southeastern China*. London: University of London, Athlone Press.
  1961–1962   The family in China, pas and present. *Pacific Affairs* 34:4.
  1966   *Chinese lineage and society: Fukien and Kwantung*. London: University of London, Athlone Press.
FREEDMAN, M., *editor*
  1970   *Family and kinship in Chinese society*. Stanford: Stanford University Press.
FRIED, M. H.
  1953   *Fabric of Chinese society*. New York: Praeger.
  1959   "The family in Communist China," in *The family: its function and destiny*. Edited by R. N. Anshen. New York: Harper.
  1961   "Trends in Chinese domestic organization," in *Symposium on economy and social problems of the Far East*. Edited by E. F. Szezepanil. Hong Kong.
GALLIN, B.
  1966   *Hsin Hsing, Taiwan: a Chinese village in change*. Berkeley and Los Angeles: University of California Press.
GAMBLE, S. D.
  1954   *Ting Hsien, a north Chinese rural community*. New York: Institute of Pacific Relations.

HO, PING-TI
  1962   *The ladder of success in Imperial China.* New York and London:
         Columbia University Press.
HSIAO, KUNG-CHUAN
  1960   *Rural China.* Seattle: University of Washington Press.
HSU, F. L. K.
  1953   The myth of Chinese family size. *American Journal of Sociology*
         48.
  1948   *Under the ancestors' shadow: Chinese culture and personality.*
         New York: Columbia University Press.
  1959   "The family in China," in *The family: its function and destiny.*
         Edited by R. N. Anshen. New York: Harper.
HSÜ, PU-YÜAN
  1932   *Hsing-fa i-li* [Annotation and cases of Chinese criminal law].
         Shanghai: Chung Hua.
HU, CH'ANG-CHING
  1946   *Chung-kuo min-fa ch'in-shu-pien* [Chinese civil code on kinship].
         Shanghai: Commercial.
KROEBER, A. L.
  1909   Classificatory system of relationship. *Journal of the Royal An-
         thropological Institute* 39.
KULP, D. H.
  1925   *Country life in south China.* New York: Columbia University
         Press.
LANG, O.
  1946   *Chinese family and society.* New Haven: Yale University Press.
LEGGE, J.
  1966   *Analects of Confucius.* Taipei: Wen Hua. (Reprinted in the Four
         Books.)
LINTON, R.
  1959   "The natural history of the family," in *The family: its function
         and destiny.* Edited by R. N. Anshen. New York: Harper.
LOWIE, R.
  1928   A note on relationship terminologies. *American Anthropologist*
         30.
LTCK
  1968   *Lao-tzu chen-ku.* Taipei: Kai Ming.
MURDOCK, G. P.
  1949   *Social structure.* New York: Macmillan.
MYRDAL, J.
  1965   *Report from a Chinese village.* New York: William Heinemann.
NAOE, HIROJI
  1967   *Chukoku no minsokugaku* [Chinese folklore]. Tokyo: Iwazaki
         Migitsusha.
NIIDA, NORBORU
  1952   *Chugoku no noson kazoku* [Rural families in China]. Tokyo: To-
         kyo University Publishing Association.

PASTERNAK, B.
1972 "The sociology of irrigation: two Taiwanese villages," in *Economic organization in Chinese society*. Edited by W. E. Willmott. Stanford: Stanford University Press.

RUEY, YEH-FU
1961 Changing structure of the Chinese family. *Bulletin of Department of Archaeology and Anthropology*, 17-18. National Taiwan University, Taipei.

SA, MENG-WU
1969 *Chung-kuo cheng-chih szu-hsiang-shih* [A history of political philosophy]. Taipei: San Min.

SCCSHPC
n.d. *Shih-chi, Chin-shih-huang pen-chi* [The record of Shih-huang-ti, in *The book of history*, volume six]. Taipei: Yee Wen.

SHIGA, SHIUZO
1967 *Chugoko Kazokuho genri* [On the principles of Chinese family law]. Tokyo: Shiobun Sha.

TAI, WANG, *editor*
1956 *Kuan-tzu chaio-cheng* [The collated text of Kuan-tzu]. Taipei: World Book.

TAI, YEN-HUI
1934 Kinsei chugoku oyobi Taiwan no Kasan Kyoyusei [On the common ownership of family property in China and Taiwan in the recent times]. *Hogaku Kyokai Zasshi* [The Magazine of the Association of Jurisprudence] 52:10. Taipei.
1963 Ching-tai tai-wan chih chia-chih chi chia-ts'an [Family system and family property of Taiwan in the Ch'ing dynasty]. *Taiwen Wen-hsien* 14:3. Taipei: Historical Research Commission of Taiwan Province.
1970 *Chung-kuo ch'in-shu-fa* [Chinese kinship law]. Taipei.

T'AO, HSI-SHENG
1934 *Hun-yin yü chia-tsu* [Marriage and the family]. Shanghai: Commercial.

TMHTP
1969 *Tai-wan min-shih hsi-kuan tiao-cha pao-kau* [Report on the investigation of civil custom in Taiwan]. Taipei: Szu-fa-hsing-cheng-pu [Ministry of Judicial Administration, Republic of China].

TWSH
1910–1911 *Taiwan shiko* [The custom law in Taiwan]. Compiled by Rinji Taiwan kyukan shosakai [The temporary committee on investigation of Taiwanese old custom]. Taipei: The Office of the Governor.

WANG, HSIEN-CH'I
1955 *Chuang-tzu chi-chieh* [Collective annotation of philosophy of Chuang-tzu]. Taipei: World Book (in Szu-pu k'an-yao).

WEBER, M.
1951 *The Religion of China*. Translated by H. H. Gerth. Glencoe: Free Press.

WITTFOGEL, K. A.
1938   *New light on Chinese society.* New York: Institute of Pacific Relations.

YANG, CH'ING-K'UN
1959a   *The Chinese family in the Communist Revolution.* Cambridge: MIT Press.
1959b   *A Chinese village in early Communist transition.* Cambridge: MIT Press.
1959c   "Some characteristics of Chinese bureaucratic behavior," in *Confucianism in action.* Edited by D. S. Nivison and A. F. Wright. Stanford: Stanford University Press.

YANG, MARTIN M. C.
1945   *A Chinese village: Taitou, Shantung Province.* New York and London: Columbia University Press.

Adolescence in a Matriarchal Society: Changing Cultural and Social Patterns After Industrialization

K. S. GOKULANATHAN

Adolescence is the period of the greatest biological and psychological transitions in an individual's life, a process highly influenced by the family and the sociocultural milieu. Adolescent problems amidst rapid sociocultural changes in industrialized societies reflect multitudes of conflicting variables, often hard to evaluate. A study of adolescence in a traditional society and an examination of the deviations incidental to sociocultural changes give insight into some of the basic issues of this complex process. Adolescence in a Nayar matriarchal society in Kerala, south India is evaluated here, first in the preindustrialized state and then after industrialization. The significance of retaining some traditional customs to lessen the adverse effects of industrialization may be observed in this society.

GEOHISTORICAL BACKGROUND

Kerala is situated between Western Ghats and the Arabian Sea, forming the southeastern border of India. The glorious past of this community, that dates back to pre-Christian times, can be deduced from its wealth of ancient literature, poetry, and sculpture, as well as from the festive occasions that are the heritage of a stable agrarian group (Padmanabha Menon 1933). Until recent times the people derived the benefits and endured the hardships of a traditionally coordinated agrarian community. Social stratification was according to castes and jobs. The land belonged to the kings, and the Nayars were advisors to the kings as well as warriors who protected the lands. They were described as the people of "eye, hand, and order." They were rewarded with lands and a secure family life, even if the individual was disabled or died in battle. Matriarchy appears to have originated in such a spartan society, where females were given the security of a home and provision was made for child care.

The matriarchal system has a matrifocal-kinship family structure and matrilineal inheritance patterns. The maternal brothers are the custodians of the family wealth and are primarily responsible for the care of the sisters and their children. The oldest brother is called the *karanavan*. The children are known by the mother's family name. The females are entitled to the house and the shared family wealth according to the number of their children. The *karanavan* plans and conducts the marriage ceremonies of his maternal kin. The women remain in the family after marriage, and their children are born there. The children become a part of the maternal extended family. They are brought up by the mother and the maternal relatives, under the supervision of the uncles and the father.

The traditional methods of child care were suited to the local conditions. Various *rites de passage* provided family and social understanding, and participation in the total care of the child as a member of society. These rites minimized the anxiety and conflicts during the process of transition and acted as a psychological stabilizer during the period of development. The mother initiated the preschool education at home; even the bedtime stories were geared to encourage the child to appreciate nature and to introduce him to the social and philosophic aspects of life.

ADOLESCENCE

Traditionally, the various phases of child growth and development are programmed in a systematic manner, providing both the desired emotional security and intellectual freedom. The children learn and accept the traditional customs and understand their implications for the welfare of the individual, the family, and the society. Adolescence is marked by the appearance of secondary sex characteristics in boys and by the onset of menstruation in girls. At this juncture there is instituted total segregation of boys and girls in the family and in social life. A *rite de passage* known as the *Kettu Kaliyanam* [pseudomarriage ceremony] is conducted when girls attain puberty. Adolescent girls join the adult females in childcare, cooking, and housekeeping. They are taught to dress modestly and to cover the front part of the body. They do not mingle with adolescent boys or adult males. The parents never discuss sex with them, and whatever sex knowledge they have is acquired from experienced housemaids. In ancient times adolescent girls were married to adults. We can only conjecture whether any serious sex problems existed at that time — without Kinsey, Masters, and Johnson and their electrodes. If problems did exist, they appear never to have retarded the massive population explosion in the last few centuries. This conclusion is supported by a comment related to sex in the local literature: "You do not teach the calf to find the udder."

While the girls are busy in the kitchen, the boys are initiated into the regimented life of study of the scriptures, administration, and the skills and tactics of warfare. There is little discussion about sex with family members. Boys obtain some knowledge from male servants or gardeners, or from obliging housemaids. The boys continue to wear the same dress as before adolescence, but now also carry a sword and shield. An adolescent boy can marry, but the marriage is consummated only years later, since the girl stays with her mother until the boy becomes an adult.

In recent years, the establishment of various industries and the influx of people of different socioeconomic levels to this area have created problems. Independence, the unification of the Indian states, and the abolition of princely states have gradually limited the Nayars' role in local administration. They have had to modify their system to accommodate the changing political and social structure of society. This has entailed the professional education of women, the movement of educated males and females to urban locales or foreign lands, and a diminution of interest in agrarian activities. In recent times one can observe complex and decisive modifications and social adjustments during adolescence, as well as modern arranged marriages.

One important trend is to assure higher education for both boys and girls. Except for a few coeducational schools, boys and girls still attend separate secondary schools. At the university level, however, there is coeducation. Here young people have more freedom to communicate with each other at arm's length. Although the total segregation of adolescents by sex has gradually disappeared in family and social life, dating is still not an accepted custom in the university community. Rather drastic changes in dress and hairstyle are common on the university campus, at times to the disgust of older people. (A vestige of the former modesty in dress is apparent in the thin band of ultratransparent synthetic fabric worn across the front part of the body by fashionable girls!) Pants fit more tightly or flare out, as the ways of the world change. Sex knowledge is readily available from experienced classmates and from the ever-increasing pornography stores.

This surge of modernism has not deterred the majority of adolescents from following traditional family and social values. They still wear the traditional dress at home and at social functions. The girls learn and share the household responsibilities, and the boys learn family administration under the direction of their elders. By far most marriages are on an arranged basis (Gokulanathan 1973). Consciousness of the joint family or *taravad* appears to persist among individuals with the traditional upbringing, despite the establishment of nuclear family units.

Adolescence in the matriarchal society embodies a symbolic retention of the contents and concepts of traditionalism amidst modernization. Young people continue to recognize the status and experience of older family members and to value their counsel in making decisions. This respect for elders is inculcated from infancy and appears to prevail among individuals at the family, school, and social levels. Emotional security under the guidance of elders, together with intellectual freedom, sets the stage for the final integration described by Erikson (1950). Emotional security, intellectual freedom, and total sex segregation during adolescence play a significant role in the orderly achievement of healthy adolescence in this society.

Adolescence in the matriarchal society represents a syncretism between cultural and traditional legacies and the demands of a technocratic life. The process of self-identification and integration into the life of the society is achieved without ego suppression and conflicts. The segregation of adolescents by sex and the nonexistence of opportunities for heterosexual experiences are accepted as social customs. The psychodynamics of this process may be a reawakening of the superego derived from the parents in earlier years and intelligent assimilation of their value systems. The persistence of these values provides a concrete basis for the initiation of a new family life. In like fashion, the traditional ceremonies connected with marriage also leave an impression on the couple psychologically favorable to the realization of some of the basic values and attitudes of the preindustrialized society. Their beneficial effects are reflected in the integrity of the family and in the child-rearing practices of Nayar families in different parts of world. Some of the traditional values and attitudes help to lessen the adverse effects of industrialization, especially on family life and child care. They may also help to retard the untoward effects of the psychological and social upheavals that take place during adolescence.

The ever-increasing problems of adolescence in industrialized societies attest to the need for a reexamination of the common cultural and traditional values of the respective preindustrialized societies. Incorporation of these values may enable the individual to understand the fundamental values of life amid technological advancements. This lingering look back to the past may give us strength and insight so essential to preserve our cultural and biological heritage for posterity.

REFERENCES

ERIKSON, E. H.
  1950 *Childhood and society*. New York: W. W. Norton.
GOKULANATHAN, K. S.
  1973 "Neomatriarchy among Nairs (Nayars) in Kerala, India: a phenomenon of social selectivity of traditionalism in child rearing." Paper presented at the IXth International Congress of Anthropological and Ethnological Sciences, Chicago.
GOKULANATHAN, K. S., K. P. VERGHESE
  1970 *Child care in a developing community* (second edition). New York: Vantage Press.
PADMANABHA MENON, K. P.
  1933 *History of Kerala*. Ernukulam: Cochin Government Press.

Problems of Socialization in Indian Families in a Changing Society

GEORGE KURIAN

This paper is a comment on the changes in the process of socialization in Indian families as a result of exposure to influences which affect traditional lifestyles. In Joan Mencher's well-known study of socialization in Malabar, she has given an appropriate description of the traditional pattern of relationships:

The traditional patterning of social relations in Kerala was noted for its extreme rigidity and minuteness of detail. Within the household all interpersonal relations were sharply delineated: roles were carefully circumscribed, and every individual always knew how he was expected to act in relation to everyone else.... All interpersonal relations within the family were carefully regulated by principles of age — an extreme structuring of role relations which found its counterpart throughout Kerala in relations between families and between caste and sub-caste groups.... While there were many rules and regulations to be learned, if one learned and abided by them all, life was simple, clearcut and harmonious (Mencher 1963).

This description of the traditional interpersonal family relations in Kerala is applicable in significant degree to most of the rural areas of India.

However, winds of change have made deep inroads in socialization patterns. As long as a person lived a fairly isolated life in a rural region mostly dependent on a rural-based economy, it was possible or, in fact, desirable to follow the accepted traditional life-style. Modern education and the opportunity to choose new occupations, however, increasingly affect the attitude of the younger generation. By and large,

The author is most grateful to Mrs. Ratna Ghosh for her invaluable contribution to the study of socialization of Indian immigrant children.

parents are adjusting to these changes and are willing to encourage some initiative in their children. As Joan Mencher rightly observed, "of significance here is the beginning of respect for initiative, which was totally lacking in the traditional large group setting."

This paper will discuss two studies. The first one, a survey done in Kerala in 1971, includes some of the comments of parents about changes in the attitudes of their youngsters. The second study deals with issues faced by some Indian families who have emigrated to Canada. Both these studies indicate the changes that are inevitable when families are faced with adjustment to a rapidly changing social environment.

PARENT-CHILD INTERACTIONS IN KERALA

A comprehensive study of 250 families in Kerala, representing all major religions and castes, was done in 1971–1972. Here we deal only with the section on the issues of socialization.

Discipline

Only 19 percent of the respondents expected their children to obey them without question. Of the people fifty-five years and older, a predominant number wanted strict obedience. Seventy-four percent of the respondents expected obedience but wanted to encourage initiative. This is a very significant, progressive view. Only 38 percent were willing to allow children to speak freely before adults, as tradition is fairly strong with regard to respect for age.

When one compares the experiences of the respondents, it is clear that there has definitely been change with regard to correction of children. While 16 percent of the respondents had received spankings when they were young, only 10 percent spanked their own children. While only 44 percent of the respondents had been corrected through persuasion, 61 percent of the respondents use this method with their own children. Generally there is now less strict disciplining of children. The benefits of the progressive attitude can be noted in the children, who show much more initiative than the children of a generation ago, when strict discipline was more common. Seventy-three percent of the respondents claimed that they have noted significant changes in the general behavior of children as compared with their own childhood. Of these respondents, 55 percent said that the youngsters demand more freedom. Only 28 percent found the children irritated by stern authority. Fifty-one percent said that their children appreciate friendly persuasion. Altogether, there is little evidence among the respondents of negative attitudes toward their children.

Class, Caste, Sex, and Schooling

Seventy-six percent of the parents were willing to allow children up to twelve years of age to play with all classes and castes, which is really a great stride from about thirty years ago when such free contacts were not encouraged. However, only 34 percent were willing to allow children of the opposite sex to play together even at this early age; such commingling was still too progressive for some people.

According to respondents, children between twelve and sixteen years of age were expected to be put under some control. Thirty percent said they should not be allowed to meet or associate with members of the opposite sex. This is a conservative attitude which indicates that there are still people who feel that freedom for teenagers means disaster. However, 66 percent were willing to give these children some freedom under supervision; only 5 percent were willing to give unrestricted freedom. Twenty-five percent wanted their boys and girls to study in separate educational institutions, while 41 percent were willing to allow them to study in the same educational institution. Answers to the remaining questions were less conclusive. It seems that the parents are not entirely certain about the desirability of heterosexual contacts in educational institutions. Only 27 percent were willing to allow children to mix freely at all levels. Sixty-two percent felt that sex education is the responsibility of both parents and schools. One should consider this very progressive in a society where sex is still not discussed in public. In the last year the investigator has noted articles appearing in newspapers and popular magazines concerning sex problems, and this is a great step forward. This makes it less difficult for parents to answer their children's questions, in view of the declining level of orthodoxy.

As for the purpose of education, most respondents held the view that knowledge in itself is satisfying; next most important were the views that education leads to the best jobs and that the country needs good leaders. Fifty-three percent of the respondents (which is the majority) expressed the opinion that it is best to allow children to make up their own minds with regard to their future career plans. The remaining questions concerning education elicited much less response. By and large, the answers show the awareness of parents that in these changing times youth should be allowed sufficient freedom to develop on their own.

The following opinions expressed by respondents about youth are interesting:

"Too much social contact leads to trouble."

"Between the ages of nine and eleven girls should be instructed about the problems of dealing with the opposite sex. My wife has given such instruction to a number of girls with good effects."

"With the collapse of the joint family system (in which I started), children are better cared for individually and they know their responsibilities better."

"The present education gives only some superficial ideas and not all are related to the realities of life."

"Before the completion of study in educational institutions, children should not be allowed to entangle themselves in politics. Similarly, political parties should not use students to achieve their selfish ends."

"I am too sensitive to instruct my children on sex matters. But I would prefer my children not to be instructed on sex matters by the present slogan-shouting teachers."

"In a poor country like India people should not imitate affluent Western society, and youth should avoid becoming hippies."

SOCIALIZATION IN CANADA

A number of Indian children have been born in Canada and are being educated there, and there are also a number of Indian families who have migrated to Canada with their children. Almost all the postwar immigrants are professional people, with such a high level of education that Indians are among the best-qualified immigrants in Canada. With this kind of background, it is interesting to observe the socialization process of Indian children.

This section will discuss some of the significant findings of a study done in Calgary, Alberta in 1969–1970. It is interesting to note the general change in attitude of the parents concerning the socialization of their children. The study is the result of replies to a questionnaire submitted to ninety respondents and of interviews with thirty families. As far as possible, both parents and children were included in this study. The sample was fairly heterogeneous in terms of language, religion, region of origin, and length of stay in Canada.

In the study there were thirty-nine Hindu, twenty-three Christian, fifteen Muslim, and thirteen Sikh families. The languages represented were Marathi, Gujerati, Hindi, Bengali, Malayalam, Punjabi, and English. The majority of the subjects were Punjabi, Bengali, and Malayalam speakers. There were nine vegetarians among the respondents. With regard to the occupational distribution of the adults, all of them were professionals such as teachers, professors, doctors, lawyers, engineers, students, and accountants. With regard to dress of the women, seven wore only Indian dress such as the sari. The remainder wore both Indian and Western dress. The Western dress of the women was almost always slacks and coats. About half of the subjects planned to stay in Canada permanently. In all, twenty children from six to fifteen years old were interviewed.

The items that represent freedom for the children are in opposition to most conservative Indian traditions. The results were relatively similar as between the different language and religious groups, and as between the responses of the father, mother, boy, or girl. Both the interview data and the questionnaire data showed that the trend is toward greater freedom for children at present than in the traditional Indian pattern, but less freedom than may be perceived in the pattern among non-Indian Canadian children. The item "to speak freely but with respect in front of adults" is a compromise between freedom of speech according to the Canadian pattern and respect for adults in the traditional Indian family. One of the mothers commented: "I have noticed that youngsters of Canada do not respect adults as much as youngsters of India" (see Table 1).

Punishment and reward items showed no significant changes among the trends in Canada as against the trends in India. On the whole, modern Indian families now tend to correct by persuasion more often, and to reward by affection and praise rather than by material things (see Table 2).

Trends show considerable opposition to parents in about the same proportion between girls and boys. While this may perhaps be evident in modern India also, it is in contradiction to the traditional Indian pattern. There is a little more opposition to the mother than to the father, perhaps because she is easier to oppose, but children's responses to the question "Who makes the decisions in the family?" lead to the conclusion that the mother is emerging as the chief authority figure in the home, in opposition to the traditional pattern and in conformity with the Canadian companionship family type. The fathers' responses,

Table 1. Childhood freedom

	Things permitted up to the age of 12				Things permitted above the age of 12			
	Mother	Father	Boy	Girl	Mother	Father	Boy	Girl
(a) To go out with friends to visit friends living close by	30	31	11	8	32	31	11	8
To visit friends in another part of the city	5	11	2	1	20	29	5	3
To see a movie	20	21	5	4	30	28	9	5
To go shopping	14	22	5	4	30	30	9	6
(b) To play or associate with children of the opposite sex: Yes	31	30	9	5	30	28	10	5
No		1	2	4	1	4	1	3
(c) To spend as they choose: allowance money	27	28	9	7	27	30	9	7
gift money	27	19	9	6	27	27	9	6
money earned	27	27	9	7	27	29	11	8
(d) To choose their own clothes without parents' suggestions	2	7		1	11	13	1	1
To choose their own clothes subject to parents' approval	31	32	11	10	30	29	12	8
To have no say in the choice of their own clothing			1	1				
(e) To speak to a limited extent and with respect in front of adults	2	4			1	4	2	
To speak freely but with respect in front of adults	30	28			31	28	10	9
To have complete freedom of speech without thought of respect for adults		1				1		

however, show resistance to this trend (see Table 3). Among the possible causes of indiscipline in children "Westernization" and "modernization" rank high (see Table 4).

In the traditional Indian family, socialization of the child is a parent-to-child training program. Modernization demands a two-way interaction between parent and child, and as a result, the modern Canadian family experiences a mixture of pleasure, satisfaction, and problems.

Table 2. A. Form of punishment

	Prevailing pattern				Possible pattern if living in India			
	Mother	Father	Boy	Girl	Mother	Father	Boy	Girl
Spank								
Never	6	9	2	5	6	9		
Sometimes	23	21	9	3	23	21		
Often	1				1			
Always								
Scold								
Never		3				3		
Sometimes	23	21	9	6	23	21		
Often	6	2	2	2		6		
Always								
Correct by persuasion								
Never								
Sometimes	10	8	4	3	8	10		
Often	17	18	5	7	17	17		
Always	6	9	3	9	10	6		
Withhold allowance								
Never	9	5	5	3				
Sometimes	10	11	1	1				
Often			1					
Always								

B. Reward for good behavior

	Prevailing pattern					Possible pattern if living in India				
	Rank	Mother	Father	Boy	Girl	Rank	Mother	Father	Boy	Girl
Affection	1	29	27			1	29	27		
Praise	2	28	25			2	28	25		
Toys/candy	3	4	2			4	3	2		
Money	5	2	1			5	2	1		
Other (gift, etc.)	4	3	2			3	4	2		

The Indian family living in Canada is confronted — not unexpectedly — with many problems of modernization: in the development of the individual personality, in school, and in social relationships that take a course not to the parents' liking. Not all of the socialization problems are postponed until adolescence, as is generally assumed. Moreover, there are aspects of Westernization that are considered desirable

Table 3.   Attitude toward decisions by parents

	Canada		India	
	Boy	Girl	Boy	Girl
A. Opposition to father's decision				
Never	2	1	3	
Sometimes	21	20	7	6
Often			2	1
Always				
B. Opposition to mother's decision				
Never			1	
Sometimes	19	17	7	7
Often	8	6	4	

C.   Person making the important
decisions in the family

		According to			
	Rank	Mother	Father	Boy	Girl
Mother	1	32	29	8	7
Father	2	29	30	6	6
Children	3	5	4	4	4
Other	4				

Table 4.   Causes of indiscipline

		According to	
	Rank	Mother	Father
Westernization	1	10	10
Modernization	2	8	6
Violence on television	3	5	2
Parents' own failure in discipline methods	4	2	2
Other*	5	3	

* Among the other causes suggested by respondents are peer-group influence and too much affection.

and hence sought after (for example, material comforts), while others are considered "corrupting." The comment of one respondent reveals this clearly: "The idea is to pick up the good habits of Canadians but at the same time not give up decent Indian customs and replace them by undesirable ones."

Data on the role of parents in deciding their sons' and daughters' careers show an adjustment from the traditional Indian pattern of choosing the career (the daughter's being that of a housewife) to the Canadian pattern of leaving the choice entirely to the son or daughter but at the same time influencing the choice, consciously and deliberate-

Table 5. Career decisions

Parent	Son's career		Daughter's career	
	Mother	Father	Mother	Father
Chooses child's career				
Influences child's choice of career	21	23	21	23
Leaves the choice entirely to the child	5	4	5	3
	Rank		Total	
Child's basis for choice of career:				
Parents will be pleased	3		2	
Friends are choosing that career	4			
The money in that career is good	2		3	
Child would enjoy that career	1		12	

ly. Children's responses also indicate trends away from the traditional pattern of pleasing the parents in the choice of a career. Interviews indicated that daughters were eager to take up a career other than that of a housewife, contrary to the traditional Indian pattern (see Table 5).

Whereas all Christian respondents named "same religion" as an important factor in choosing a spouse, they also consistently preferred a marriage ceremony in their traditional religious style. While one might be tempted to explain this by pointing out the similarity of their traditional religious style to the Canadian religious style, it was found, contrary to expectation, that the majority of the other religious groups, including their boys and girls, showed a preference for a marriage ceremony in their own traditional religious styles.

The data on arrangement of marriages shows a tendency to shift from the traditional pattern of marriages arranged by parents without consulting the couple to the Canadian pattern of marriages arranged by the couple on their own. The prevailing pattern at the time of the study was one of compromise (see Table 6).

Among the socialization practices of Western culture, perhaps the most controversial for Indian parents is dating and the association of adolescent boys and girls. While the response that adolescents should be allowed to meet with the opposite sex under supervision is an attempt to adjust to this great problem, some respondents are clearly conservative in this regard, although an almost equal number (a greater number among the adolescents themselves) show the influence of Canadian practices. Data on dating show that most Indian parents, no matter what their religion or language, are not anxious to let their boys and girls date. Both parents are more willing to let their sons date than they are their daughters. Fewer mothers than fathers are willing to let their teenage girls date, while mothers are more willing than fathers to let their grown-up daughters date.

Table 6.   Marriage and dating

	Rank	Mother	Father	Boy	Girl
A. Spouse should					
have the same religion	2	16	13	4	2
speak the same language	4	8	7	3	1
be any suitable Indian	1	27	26	3	1
be a North American/European	5	2	1	1	1
have other qualities*	3	7	15		1
B. Marriage ceremony should be					
in traditional religious style	1	28	20	6	4
in a civil court, by registration	2	9	9	1	
C. Marriage should be arranged by					
parents without consulting the couple				1	
parents with the consent of the couple		27	26	3	3
the couple on their own		10	4	7	4
D. Adolescents should					
not be allowed to associate with members of the opposite sex		4	2	1	1
be allowed to meet members of the opposite sex under supervision		28	25	4	2
be allowed to associate freely and without supervision		3	4	6	4
E. Dating all right for					
teenage girls Yes		5	8		4
No		27	25		2
teenage boys Yes		7	9	7	
No		25	20	1	
grown-up girls Yes		10	8		4
No		15	25		2

*   Respondents named education, character, culture, and career as factors.

The treatment of old parents is another aspect of Westernization that is looked upon with disapproval. Data show that with the exception of one girl (in the six-ten age group), none of the parents or children agree with the Canadian idea of spending old age in a home for senior citizens (see Table 7).

While some of the children would like their parents to live with them, interviews revealed their lack of knowledge of the problems that might arise. Parents, on the other hand, are fully aware of the problems, and the majority want to live near their children but not with them (as in the traditional pattern).

Data indicate that of the social customs of the dominant Canadian culture listed above, which are new to the Indian families, most have been adopted by their children. Interviews reveal that parents encourage this and that children enjoy it because of greater acceptance by their peer group (see Table 8).

Table 7. Old age

	Mother	Father	Boy	Girl
Parents in their old age should				
live in a home for senior citizens				1
live with their children	5	2	7	6
live on their own but near their children	29	27	3	2
return to India and live close to relatives	3	3		
live in some other place (with a warmer climate)		2		

Table 8. Adoption of Canadian ways

	Mother	Father	Boy	Girl
A. New social customs adopted:				
Halloween	17	16	8	7
Thanksgiving	11	11	3	3
Sunday school	9	9	2	1
Valentine's Day	12	17	7	7
Other (Christmas, Easter)	14	15	8	7

	Mother	Father	Girl
B. As adults, girls should always			
wear the sari/salwar			2
wear these on special occasions	9	4	5
wear these when convenient	15	20	1
wear Western dress all the time		2	

Opinion on dress is governed by both practical and aesthetic considerations. The sari is still considered a very feminine and beautiful dress and is worn on all festive occasions. However, it is not considered practical for some kinds of work or for extreme weather conditions. A compromise has been reached by wearing both types of dress, as and when necessary. The younger girls show a preference for Western dress except on special occasions.

The fact that Indian parents are almost all anxious to make their children knowledgeable about their own culture and encourage frequent visits of their children to India indicates the desire to retain their culture. The twice-a-month movie shows arranged by the Indian Students' Association and the turn-out of children and parents to see them testify to the fact that the children are encouraged to see Indian movies. The children enjoy these and other cultural and religious shows. Their own responses reveal an interest in India. While most of the parents are not insistent on their own religious values, all the Christian parents are strict about seeing that their children learn and practice their own religion (see Table 9).

Table 9.   Perpetuation of own culture/religion

Culture		Mother	Father
A. Parents are willing to make children knowledgeable about their own culture			
Yes		31	31
No		1	

	Rank	Mother	Father
B. To make children knowledgeable about their own culture parents encourage			
reading and attendance at movies on India	1	30	29
send them to India for frequent visits	2	26	20
send them to India for education	4	4	4
use other means*	3	6	7

	Girls	Boys
C. Children are willing to go to school in India		
Yes	7	8
No	1	2
D. Children are eager to		
learn about India	6	7
read and see movies on India	6	8
stay in Canada all the time	2	5
see Western movies	6	7

Religion	Mother	Father
E. Parents		
are strict about having children learn and practice their own religion	13	12
are not insistent on their own religious values	20	19
want children to accept prevailing Western values		1

	Girls	Boys
B. Children		
are interested in knowing and learning about their own religion	6	5
are not interested in their own religion		
want to accept the prevalent Canadian religious values		

*   These may be association with Indian families, or parental training.

While the children choose to be influenced more by what the parents say, both interviews and observations indicate their strong desire to be accepted by their peer group. Data show that most children have more Canadian than Indian friends. Peer groups exert strong pressures for "uniformity" within the group, and actual differences in achievement and status tend to be minimized. The language used, for example, although directly related to length of stay in Canada, tends to be more often English, rather than the mother tongue together with English. While some children understand the mother tongue, all of them tend to speak English. Most, however, forget the mother tongue, and their sporadic visits to India only confuse them.

Table 10.   Adjusting to Canadian society

		Girls	Boys
A. Children choose to do what the peer group does			
what the parents say		7	8
what the teacher says		2	1

	Mother	Father	Boy	Girl
B. Parents and children reconcile social and religious conflict by upholding Canadian (non-Indian) ideas				
and rejecting Indian ones that conflict		1		1
by adjusting to a complex mixture of Canadian and Indian ideas	32	30	8	7
by rejecting Canadian ideas and reinforcing Indian ones	1	2		1

Table 10 supports the hypothesis presented in this paper that in socializing their children, the Indian families living in Canada tend to adjust to a cultural conflict by a complex mixture of Canadian and Indian ideas.

SUMMARY

The Indian immigrant family is changing its socialization patterns rapidly, and the changes are away from the institutional and traditional family pattern toward a conjugal type. The changes are not parallel to those in the modern progressive family in India because in Canada the families are adjusting to Canadian influences, although they are not becoming completely Canadian. Changes in certain ideals and practices interact with and react upon others to produce new structures. The pattern of the Indian families in Canada today represents a continuing process of creative adjustment, and the directions of change are partly toward the Canadian pattern, partly in opposition to it, and partly in compliance with traditional sentiments.

It was expected and found that many of the respondents and interviewees had accepted some new patterns of behavior with ease (e.g. social customs such as Halloween), others with difficulty (e.g. dress), while still others had been resisted altogether (e.g. dating). This shows that individuals, like institutions, do not change rationally or consistently; rather they may accept changes in areas to which they are open, stubbornly reject other changes, and adjust to still others in varying degree.

The subtle factors that bind people together in groups are extremely hard to break down into measurable units. People often express group attitudes rather than their own, so that sometimes it is only through their actions (rather than their words) that one may judge their true feelings. Expressions of intense inner conflict and guilt were observed in the case of interviewees who did not live up to the traditional expectations of obligation (e.g. when old parents had been left behind in India, or when beef had been eaten by Indians coming from an orthodox Hindu background or pork by Muslims), showing the dilemma of people when the pressure of circumstances causes them to alter their deeply ingrained patterns of behavior.

Perhaps the greatest change is taking place in the socialization patterns affecting relations between men and women. In the emancipation of children, in the crucial aspect of the hierarchy of power and control, it is found that the Indian family does not accept complete emancipation (neither in choice of career nor in the selection of a spouse). The emerging independence of the young Indians in Canadian society will be supported by their peers and reinforced by the media of mass communication, and problems will result for the Indian family. The new roles the young people learn to play in the course of their Canadian education may conflict with those of their parents. In industrialized societies the knowledge, experience, and skills of older people no longer relate to the present, for it becomes difficult for them to keep pace with a dynamically changing society. The authority, responsibility, and prestige of older people thus decline in importance. These changes bring older people many frustrations and anxieties; they experience a loss of self-esteem, and may even feel intense social isolation.

These, then, are some of the many probleems that seem to be arising in the socialization patterns of the Indian children living in Canada. This study is at best partial and tentative, and its value, if any, is perhaps rather in questions raised than in questions answered. The Indian families in Canada (and there is evidence to support this thesis) are adapting to a new way of life that will enable them to socialize their children to become successful citizens in a dynamic society while retaining some of their Indian identity, thereby contributing an element of brightness to the mosaic that is Canada.

REFERENCES

MENCHER, JOAN
1963   Growing up in South Malabar. *Human Organization* (Winter).

Psychological Correlates of Family Socialization in the United States and Korea

BELA C. MADAY and LORAND B. SZALAY

R. Pinot once said that "Every day society is submitted to a terrible invasion: within it a multitude of small barbarians are born. They would quickly overthrow the whole social order and all institutions of the society, if they were not disciplined and educated." In other words, it is socialization, and mainly that received in the family setting, that saves existing societies from destruction each time a new generation grows up.

In the process of socialization, the family appears to be still the most important agent, provider of a mold for the development of the social self. The family has an overwhelming influence in simple societies, and retains considerable influence in complex cultures as well. Bruner (1961), quoting Hauser (1957), said that "we find in many Asian cities that society does not become secularized, the person does not become isolated, kinship organizations do not break down, nor do social relationships in the urban environment become impersonal, superficial, and utilitarian."

The perpetuation of family organization seems to argue for per-petuation of the individual's concept of self and his relationship to the social environment as determined by family socialization. Of course, a degree of adjustment can and does take place during the adult lifespan, but this adjustment is highly preconditioned by the socialization ex-perience of early years. A signal finding of Bloom (1964: 214-215) was that "there is a negatively accelerated curve of [cognitive] development which reaches its midpoint before age five."

Characteristics of cognitive development and intelligence seem to be universal in appearance. What differs is the content and intensity of the family socialization process from one culture to another. The process is universally supposed to enable members of a society to function properly during their adult life within the space and time perimeters of their culture and age. Once removed outside these perimeters and into a culture in which the selfconcept is differently conceived, where the rules of the game are different, difficulties of adjustment or even of survival may arise.

Francis Hsu (1970) said that social structure is one form of expressing a value system pertinent to the self. He argues vigorously that the self-concept is not only acquired through the social structure into which a person is socialized, but also is maintained throughout life by this structure — in other words, that variation in social structure results in varying patterns of selfconcepts. Thus, in the Chinese, Japanese, and Korean conceptualization the self is always a part of a larger kinship network, while in the American or European concept of self the person stands alone; his place in the family is weakened if not altogether denied after reaching maturation.

In this paper we try to match Hsu's hypothesis against empirical data derived from the application of the Associative Group Analysis (AGA) method to groups of Koreans and Americans (Szalay and Brent 1967). Each culture group (the sample, $N = 150$) consisted of male students (S), workers (W), and farmers (F).

The Associative Group Analysis method can be used to draw inferences on cultural meanings, attitude, cognitive organization, and subjective culture from the distributions of verbal associations (Szalay and Brent 1967: Szalay, Windle, and Lysne 1970; Szalay and D'Andrade 1972; Szalay and Maday 1973). Members of representative samples ($N = 50$–100) produce verbal associations in continued association tasks; they give to selected themes as many responses as they can think of in one minute. The responses are then weighted, based on the rank order of their emission. The weights, beginning with the first response, are $6, 5, 4, 3, 3, 3, 3, 2, 2, 1, 1, 1, \ldots$ In this study, the responses were categorized by United States and Korean coders. The total response scores obtained for the categories, or meaning components, are presented in visual form in the "semantograph." To keep the presentation as short as possible, only two of the components are discussed for each of the themes; the semantographs are followed by tables giving the responses in tabular form.

In analyzing the results, we make use only of associations given to four stimulus words: SELF, FAMILY, RELATIVES, and ANCESTORS, of the sixty words administered to the groups. We first present data relevant to the Korean and American view of self in the context of the family, and then examine a few selected family-related concepts that bear responsibility historically for having shaped family relations and structure.

Semantograph 1.   United States and Korean meanings

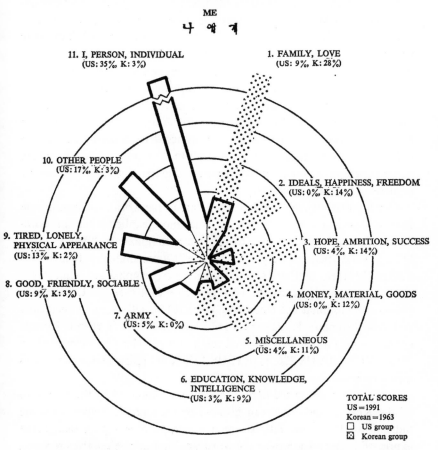

ME

나 에 게

11. I, PERSON, INDIVIDUAL
(US: 35%, K: 3%)

1. FAMILY, LOVE
(US: 9%, K: 28%)

10. OTHER PEOPLE
(US: 17%, K: 3%)

2. IDEALS, HAPPINESS, FREEDOM
(US: 0%, K: 14%)

9. TIRED, LONELY,
PHYSICAL APPEARANCE
(US: 13%, K: 2%)

3. HOPE, AMBITION, SUCCESS
(US: 4%, K: 14%)

8. GOOD, FRIENDLY, SOCIABLE
(US: 9%, K: 3%)

4. MONEY, MATERIAL, GOODS
(US: 0%, K: 12%)

7. ARMY
(US: 5%, K: 0%)

5. MISCELLANEOUS
(US: 4%, K: 11%)

6. EDUCATION, KNOWLEDGE,
INTELLIGENCE
(US: 3%, K: 9%)

TOTAL SCORES
US = 1991
Korean = 1963
☐ US group
☒ Korean group

Even a cursory view of Semantograph 1, which summarizes associations expressed in response to the stimulus word ME, clearly shows cultural differences of diametrically-opposed character. Korean (K) responses cluster around family, love, ideals, success, and material goods, while American (US) responses show a convergence around the individual and his physical and emotional conditions, and around people other than relatives.

The responses indicate that the Korean respondents view themselves as inseparable from their family group, of which they express a clear concept. It is the family that matters when the self is examined. In association with ME, 28 percent of the Korean responses referred to family and love, compared to only 9 percent of the American responses. Only 3 percent of the Korean responses referred to the self as an individual, in contrast to 35 percent of the American responses.

The American responses stress the first person singular, an individual detached from kin affiliation, standing alone in the crowd of unrelated persons. He feels surrounded by "other people" to whom he has to relate without the assistance of his family. This effort is accompanied by loneliness, concern with physical appearance, and with positive attitudes toward others with whom he may have to team up to assure success.

Both the Korean and the American have to prove themselves in life, but to two different audiences. The American has to "sell" his worth to strangers, hence the emphasis on appearance, friendliness, and sociable behavior; the Korean has to prove himself to his family, to his kin group, hence the emphasis on ambition, ideals, and material goods in the course of striving to achieve success.

The contrast between the American "me in the world," as against the Korean "me in the family" view becomes more explicit when one compares the details of responses to two main components, "family, love" (Table 1) and "person, individual" (Table 2). Immediate family members (father, brother, mother, sister, parent) were emphasized almost exclusively by the Koreans (K $18 + 29 + 59 + 51 + 6 = 163$, US 6). Emphasis on emotional ties (especially love: K 154, US 44; and sweetheart, girl, and woman: K $92 + 52 = 144$, US $11 + 6 = 17$) reflect Korean concern with intimacy in personal relationships. The American concern with self (myself: US 286, K 0; I: US 167, K 46) reflects strong individualistic orientation.

What differences in the family concept are expressed by the responses of the Korean and American groups? Semantograph 2 gives us some indications. Here associations are much more overlapping than those expressed in the responses to the word ME. First-degree relatives received almost the same attention from both groups (K 1577, US 1544), but within this category significant differences exist. The American cluster is somewhat narrower, emphasizing mother and father, while the Korean cluster is broader and includes child, brother, sister. Mother and wife have relatively greater salience for the American respondents, while father has more for the Koreans. These shades of difference seem to underline the differences between the Korean and American social structures, differences in the role of the male and in the father-son relationship, as described by Hsu for the traditional Chinese family (1963).

The broader Korean concept of the family includes members of the

Table 1. Theme: ME; meaning component: FAMILY, LOVE

Responses	US groups			Korean groups			Totals	
	S	W	F	S	W	F	US	K
father	–	–	–	6	–	12	–	18
brother	–	–	–	6	7	16	–	29
mother	–	–	–	11	29	19	–	59
parent	–	6	–	11	12	28	6	51
brother and sister	–	–	–	–	6	–	–	6
family	5	–	13	–	–	–	18	–
home, house	–	12	12	11	8	7	24	26
marry, married	7	–	9	–	–	–	16	–
wife	–	10	–	–	–	–	10	–
husband	7	–	–	–	–	–	7	–
sweetheart	–	–	–	33	29	30	–	92
girl	–	11	–	–	–	–	11	–
woman	6	–	–	22	17	13	6	52
love, lover, lovely, loving, love affair	14	24	6	71	52	31	44	154
life, live	8	–	8	–	4	–	16	4
health	6	–	–	11	–	9	6	20
friend	–	11	9	14	–	20	20	34
Total	53	74	57	196	164	185	184	545
(percent)	(29)	(40)	(3)	(36)	(30)	(34)	(9)	(28)

Table 2. Theme ME; meaning component: I, PERSON, INDIVIDUAL

Responses	US groups			Korean groups			Totals	
	S	W	F	S	W	F	US	K
I	69	40	58	7	12	27	167	46
self	27	–	–	–	–	–	27	–
myself	95	92	99	–	–	–	286	–
mine	11	–	–	–	–	–	11	–
me	5	6	–	–	–	–	11	–
individual	30	–	14	–	–	–	44	–
person	23	21	16	–	15	–	60	15
man	24	14	27	–	–	–	65	–
other[1]	21	–	–	–	–	–	21	–
Total	305	173	214	7	27	27	692	61
(percent)	(44)	(25)	(31)	(11)	(44)	(44)	(35)	(3)

[1] United States: ego, being, one.

extended family, hence, the "relatives" component of the semantograph is twice as large for the Koreans as for the Americans. It is also interesting to observe the greater Korean concern with the older generation, as

Semantograph 2.   United States and Korean meanings

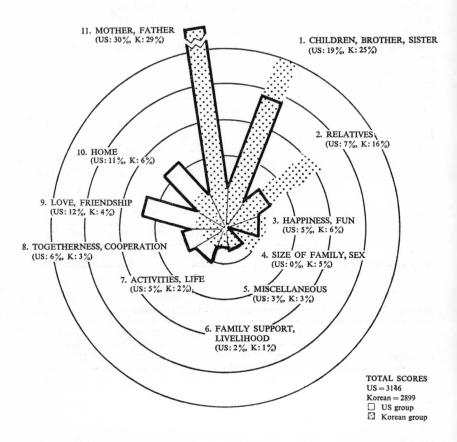

FAMILY

가 족

11. MOTHER, FATHER
(US: 30%, K: 29%)

1. CHILDREN, BROTHER, SISTER
(US: 19%, K: 25%)

2. RELATIVES
(US: 7%, K: 16%)

10. HOME
(US: 11%, K: 6%)

9. LOVE, FRIENDSHIP
(US: 12%, K: 4%)

3. HAPPINESS, FUN
(US: 5%, K: 6%)

8. TOGETHERNESS, COOPERATION
(US: 6%, K: 3%)

4. SIZE OF FAMILY, SEX
(US: 0%, K: 5%)

7. ACTIVITIES, LIFE
(US: 5%, K: 2%)

5. MISCELLANEOUS
(US: 3%, K: 3%)

6. FAMILY SUPPORT,
LIVELIHOOD
(US: 2%, K: 1%)

TOTAL SCORES
US = 3146
Korean = 2899
☐ US group
⊠ Korean group

shown in Table 3 (grandparents: K 61 + 74 + 15 = 150, US 13 + 8 + 6 = 27) in contrast to the American concern with children as shown in Table 4 (US 133 + 7 = 140, K 19 + 7 = 26).

Another aspect of the comparison shows that the Korean concept of family lies strictly in the dimension of people (relatives), while the American concept places heavy emphasis on the place (nest) of the family and on the intimate relationships that the family provides.

Another theme for which associations were elicited was RELATIVES (Semantograph 3). Both the Korean and the American respondents identified siblings of their parents and the children of these siblings as

Table 3.   Theme: FAMILY; meaning component: RELATIVES

Responses	US groups			Korean groups			Totals	
	S	W	F	S	W	F	US	K
grandmother	3	5	5	24	32	5	13	61
grandfather	–	4	4	21	43	10	8	74
grandparents	–	3	3	3	6	6	6	15
uncle	6	11	11	–	6	7	28	13
aunt	–	12	14	–	–	–	26	–
cousin	–	7	6	–	–	–	13	–
nephew	–	2	–	10	10	10	2	30
niece	–	6	–	–	–	–	6	–
relatives, relation (blood)	47	15	21	34	28	42	83	104
brother-in-law	–	6	–	–	–	–	6	–
family member	–	–	–	30	48	90	–	168
family tree	14	8	5	–	–	–	27	–
Total	70	79	69	122	173	170	218	465
(percent)	(32)	(36)	(32)	(26)	(37)	(37)	(7)	(16)

Table 4.   Theme: FAMILY; meaning component: CHILDREN, BROTHER, SISTER

Responses	US groups			Korean groups			Totals	
	S	W	F	S	W	F	US	K
sister	55	61	90	25	49	31	206	105
brother	55	87	84	67	12	81	226	270
sibling	–	–	–	68	98	85	–	251
child, children, kids	54	29	50	7	12	–	133	19
son	–	–	7	–	–	7	7	7
me, mine, myself	–	17	–	31	21	21	17	73
other[1]	–	–	4	5	–	7	4	12
Total	164	194	235	203	302	232	593	737
(percent)	(28)	(33)	(40)	(28)	(41)	(31)	(19)	(25)

[1] United States: baby; Korean: son and daughter, daughter.

the principal group constituting relatives. But here the similarity ends. While both groups emphasize the family in association with relatives, we know from previous data that the two groups conceive the family in quite different terms. This difference is illustrated by the 175 Korean responses emphasizing "one family" (Table 5), as contrasted with none for the Americans. The Korean emphasis on family is stronger, and unity and cohesion of relatives with the family are stressed. The United States references to family are fewer and do not emphasize unity or cohesion.

The focus and scope of the American concept of relatives is also shown by the stress given to mother, father, and child. In contrast, the Korean

Table 5.   Theme: RELATIVES; meaning component: FAMILY, KINSHIP

Responses	US groups			Korean groups			Totals	
	S	W	F	S	W	F	US	K
family	84	62	32	33	43	65	178	141
kin, kinship	18	9	32	–	–	27	59	27
related, relation (blood)	48	12	63	–	–	–	123	–
sister-in-law	37	20	11	–	–	–	68	–
clan	–	–	–	–	11	8	–	19
flesh and blood	–	–	–	–	8	14	–	22
genealogical, -table	–	–	–	6	7	–	–	13
family system	–	–	–	9	–	–	–	9
family name	–	–	–	12	28	17	–	57
mother's family	–	–	–	20	49	23	–	92
one family	–	–	–	24	60	91	–	175
Total	187	103	138	104	206	245	428	555
(percent)	(44)	(24)	(32)	(19)	(37)	(44)	(14)	(25)

Table 6.   Theme: RELATIVES; meaning component: MOTHER, FATHER, CHILDREN

Responses	US groups			Korean groups			Totals	
	S	W	F	S	W	F	US	K
father	41	39	68	10	7	6	148	23
mother	47	60	85	7	3	5	192	15
parent	46	18	7	–	–	–	71	–
brother	38	40	44	–	6	8	122	14
sister	38	37	56	–	9	–	131	9
brother and sister	–	–	–	16	33	46	–	95
wife	44	41	18	–	–	–	103	–
child	18	–	–	–	–	–	18	–
son	5	–	–	–	–	–	5	–
daughter	4	–	–	–	–	–	4	–
home, house	16	25	6	–	–	–	47	–
Total	297	260	284	33	58	65	841	156
(percent)	(35)	(31)	(34)	(21)	(37)	(42)	(28)	(7)

concept of relatives does not include parents and children, nor does it include grandparents. All these are too close to the individual to be thought of as just relatives; they belong to the innermost circle of the individual. Especially clear is the contrast in the case of the wife, who is considered a relative by Americans but who is not mentioned by Koreans at all (US 103, K 0) (Table 6). Though summation of a complex range of responses carries some danger, it is interesting to observe the overall difference in emphasis on first-degree relatives: Americans 841, Koreans 156.

Semantograph 3.   United States and Korean meanings

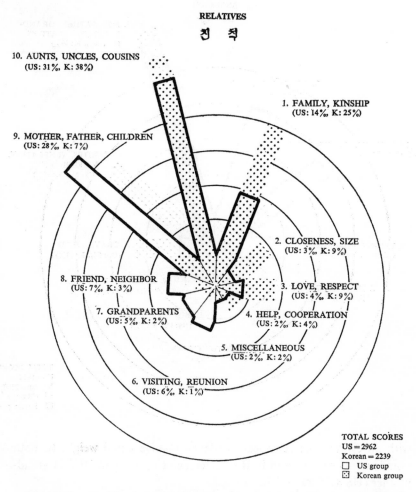

RELATIVES

친   척

10. AUNTS, UNCLES, COUSINS
(US: 31%, K: 38%)

1. FAMILY, KINSHIP
(US: 14%, K: 25%)

9. MOTHER, FATHER, CHILDREN
(US: 28%, K: 7%)

2. CLOSENESS, SIZE
(US: 3%, K: 9%)

8. FRIEND, NEIGHBOR
(US: 7%, K: 3%)

3. LOVE, RESPECT
(US: 4%, K: 9%)

7. GRANDPARENTS
(US: 5%, K: 2%)

4. HELP, COOPERATION
(US: 2%, K: 4%)

5. MISCELLANEOUS
(US: 2%, K: 2%)

6. VISITING, REUNION
(US: 6%, K: 1%)

TOTAL SCORES
US = 2962
Korean = 2239
☐ US group
☒ Korean group

Associations with the stimulus word ANCESTORS (Semantograph 4) seem to follow the same pattern as those for RELATIVES: one strong overlapping category, and a number of divergent associations. When analyzed, the overlapping category also shows significant internal divergence. Both the Korean and the United States respondents named grandfather as the single most important ancestor, but the weight of this association for the Koreans (420) is more than three times that for the Americans (126), emphasizing also the importance of a male-dominated social structure, as expressed by the patriarchal family system (Table 7). The Korean emphasis on male progenitors becomes further apparent from the fact that they did not associate grandmother or grandparents

Semantograph 4.   United States and Korean meanings

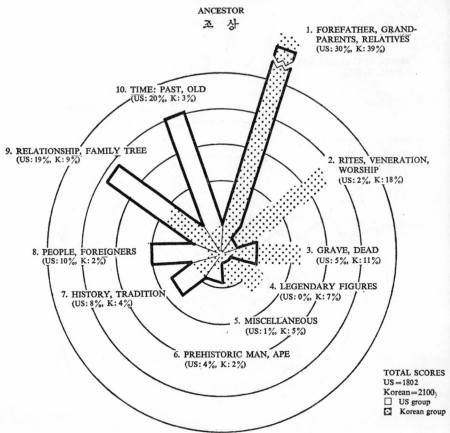

ANCESTOR

조 상

1. FOREFATHER, GRAND-
PARENTS, RELATIVES
(US: 30%, K: 39%)

10. TIME: PAST, OLD
(US: 20%, K: 3%)

9. RELATIONSHIP, FAMILY TREE
(US: 19%, K: 9%)

2. RITES, VENERATION,
WORSHIP
(US: 2%, K: 18%)

8. PEOPLE, FOREIGNERS
(US: 10%, K: 2%)

3. GRAVE, DEAD
(US: 5%, K: 11%)

7. HISTORY, TRADITION
(US: 8%, K: 4%)

4. LEGENDARY FIGURES
(US: 0%, K: 7%)

5. MISCELLANEOUS
(US: 1%, K: 5%)

6. PREHISTORIC MAN, APE
(US: 4%, K: 2%)

TOTAL SCORES
US = 1802
Korean = 2100
☐ US group
☒ Korean group

with ancestors. The American tendency to give equal weight to both grandparents can be seen in their reference to grandparents and grandmother (US $47 + 88 = 135$).

Another difference that appears within this category involves the role of age. The Koreans strongly associate ancestors with elders and seniors, while the American sample makes no reference to age.

When we examine the other elements of this category, we find a strong American association of ancestors with deceased blood relatives, foreign immigrants, historical figures, and history itself. Though blood relations are explicitly mentioned by the United States respondents, ancestors also seem to include all ancestors of the human race, including prehistoric man and apes. These strong references to time and history suggest that the American's relationship to ancestors is vague and weak. For the Koreans, ancestors are more real, more immediate persons, who in-

Table 7.   Theme: ANCESTOR; meaning component: FOREFATHERS, GRANDPARENTS, RELATIVES

Responses	US groups			Korean groups			Totals	
	S	W	F	S	W	F	US	K
grandfather	47	42	37	133	157	130	126	420
great-grandfather	11	4	–	23	11	43	15	77
father	11	11	12	9	22	27	34	58
forefather	37	21	17	28	47	50	75	125
grandmother, great-grandmother	–	31	16	–	–	–	47	–
grandparent, great-grandparent	41	34	13	–	–	–	88	–
elders	–	–	–	6	42	34	–	82
senior	–	–	–	–	11	–	–	11
family, family life	55	21	14	12	6	10	90	28
forebears	16	–	–	–	–	–	16	–
predecessor	45	–	–	–	–	–	45	–
other[1]	3	7	–	–	–	23	10	23
Total	266	171	109	211	296	317	546	824
(percent)	(49)	(31)	(20)	(26)	(36)	(38)	(30)	(39)

[1] United States: uncle, parent; Korean: mother, brother, parent.

Table 8.   Theme: ANCESTOR; meaning component: RITES, VENERATION, WORSHIP

Responses	US groups			Korean groups			Totals	
	S	W	F	S	W	F	US	K
worship	10	–	–	–	–	–	10	–
respect	6	–	–	27	7	–	6	34
veneration	–	–	–	37	12	35	–	84
serve	–	–	–	11	6	7	–	24
great	–	10	7	–	–	–	17	–
rite	–	–	–	105	58	35	–	198
other[1]	6	–	–	35	–	9	6	44
Total	22	10	7	215	83	86	39	384
(percent)	(56)	(26)	(18)	(56)	(22)	(22)	(2)	(18)

[1] United States: pride; Korean: authority, authoritarian, bow, *chusok*, filial duty, gratitude, solemnity.

fluence their decisions, and in this sense are a part of their daily lives. This connection is reflected by rites, veneration, worship — that is, activities that are obligations which constitute a part of the Korean's daily existence.

Koreans not only see ancestors as involving a somewhat different category of people, but their relationship to ancestors is also different from that of the Americans. A strong Korean association with ancestors is rite, as shown in Table 8 (K 198, US 0), which carries clear religious connotations, followed closely by associations with grave (K 106, US 0). According to Confucian beliefs, ancestor worship, including ritual mourning for the dead parent, is part of one's filial duty. T'ae-gil Kim (1969: 14–15) says that "the filial duty of a son does not terminate when his parents die. Both the funeral and memorial services are held to be very important parts of that duty ... the memorial service is supposed to be held not only for one's own parents but also for one's remote ancestors." The validity of these traditional concepts for the contemporary Korean has been an issue of controversy. The sizable responses in the category of rite, veneration, worship, and respect (K 384, US 39) could positively assist in the settlement of this argument.

SUMMARY

There seems to be ample evidence that even if the family is gradually diminishing in size, its role in the socialization process remains dominant, and its responsibility for maintaining cultural differences, decisive. The concomitants to the transition from extended to nuclear, from rural to urban, from simple to complex life patterns are highly influenced by family socialization, and therefore differ from one culture to another.

Family socialization, influenced by family structure, seems to have an impact on the development of the self-concept and is producing culture-specific patterns in shaping the individual's relationship to his social environment. Hsu (1970) suggests that in the Chinese conceptualization, self is part of a larger kinship network, while in contrast, the American concept of self is rooted in individualism.

The results of the study provide empirical evidence supporting Hsu's hypotheses. Associations with the stimulus words ME, FAMILY, RELATIVES, and ANCESTORS show contrasting self-concepts as between the American individualist "me in the world" concept and the Korean familist "me in the family" concept. The associations also show differences in the concept of family structure and intrafamily relationships. The American concept is more horizontally-structured and narrower in scope, while the Korean concept is more hierarchical and wider. The American concept is bilateral and sexually egalitarian; the Korean does not exclude female members but assigns them a less prominent status than men. The Korean seems to be more concerned with elders; the American, more with children.

The circles of relatives and their hierarchical arrangement are well-defined in the Korean mind, and relatives are conceptualized as an extension of the intimate group of family members living under the same roof. The American concept of relatives focuses more on the closer circle and tends to include only the closest family members, such as wife, husband, parents.

The extension of the concept of relatives leads to the concept of ancestors. For the Koreans, ancestors are an extension of the family and are viewed as elderly and male, that is, having the qualities that rank high in the social and family hierarchy. Although they do not exist in the physical world, ancestors represent people very much alive and present; they are worshipped, venerated, and remembered, and, thus, are an important part of the Korean's daily living. For the Americans, ancestors are people belonging to the past, historic or even prehistoric, with little or no direct relationship to the living. This association seems to underline the general American impersonal or more abstract conceptualization of ancestors, as compared to the person-centered Korean conceptualization.

REFERENCES

BLOOM, BENJAMIN S.
   1964   *Stability and change in human characteristics*. New York: J. Wiley and Sons.
BRUNER, EDWARD
   1961   Urbanization and ethnic identity in North Sumatra. *American Anthropologist* 63:50.
HAUSER, PHILIP M., *editor*
   1957   *Urbanization: Asia and the Far East*. Tensions and Technology Series. Calcutta: UNESCO (United Nations Educational, Scientific, and Cultural Organization).
HSU, FRANCIS L. K.
   1963   "Kinship and ways of life," in *Psychological anthropology*. Edited by Francis L. K. Hsu. Cambridge: Schenkman.
   1970   *Americans and Chinese: purpose and fulfillment in great civilizations*. New York: Doubleday.
KIM, T'AE-GIL
   1969   "How to harmonize the traditional moral values and present-day needs in Korea," in *Aspects of social change in Korea*. Edited by C. I. Eugene Kim and Ch'angbok Chee. Kalamazoo, Michigan: The Korea Research and Publications.
NORBECK, EDWARD
   1965   *Changing Japan*. New York: Holt, Rinehart and Winston.
SZALAY, L. B., J. BRENT
   1967   The analysis of cultural meanings through free verbal associations. *Journal of Social Psychology* 72:161–187.

SZALAY, L. B., R. D'ANDRADE
   1972   Similarity scaling and content analysis in the interpretation of word associations. *Southwestern Journal of Anthropology* 50–68.
SZALAY, L. B., B. C. MADAY
   1973   Verbal associations in the analysis of subjective culture. *Current Anthropology* 14:33–50.
SZALAY, L. B., C. WINDLE, D. A. LYSNE
   1970   Attitude measurement by free verbal associations. *Journal of Social Psychology* 82:43–55.

Intragroup Competitive Pressures and the Selection of Social Strategies: Neglected Paradigms in the Study of Adolescent Socialization

COLIN LACEY

This paper is a brief discussion of the findings of two pieces of research into adolescent and early-adult socialization. Both researches were heavily dependent on social anthropological fieldwork methods extending over a number of years, carried out in urban areas in a modern industrial society (the United Kingdom). In both cases I moved into the area of the institution I studied, lived in its environment, and participated as fully as possible in its inner social life. The first institution was an English grammar school (pupils are aged eleven to eighteen and are selected on a meritocratic academic basis), the second a graduate teacher-education course (students' ages ranged from twenty-one to twenty-four and over).

The discussion of findings raises a number of theoretical issues concerning the nature of socialization and the construction of concepts to encapsulate the notions introduced into the discussion. The implications of these ideas for the interpretation of earlier work in the field and the design of future research are also discussed.

In 1963 George Spindler wrote:

... education was not even listed as an area of application for anthropology in the encyclopedic inventory, *Anthropology today* (Kroeber 1953). Education is not in the subject index of the Decennial Index 1949—1958 of the *American Anthropologist* .... Only a handful of joint appointments in education and anthropology exist in American colleges and universities. Very few anthropologists have attempted to study the educational process in our society (Spindler 1963: 53).

The last ten years have done much to remedy this situation in the United States. In Britain, however, the present situation does not as yet allow the writer to talk about even "a handful of joint appointments in education and anthropology." To my knowledge there are none. It is still axiomatic that any young anthropologist who wishes to study education within his own culture becomes a sociologist.

Coincidentally, it was in 1963 that I began my fieldwork in a sector of the greater Manchester conurbation that in other publications I have called Hightown. Despite my earlier years in training as a social anthropologist, I became known almost immediately as a sociologist. Yet quite obviously my study of Hightown Grammar School contains all the major elements of the social anthropological approach to the study of a social system.

The major elements of the anthropological approach, which then distinguished it from contemporary British sociology,[1] were the methodological commitment to participant observation and the theoretical concern with social structures viewed as systems. There was, however, at the time an important challenge to classical anthropological theory. Growing criticism among younger anthropologists of classical and of some contemporary studies challenged the presentation of analyses as functionally "closed" systems — systems that were purported to be in dynamic equilibrium, with change seen in terms of cycles of fission and fusion. To younger anthropologists it seemed that these systems were in fact in the throes of the most rapid, open-ended revolutionary change the world had yet seen.

The classical concern with the recreation of timeless systems led to a number of shortcomings in the contemporary literature:

1. Relationships with external systems, especially rapidly changing (modern) systems were neglected.

2. An emphasis on notions of structure and function led to neglect of emergent social processes.

3. There was a simplistic view of socialization, with initiation ceremonies given a predominant place, and a preoccupation with the "continuity of culture,"[2] at the expense of emergent and changing cultures developing among the younger generation.

In my study of Hightown Grammar, I was concerned to avoid these pitfalls. The school was, therefore, viewed in the context of the community it served, and the study was given a historical dimension by tracing the changing function, within the community, of the education

---

[1]   There have been substantial changes in British sociology over the last ten years. These distinctions no longer exist in the way they did ten years ago.

[2]   There are notable exceptions to this general rule, but mainly outside British anthropology.

offered by the school. The major emphasis of the study was, however, the detailed examination of the social processes within the school. These processes, once identified, were traced at a variety of levels: first at the level of the total cohort or year group within the school; then at the level of a single class; and, finally, within the class, at the level of cliques and individual case studies. The notion of structure was neglected, so that a picture of a moving, developing process, in which further changes were possible and perhaps imminent, could emerge from the analysis.

The material presented in this discussion relates to the identification of the social processes of differentiation and polarization within this student body. I wish to bring out some of the implications for the process of socialization that seem to be implicit in these findings.

In the second part of the paper, some of these concerns are carried over into an examination of professional socialization among student teachers. The study referred to here is a recently completed study of an innovative teacher-education scheme at Sussex University. An emerging characteristic of adolescent socialization, identified in the review of the Hightown material, seems to have become an important or even determinant characteristic of early professional socialization by this stage.

HIGHTOWN GRAMMAR SCHOOL

Hightown Grammar is an exclusive secondary school for boys in a predominantly working-class urban community. At the age of ten all pupils in the Hightown junior schools took an examination which determined which secondary schools they would enter. Because of its academic standing, Hightown Grammar attracted a high proportion of the most able pupils in the town. It represented the educational goal for most parents with academic ambitions for their boys, and competition for entry was often fierce.[3] Within the state system, this school represented the major avenue into the universities and the professions.

An examination of the junior-school records of the boys in the school revealed that the vast majority of the entering students had been "good pupils" in their junior schools. They had been monitors and prefects, and only a few had not been placed regularly in the top half of their class.

---

[3]   The majority of its pupils came from the top 10 percent of the final examination ranking for the whole of Hightown. About 60 percent of its entering students came from middle-class parents, although the community was predominantly working class.

The curriculum at Hightown Grammar School represented an extension of academic studies for these pupils. Their timetables included subjects like physics, chemistry, biology, and foreign languages. Mathematics quickly moved from arithmetic to algebra, geometry, and calculus. There was some project teaching in the first two or three years, principally in English, geography, and history, but the bulk of the teaching became narrative- and textbook-oriented. The academic pressures implicit in the organization of the curriculum, the method of classroom teaching, and the volume of homework found explicit and sometimes ritual expression in the public award of academic prizes[4] and the weekly house-point competition. In other publications, I have described these characteristics of the school as amounting to a "pressured academic environment." The child entering this environment could expect pressures toward academic achievement from the school, his parents, and his peers, and also from his own image of himself and his past record of academic success at his junior school and in the selection examination. I have described these pressures toward academic achievement in some detail because they seem to me to be an important factor in the phenomenon I will describe here. In my experience they would be difficult to match in an American setting.

After observing and teaching in the school for a relatively short time, it became clear that although initially each cohort had been artificially more or less homogeneous as a result of the selection procedures, after they had been in the school a new heterogeneity in their school relations had begun to develop. This development was particularly noticeable among first-year boys, for, although they were generally more conformist and more enthusiastic and responsive to the teacher than the boys in other years, they had nevertheless begun to develop a set of expectations about particular boys who performed or behaved differently from the norm. At various times I noticed that not only did the class obviously anticipate particular attitudes or behaviors from certain of the boys, but their own behavior helped to bring them about:

On one occasion, for example, a master asked three boys to stay behind after the lesson to help him with a task calling for a sense of responsibility and co-operation. He called out "Williams, Maun and Sherring." The class burst into spontaneous laughter, and there were unbelieving cries of "What! Sherring?" The master corrected himself. "No, not Sherring, Shadwell." From the context of the incident, it was clear that Sherring's reputation was already inconsistent with the qualities expected of a monitor.

4   As with many grammar schools, great prominence was given to outside academic honors won by pupils and former pupils. Scholarships to Oxford and Cambridge topped the hierarchy of honors.

On another occasion, Priestley was asked to read, and the whole class groaned and laughed. A fat boy, he had been kept down from the previous year because of ill-health (catarrh and asthma) and poor work. He grinned apprehensively, wiped his face with a huge white handkerchief and started to read very nervously. For a few moments the class was absolutely quiet, then one boy tittered; Priestley made a silly mistake, partly because he was looking up to smile at the boy who was giggling, and the whole class burst into laughter. Priestley blew his nose loudly and smiled nervously at the class. The teacher quieted them and Priestley continued to read. Three lines later a marked mispronunciation started everyone laughing again. This performance continued, with Priestley getting more and more nervous, mopping his brow and blowing his nose. Finally, the master snapped, with obvious annoyance, "All right, Priestley, that's enough!" (Lacey 1970: 53).

In other words, the boys in the class collectively reinforced certain reputations. In the case of Sherring, they were actually policing the system of relationships established and recognized by the teacher.

Within the grammar school it was possible to see two distinguishable processes at work, structuring the relationships within the classroom and the year group — differentiation and polarization:

By DIFFERENTIATION I mean the separation and ranking of students accord-to a multiple set of criteria which makes up the normative, academically-orientated value system of the grammar school. Differentiation is defined here as being largely carried out by teachers in the course of their normal duties (1970: 57).

Differentiation proceeds through the teacher distributing rewards and punishments. I have called one class of rewards "short-term gratifications," because I wish to make clear that I am describing a flow of rewards that are more or less implicit in every situation. They can range from a smile or an approving nod to a five-minute eulogy on how well a boy has done in an examination. Rewards and punishments flow "differentially" to various boys in the class:

POLARISATION, on the other hand, takes place within the student body, partly as a result of differentiation, but influenced by external factors and with an autonomy of its own. It is a process of sub-culture formation in which the school-dominated, normative culture is opposed by an alternative culture which I refer to as the "anti-group" culture. The content of the anti-group culture will, of course, be very much influenced by the school and its social setting. For example, it may range from a folk music CND group in a minor public school to a delinquent sub-culture at a secondary modern school in an old urban area. In Hightown Grammar School it fell between these extremes and was influenced by the large working-class and Jewish communities of Hightown (1970: 57).

Polarization proceeds to a large extent outside the classroom, in conversations and interaction concerning the classroom and what the teacher has said or done. It develops where relatively unfettered and unpoliced interaction between boys can take place. The "antigroup" subculture is therefore an "underground" or "reactive" subculture which, nevertheless, increasingly makes itself felt within the classroom. Although the evidence for these two processes has been presented in detail elsewhere, I will recount some of it here, inasmuch as the pertinent publications are not generally available outside of England and inasmuch as the evidence reveals some of the characteristics of the processes under discussion.

Figure 1 represents the passage of a cohort of students through the the school in terms of their differentiation and polarization. The regrouping of pupils at the end of the first year, with the brightest 25 percent from each class going into the top stream (2 Express, or 2E), produces a new homogeneity which proceeds to be differentiated further during the second year.

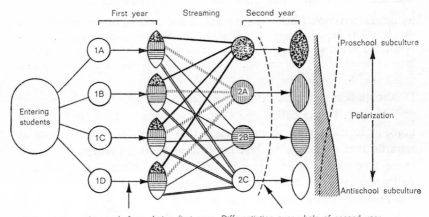

Figure 1.   Differentiation and polarization associated with the streaming that takes place at the end of the first year

Quantitative Indices

The indices developed below were prepared from two questionnaires completed by all students who entered the school in 1962. One questionnaire was given at the end of the first year and one at the end of the second. The indices are designed to illustrate the processes of differentiation and polarization. On both occasions the boys were asked who had been their close friends over the last year. Unless they felt that they definitely could not do so, they were asked to restrict themselves to boys in the school and to six choices.

In the four UNSTREAMED first-year classes there was virtually no difference in the average number of times each boy was chosen (Table 1).

Table 1. Average number of times each boy in each first-year class was chosen as a friend *

Class	Choices per boy
1A	4.1
1B	4.1
1C	4.2
1D	4.5

* The choices were by boys in their own class and in the other first-year classes.

Table 2. Average number of times each boy in each second-year class was chosen as a friend

Class	(a) First year *	(b) Second year
2E	4.8	4.8
2A	4.5	4.6
2B	3.9	4.0
2C	3.3	4.3

* The choices in column (a) were made at the end of the first year and are the same as those shown in Table 1, but here they have been averaged for the class that each pupil was about to enter. The choices in column (b) were made at the end of the second year and have been averaged for the class in which the pupil had spent the year.

At the end of the first year, the higher up in the academic scale a boy was placed, the more likely he was to be chosen as a friend by a large number of his schoolmates.

At the end of the second year, when the boys were asked the same question, their responses revealed striking differences, and these differences were related to academic achievement. Column (b) of Table 2 shows that the year spent in a new class had hardly changed the overall positions of boys in 2E, 2A, and 2B, although the actual friendship choices for any one boy would have undergone considerable change. In contrast, the choices in class 2C had undergone a substantial change. In a class of thirty boys, the increase from 3.3 to 4.3 in the case of 2C represents an increase of something like thirty choices. That the new popularity of boys in 2C was brought about by the growth of a new set of norms and values, or the beginnings of the antigroup subculture, is demonstrated by Table 3. At this stage, the boys of 2C had become popular for the very reasons that they had been unpopular in the first year.

Table 3.   Distribution of friendship choices according to class: second year, 1963 *

Read ACROSS for choices made, DOWN for choices received by each class.

Class (number in each class in brackets)	2E	2A	2B	2C	Others	Total of choices made	Percentage of choices in own class
2E (31)	91	26	14	7	12	150	60.7
2A (31)	28	94	16	6	14	158	59.5
2B (28)	20	17	63	23	20	143	44.0
2C (30)	9	4	18	92	13	136	67.7
Total (of choices received)	148	141	111	128	58	588	

* Figures are for students who entered in 1962, at the end of their second year.

The boys of 2E and 2A had proved academically successful, as reflected in their academic grading, and according to our hypothesis, they SHOULD have been influenced positively by it. Table 3 shows that academic standing did, indeed, have a marked positive influence on their choice of friends (e.g. 2E made twenty-six choices from among boys in 2A, fourteen choices from among boys in 2B, but only seven from among boys in 2C). There was no element in the organization of the school that could have brought about this result. Similarly, 2A made twenty-eight choices from 2E, sixteen from 2B, but only six from 2C.

This analysis was confirmed by another set of data which are, in many ways, complementary to the first. The second-year questionnaire asked, "What boys do you find it difficult to get on with?" Once again, the subjects were allowed to give up to six names, unless they felt that they could not possibly confine themselves to six. This time, however, many boys refrained from putting any names down, and only a few put down as many as six. Enough names were mentioned, however, to establish a pattern of unpopularity. Once again, the largest number of choices were made from among boys in the informants' own class (Table 4). The number of choices from other classes was always fewer than seven, with one notable exception: boys in 2C were named twenty-six times by boys in 2E, nine times by boys in 2A, and twenty times by boys in 2B, thereby eliciting the highest number of unpopularity choices, ninety-seven — compared with fifty-three for 2E, the next highest.

Table 4.   Distribution of choices of unpopular boys: second year, 1963

Class	2E	2A	2B	2C	Others	Pre-fects	Total of choices made	Average number of choices received
2E	38	4	4	26	3	0	75	1.71
2A	5	33	1	9	22	1	51	1.45
2B	7	4	24	20	1	0	56	1.14
2C	3	4	3	42	3	6	61	3.23
Total (of choices received)	53	45	32	97	29	7	243	

Table 5.   Sociomatrix: friendship choices within class 3E: third year, 1964*

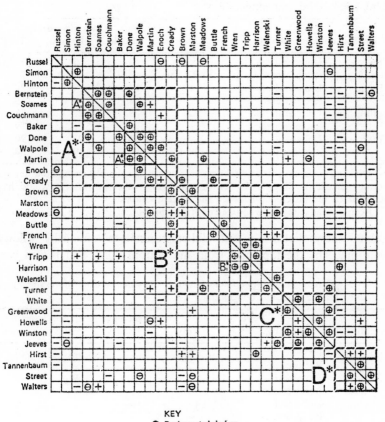

KEY
⊕ Reciprocated choices
+ Unreciprocated choices
− Dislikes (can't get on with)
⊖ Reciprocated dislikes
▭ Friendship areas
☐ Cliques

*   Students who entered in 1962.

The preponderance of unpopularity choices from 2C is to be explained by the antigroup development in 2C. These boys were now regarded as bullies and "tough eggs," who, in Badman's terminology, would rather be hooligans and have a good time than be nice little boys. They were aggressive and loudmouthed and were feared by many boys who were successful in terms of the dominant school norms. In Tables 5 and 6, there were no reciprocated choices between the top-third and bottom-third groups. This in itself does not prove polarity. We must show that this linear arrangement also concentrates "can't get on with" choices between the two extremes.

Table 6. Friendship choices between the three sections of the sociogram: top third, middle third, and bottom third*

Friendship choices made by		Friendship choices made from			
		Top	Middle	Bottom	Total
Top	Unilateral	25	2	1	28
	Reciprocated †	22	2	–	24
Middle	Unilateral	6	19	4	29
	Reciprocated	2	14	3	19
Bottom	Unilateral	3	8	22	33
	Reciprocated	–	3	16	19
Total:	Unilateral	34	29	27	90
	Reciprocated	24	19	19	34

* Dividing lines were drawn arbitrarily between the top eleven, middle ten, and bottom ten. If the lines had been drawn in any other position, it would have accentuated the difference between the three divisions.
† Reciprocated choices are counted each time they occur, i.e. not as pairs.

Table 7 shows that this polarity did exist: nineteen "animosity" choices were made by the top third from the bottom third, and fifteen were

Table 7. "Can't get on with" choices between the three sections of the sociogram: Top third, middle third, and bottom third

Negative choices made by		"Can't get on with" choices from			
		Top	Middle	Bottom	Total
Top	Unilateral	5	2	19	26
	Reciprocated	2	2	4	8
Middle	Unilateral	3	1	9	13
	Reciprocated	2	–	2	4
Bottom	Unilateral	15	6	5	26
	Reciprocated	4	2	–	6
Total:	Unilateral	23	9	33	65
	Reciprocated	8	4	6	18

made by the bottom third from the top third. The next highest figure was nine, made by the middle group from the bottom group. It is important to examine the nature of this polarity and get some idea of the characteristics that are associated with the members of each of these groups.

SOCIAL CLASS   The distribution of social-class background was very different among the three groups (Table 8). The table shows that boys in the "top third" were predominantly middle class, while those in the "bottom third" were predominantly working class.

Table 8. Distribution of manual and nonmanual parental occupations in the top third, middle third, and bottom third of the 3E sociomatrix

	Top	Middle	Bottom	Total
Parents with nonmanual occupation	9	5	3	17
Parents with manual occupation	2	5	7	14
Total	11	10	10	31

CLUB MEMBERSHIP   Membership in social clubs can be used as one index of whether a boy is oriented toward the normative adult-dominated school culture or toward the antiacademic, adolescent-dominated culture. Clubs were categorized in the following way:

1. PROSCHOOL, ADULT-DOMINATED — school clubs, scouts, religious bodies and their youth clubs, libraries, golf and tennis clubs, etc.

2. ANTISCHOOL, ADOLESCENT-DOMINATED — coffee-bar clubs, snooker and billards clubs.

Table 9 shows dramatically the extent to which the behavior of the three groups differed in this respect.

Table 9. Membership in clubs, categories 1 and 2, of pupils in the top third, middle third, and bottom third of the 3E sociomatrix

	Club membership			
	Top	Middle	Bottom	Total
Category 1 Proschool, adult-dominated	34	26	8	68
Category 2 Antischool, adolescent-dominated	1	1	14	16
Total	35	27	22	84

Theoretical Implications

Let us now take a step back from the concrete detail of the empirical situation and begin to examine in broader terms the process being illustrated and its implications for a view of socialization.

Dennis Wrong summarizes the sociological answers to the Hobbesian question of order in a twofold classification that also effectively summarizes the two main roots of socialization theory:

> The first answer is summed up in the notion of the "internalisation of social norms." The second, more commonly employed or assumed in empirical research, is the view that man is essentially motivated by the desire to achieve a positive image of self by winning acceptance or status in the eyes of others (Wrong 1961: 185).

In his influential article, Wrong elegantly and persuasively puts the case that the model of human nature implicit in these statements portrays an oversocialized conception of man. But he terminates the discussion at a crucial point. Man, he argues, is a neurotic, discontented animal for whom culture is a violation of his socialized bodily drives. Even though Wrong's apologies for a psychological view of man have the virtue of making the assumptions underlying this view explicit, we are left, nevertheless, without having examined the sociological advantages inherent in this powerful critique.

To me, the main benefit seems to be that our attention is forced to an awareness of the imperfect or partial nature of socialization and the existence of an essential element in man that remains outside both the processes of internalization of social norms and the conforming needs of his personality. I do not think that in theorizing about this element, sociologists or anthropologists need necessarily ascribe a psychological nature to it; in fact, following Gluckman (1964), I feel that it is important for us to remain naive about it. On the other hand, we should make our naive assumptions clear, describe our conceptions, and look for room in the theoretical sociological models we adopt to allow for the testing and refinement of these conceptions. We are, therefore, proposing that there is an element in man that stands above the usual socializing process as conceived by sociologists and that acts as commentator, judge, or director.[5] This "protected" self may even remain silent during the flow of interactions and impressions experienced by the individual. What I am saying is that man has purpose and will, and that sociologists and anthropologists must make room for them (a positive place — why make exceptions?), both in their models of the social process and in particular models of socialization.

---

[5] Margaret Mead's writings, for example, illustrate that this is by no means a new proposal in theoretical works. It is, however, new in relation to empirical sociology.

Let us do this, in our case, by examining the processes of differentiation and polarization in the light of the two major strands of socialization theory outlined by Wrong.

It is quite clear from the earlier description that first-year boys are highly conformist with respect to teacher definitions of the appropriate behavioral norm (in dress, manners, etc.). And, interestingly enough, the friendship-choice analysis reveals that status in friendship is also correlated with academic achievement, suggesting that these pupils also accept the fact that academic differentiation provides them with a criterion for valued friendships.

At this stage, therefore, it looks like a straightforward matter of internalization. However, a problem emerges with the subsequent development of a subculture, for although some pupils proceed according to prediction and continue to conform to the "internalized" conceptions of behavior and academic performance, some start to behave in ways that suggest a rejection of these "internalized" values. Internalization as a way of "understanding" this phenomenon requires some elaboration.[6] Similarly, conformity with the expectations of friends needs considerable elaboration to explain why, among the boys who develop the subculture, there is a shift away from friendships with the more academic boys.

Two additional notions are required to explain these developments:
1. The Hightown Grammar School classroom is a relatively "closed" system of relationships, with limited teacher resources and rewards in terms of both short-term gratification (e.g. praise from the teacher) and longer-term successes (e.g. examination successes or admission to a university). I have used the term "competitive arena" to describe this aspect of the classroom.

Table 10 illustrates the way the classroom becomes a self-contained

Table 10. Personal estimate of success in second year

Class	Regarded the past year as a success	Couldn't say	Regarded the past year as unsuccessful
2E	19	1	11
2A	24	–	7
2B	21	–	7
2C	24	2	4
Total	88	3	29

[6] See Parsons (1951: 252 ff.) for one theoretical classification of possible elaborations.

"competitive arena" in which pupils compare themselves against each other. It shows that in 2E, eleven pupils regarded themselves as unsuccessful, despite the fact that they were in the top group, compared with only four pupils in 2C, who were in the bottom group. The difference can be accounted for only by the past experience of the two groups, the different sets of standards they have acquired, and the way in which their new experiences measure up to those standards. This view is confirmed by an analysis of the experience of the eleven boys who regarded themselves as unsuccessful in 2E. On the average, they dropped sixteen places in their second-year examinations compared with their first-year ones. The rest of the class dropped eight places on the average. During the year two of these boys had been considerably disturbed emotionally, crying during lessons, crying before school, and refusing to come to school. A third went through a similar period, and his father wrote to the school complaining that "the boy is utterly demoralized."

2. The extreme competitive pressures described earlier highlight success and failure within the system. Success or failure is readily understood in terms that the classroom has established for itself and becomes knowledge that is immediately available to all members of the group.

Let us go back to the group of thirty boys entering the school. As soon as formal work begins, each action by the pupil (academic or behavioral) has meaning (1) in relation to the master and (2) in relation to what the other twenty-nine boys in the class can do.

Our friend Billy Green might be quite good at English, but if fifteen other boys in the class are better and maintain their advantage, no matter how much Billy Green tries to improve, he remains sixteenth, and his strategy for excelling at English fails. In fact, Billy Green's efforts to improve his own position can become part of the pressure that encourages the other fifteen to improve theirs. As we have seen, many of these pupils had been accustomed to playing the "good pupil" role in their junior schools. For a large number of these pupils this role is NECESSARILY no longer available. In our example, Billy Green's efforts in English and in other subjects are thwarted by his classmates and by the structure of rewards set up by the teacher.

The antigroup subculture is CREATED in the search for solutions to this type of problem, posed by intragroup competitive pressures.[7] Indi-

---

[7]   This analysis suggests that each cohort "creates" an antigroup subculture; there is little or no evidence that it is "learned" from older cohorts. For example, first-year boys make very few friendship choices from among boys in the second year, second-year boys have few friends in the third year, etc.

vidual pupils adopt strategies that they hope will provide personal solutions, and since there is a commonly recurring concern with the problem of "relative failure," there is sufficient coalescence, sufficient common ground in these adaptive strategies, to give rise to a recognizable subculture. Without some of the structural parameters that I have described, it is doubtful whether a similar development would take place. For example, in a Steiner school, with an explicit philosophy of cooperation and support within the classroom, no similar development takes place.[8] The sociogram reveals a loosely integrated classroom structure without distinct inclusive/exclusive cliques, in which half a dozen children who are either late arrivals or children with fairly marked behavioral problems are given the support of the "community" of the others.

The emergence of the antigroup subculture marks the emergence of the first "underground" culture expressed by this group of boys. That is, there comes into existence a second set of sufficiently coherent behavioral norms, sufficient mutual understanding which the boys are able to anticipate and manipulate to establish alternative reputations. For example, by the second or third year, a boy could make a statement like "Let's borrow your math book" and not elicit the response, "What do you want it for?" said in a surprised and hurt tone. Instead, the book would be tossed almost carelessly to the person making the request. It would be understood that THAT boy had made the request in order to copy the homework. By acceding to his request, the boy who supplies the book can enjoy the feeling of being "one of the boys" — of being openhanded and devil-may-care, even if he himself would never dare to come to school without the work completed. (Some boys, of course, would never be asked, and some would never make that sort of request.)

The existence of the antigroup subculture after the first year of school creates a new situation. Now most of the boys are put in the position at one time or another of choosing which shared meanings, which set of understood rules to adhere to in a given situation. A most dramatic example of this sort of choice was, in fact, demonstrated by a fifth-year boy:

Sherman was frequently top in 5B. He rarely misbehaved in class and was prominent in cooperating with teachers during lessons. On one occasion,

---

[8]   The sociometric data were collected by Murray Webster for a master's dissertation. It is one of a number of school and classroom studies being undertaken at Sussex by graduate students.

however, I observed that after a lesson in which he was conspicuous for his enthusiastic participation, he waited until the master had left the room, then immediately grabbed an innocuous classmate's satchel and in a few moments had organised a sort of piggy-in-the-middle game. He passed the bag across the room, while the owner stood helplessly by, occasionally trying to intercept or picking up a fallen book. The initiation of this activity so soon after the lesson seemed to be a conscious demonstration of his status within the informal structure of the class. He was indicating that, although he was good at work, he was not a swot and would not be excluded from groups based on other than academic values (Lacey 1970: 86).

It was interesting to note how different boys reacted to having the satchel flung at them. Some entered eagerly into the "tease" and made fun of the luckless owner, while others tried to ignore its arrival — on their desk or at their feet. These boys were quickly brought into the game by the shouts or jeers of their classmates. To throw the satchel was likely to get them into trouble if a master came through the door; to ignore it was likely to get them the reputation of a "soft-arsed mard." Pupils found that both sets of values were important to them.

The manipulation of social strategies in situations of this sort brings to many adolescents a new awareness. The first step is the conscious manipulation of situations in terms of one or another set of subcultural norms. The next step is the awareness of that manipulation, and, therefore, the self-conscious recognition of an aspect of the self (the protected self) that lies outside the socialization influences of situation and biography.[9]

In the following quotation from the diary of a fourth-year boy he comes fairly close to recognizing this dualism and protected self in another boy, a newcomer to the school. After describing in detail the boy's various strategies, he writes, by way of explanation: "He is not naturally stupid, he is just a little cleverer than most people in deception. He is not clever enough, though, to maintain both an image [a good image] and a full-scale deceptive network. Enoch is, though." The good image corresponds to the boy's place in the proschool subculture, while the deceptive network represents his place in the antigroup subculture. The author of the diary correctly diagnoses Enoch as being relatively successful in this respect.

---

[9]   I am not postulating that there is a regular, or even a progressive, realization of the existence of the protected self by all individuals. I have observed, however, that there is a far greater consciousness of this self among university postgraduate students than among grammar-school pupils.

SUSSEX TEACHER-EDUCATION COURSE

The above-described review of some of the original findings of the Hightown research came about as a result of the insights obtained in a second piece of research, into the professional socialization of teachers. Certain features of the socialization process at Hightown, described above, were highlighted by some of the features noted also in early-adult socialization—in particular, the selection or creation of strategies to deal with different situations. The teacher-education research contained both macro and micro approaches to the study of change. Briefly, it was a study of the Sussex postgraduate-certificate-in-education course, against a background of four other teacher-education courses, chosen in order to represent some courses like and some unlike the Sussex course. Two of the schools (like Sussex) were innovative — York New Northern University and Brunel New Southern University; two were traditional — Soton Provincial South Coast University and Kings Metropolitan University (see Table 11). The material quoted in this paper is predominantly from the intensive study of the Sussex course.[10]

Table 11. Universities chosen by students who also chose Sussex

	Innovative	Traditional
Yes	York New Northern	Soton Provincial South Coast
No	Brunel New Southern	Kings Metropolitan

The Sussex course was designed to involve students concurrently in the two worlds of "the school" and "the university." Student-teachers were, therefore, assigned to schools in which they taught for three days a week under the guidance of teachers from the school (teacher-tutors, or T-tutors). During the other two days a week they attended university seminars in which they discussed their teaching experiences and examined theoretical approaches to education. In these university sessions they participated in two main types of groups: (1) the subject group, made up of all students teaching that school subject (twelve in number), supervised by a specialist in that subject (E-tutor); (2) the mixed group, made up of students from a variety of disciplines (also twelve), super-

---

[10] The 1970–1971 cohort studied was followed up for a year of their teaching career after their one year at Sussex.

vised by various theory tutors. The design of the Sussex course thus enabled the researchers to observe student-teachers in three different settings, all of which recurred every week.

In all four of the other university courses that were studied, school and university experiences were separated into discrete blocks of time. This separation enabled the students to adjust to the school and university situations over fairly long periods of time (one or two months).

My first insight into the effects of the different settings within the Sussex University course came as I attended seminars of the biology group and then met some of the biologists in their mixed-subject seminars. There was one biologist in the biology seminar who played what could be described as a "progressive" role, advocating child-centered techniques and liberal educational reforms; in the mixed seminar he became an advocate of formal academic standards and firm discipline. When I questioned him about this reversal, he found it difficult to accept that it had occurred, until I was able to detail some of the statements he had made and the context of the discussions. After much perplexed heart-searching, he resolved the problem by remarking that in the mixed seminar there were a couple of primary students "who really get my goat." It appeared to him that they were unrealistic in their outlook and needed to be brought back to earth. It became apparent that he felt that the biologists in his subject group were different. He could rely on their common sense and understand their outlook and problems — he therefore felt free to espouse progressive causes in the biology seminar.

In other words, the student composition of the seminar became a situational determinant of individual behavior, giving rise to two recognizable and different strategies. In this case, the emergence of distinct strategies pointed to the existence of a set of understood values and orientations within the biology group (a subject culture) that did not exist among the students in the mixed group. These incidents and many others like them encouraged me to look for more evidence of subject-culture differences and more examples of situationally determined strategies.

Attitudes Toward Tutors

The main situational difference was between the school and the university. To evaluate this difference, the students of all five universities were asked in the "end-of-year" questionnaire whether they felt that their T-tutors (school tutors) and their E-tutors (university tutors) differed in their ideas relating to five aspects of education, and whether they (the students) agreed with one or the other or both. The aspects were the following:

a. General views on the aims of education
b. Acceptance of new ideas
c. Curriculum
d. Relationships with pupils
e. The appearance of the teacher (dress, manner, etc.)
   The students were allowed five different responses:
1. Tutors did not differ
   If tutors DID differ,
2. student generally agreed with the teacher-tutor
3. student generally agreed with the university tutors
4. at different times student agreed with one tutor or the other
5. student resorted to some other method of coping with the difference.
In all five universities the students tended to agree with their university tutors rather than with their school tutors in the matters in question. The proportion of students who perceived differences in views between their E-tutors and their T-tutors, and who agreed sometimes with one, sometimes with the other, was consistently higher at Sussex than at the other universities. In other words, the Sussex course seems to produce some clear-cut differences in the perceptions of Sussex students, as compared with the rest.

Table 12. Students' perception of teacher-tutor/University-tutor differences regarding five aspects of education

(a) Average percentage who perceived differences

Sussex	York	Brunel	Soton	Kings
65.4	59.7	54.5	58.2	53.4

(b) Percentage of students who agreed with one tutor or the other at different times

Sussex	York	Brunel	Soton	Kings
29.2	18.5	20.9	19.8	16.6

(c) Above percentages (b) expressed as a percentage of those who perceived differences (a)

Sussex	York	Brunel	Soton	Kings
44.6	30.5	41.0	34.1	31.1

$x^2 = 12.88$
4DF.   P $<$ 2.5

It seems probable that the weekly cycle that includes both school and university experiences makes it possible for Sussex students to discern that differences exist. This perception is maintained throughout the year — because the school-university cycle is maintained throughout the year. Sussex students are under some pressure to find a way to live with these differences, and they seem to manage by agreeing with "both [the E-tutor and the T-tutor] at different times." Table 12 shows that not only do they follow this strategy to a greater extent than do students at the other universities (b), but that the greater incidence of this strategy is due both to the greater perception of differences and to the greater incidence of this strategy among those who perceive differences (c).

Let us look at some of the content of these strategies as reported by the students when they answered that there were differences and told how they coped with them:

1. IGNORING T-TUTOR: (a) [The tutors disagreed on] the role of English in the curriculum. I coped with [their difference of opinion] by ignoring my teacher-tutor. (b) Often it wasn't worth bringing the conflict with the teacher-tutor to a head, since there was a definite noncommunication and it was a waste of precious school time. It was more useful and peaceful to go away and do your own thing quietly.

2. DECEIVING T-TUTOR: (a) [I followed a policy of] evasion. (b) Although I disagreed with my teacher-tutor in [such matters as] discipline of children, approach to timetable, art work, and the importance of art and the story in the curriculum, the only way to cope was to concur with her when she was present.

3. DISAGREEING WITH BOTH TUTORS: (a) On most things they were [of] different [opinions], and I was [of an opinion] different from them both. It's too long to explain. (b) The teacher-tutor was at all times more recognizant of the concrete teaching situation, whereas the E-tutor preferred to talk in theoretical terms. I balanced the two viewpoints by recognizing the constraints which governed the thinking of each of them.

4. IGNORING E-TUTOR: (a) The teacher-tutor was, of necessity, more in favor of audio-visual methods than the E-tutor. This simply meant that in practical terms one used those aspects of the method in class which produced the best response, and discussed the philosophical impossibility of the entire exercise with the E-tutor. (b) [Concerning] introduction of the Nuffield A-level biology syllabus, the E-tutor favored it, while the T-tutor [received it with] qualified enthusiasm, preferring gradual incorporation of some curriculum material [from the syllabus] but not changing [to the new] syllabus [entirely]. I agreed with E in PRINCIPLE, but with T in practice.

The sense of "distance," and the sense of "I," as being apart from both "school" and "university," come through very clearly from these quotations. In only a very few cases did the student identify clearly with either the E- or the T-tutor, as in this example: "Teacher-tutor thinks that organizing and interesting children is of prime importance, and [that] our teaching must be centered around this more than around the [individual] child." This case was almost unique at Sussex, as evident in the replies to the student questionnaires. Yet in the seminars one frequently got the impression that students were agreeing and going along with members of the staff. At times it was evident that if the student felt the tutor was "unable to take" disagreement, the only way to cope was to "concur with her when she was present."

These strategies, common at this level of socialization, not only give the semblance of agreement concerning norms and procedures when there is no agreement but also allow the student to maintain a "view of the self" different from the views implied by some of his outward behavior. The model of socialization that emerges goes a long way toward explaining the very rapid changes that have taken place in some British schools after decades of relatively stable practice.

There is one final point to be made from these results. Let us examine the effects of an oversimplified view of socialization in predicting human behavior. Stones and Morris (1972) have criticized teacher-training schemes that emphasize school experience, holding that by keeping the student in school for longer periods of time and by putting more power into the hands of the practicing teacher, "all the pressures on the student are in the direction of conforming to the unadventurous stereotype" — the "sitting-with-Nellie" objection.

The Sussex scheme does both these things that Stones and Morris deplore. Sussex teacher-tutors are paid to give tutorials, and they also 'have an important role in the assessment of student-teachers. Sussex student-teachers spend more time in school than do students in any of the other four courses studied.

Stones and Morris assume that in these circumstances socialization proceeds by a simple process of identification and internalization. I hope I have given evidence to show that this is not necessarily the case. When he is put in a situation in which he is alternately viewing one institution from the standpoint of another and is constrained to exercise choices in his selection of strategies, the student becomes more aware of differences, more aware of "self" in relation to the selection of his strategies, and (I now add) both more critical and more radically critical in his approach to education.

Attitudes Toward Education

Evidence in support of the statement at the close of the last section may be found in the comparative study by questionnaire of attitudes toward education. The evidence, based on the following scales, indicates that, far from conforming, Sussex students adopt attitudes that constitute a radical criticism of schools as they are, and that they do so to a greater extent than any other group of students included in the study. The first three of the five scales used were developed in the 1950's by Oliver and Butcher (1962) and were widely used in the 1960's in research concerning teachers' attitudes. These scales — Radicalism (R), Naturalism (N), and Tender-mindedness (T) — are described briefly below. The last two scales — Liberalism and Progressivism — were developed more recently.

NATURALISM   Naturalism presumes the existence of natural standards that reside within the child and emerge in a relationship with the child. It is, therefore, opposed to the imposition of external (absolute) standards in the moral, cultural, or academic sphere. Agreement with such statements in the questionnaire as "Naturalness is more important than good manners in children" and "The teacher should not stand in the way of a child's efforts to learn in his own fashion" is balanced against disagreement with statements such as "Character training is impossible

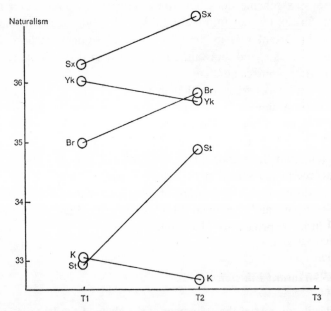

Figure 2.   Naturalism attitude scores of Sussex, York, Brunel, Soton, and Kings students (based on scales developed by Oliver and Butcher 1962)

if there is no formal standard of right or wrong" to give a positive score on the Naturalism scale (see Figure 2).

RADICALISM   Radicalism is concerned with the allocation of resources to education and the distribution and availability of education. In general, more education, more equally distributed, is at the center of the concept. For example, option for "more nursery schools," "increased expenditure on adult education," and "comprehensive schools to be the normal form of secondary education" would give a positive score on the Radicalism scale (see Figure 3).

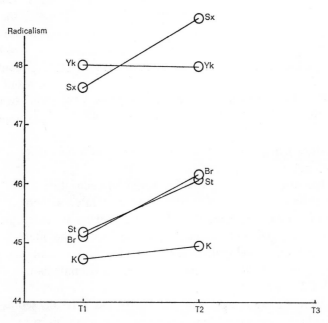

Figure 3.   Radicalism attitude scores of Sussex, York, Brunel, Soton, and Kings students (based on scales developed by Oliver and Butcher 1962)

TENDER-MINDEDNESS   Tender-mindedness is OPPOSED to narrowly conceived vocationalism and instrumentalism in education, and OPPOSED to efficiency in fitting children into the "system." It is, therefore, a very negative concept and can only be viewed as an attitude in favor of protecting children from the demands of the future and of the "system." The tender-minded person would reject the statement "A scientific training offers good prospects for a career" as a reason for teaching science, and would reject the statement "A study of international affairs

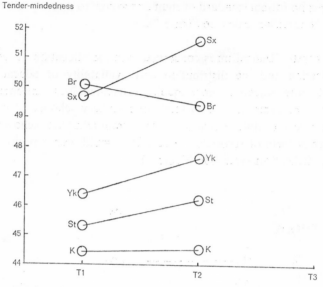

Figure 4.   Tender-mindedness attitude scores of Sussex, York, Brunel, Soton, and Kings students (based on scales developed by Oliver and Butcher 1962)

should show which countries are our friends" as a reason for teaching international understanding (see Figure 4).

In other words, "a tender-minded attitude to education is one which regards children and others as persons to be treated as ends in themselves rather than as serving the interests of others, as represented, for example, by the demands of vocational efficiency or the interests of the State." Since the development of these scales, both educational policy and educational practice have moved considerably, and this has affected the scales. For example, some issues that had been controversial in the 1950's were widely accepted by the 1970's. As a result, scores made by individuals who would have been considered radical in the 1950's, in the 1970's were clustering near the top of the scale, giving a skewed distribution and thereby reducing the possibility for high-scoring individuals to register gain on the Radicalism scale.

Because we were particularly interested in change, we decided to augment the Radicalism scale with items more closely related to current preoccupations and more challenging to high-scoring radicals. The original intention of incorporating such items into the Radicalism scale was abandoned, due partly to lack of time and partly to the observation that the new items under consideration moved the focus of attention away from the politico-administrative level and towards the notions of participation and democracy in the school. This observation was borne out when the initial scores were seen to be as closely related to Naturalism as to Radicalism: Sussex R.49, N.45; York R.52, N.57; Brunel R.64, N.71; Southampton R.56, N.58; Kings R.61, N.47. The term Liberalism (in education), therefore, seemed appropriate to this new scale.

LIBERALISM   While this scale was initially conceived as a way of bringing the Oliver and Butcher Radicalism scale up to date, it was also thought relevant to bring in the issues of pupil participation (democracy), streaming (competition), and the issue of the unequal division of resources in favor of the poorer areas (compensation). A "disagree" response to "Children learn best in a highly competitive situation" and an "agree" response to "Older children should be allowed to make decisions in the running of the school" would give a positive score on the Liberalism scale (see Figure 5).

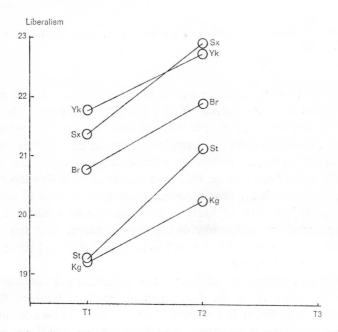

Figure 5.   Liberalism attitude scores of Sussex, York, Brunel, Soton, and Kings students

PROGRESSIVISM   The "relationships in teaching" question was designed to measure those attitudes toward the teacher-pupil relationship that seemed to typify the Sussex approach. The items were generated from

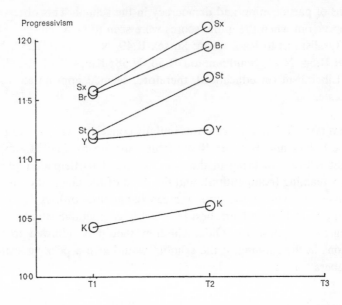

Figure 6. Progressivism attitude scores of Sussex, York, Brunel, Soton, and Kings students

notes taken during seminars and at keynote lectures, and an attempt was made to select aspects of the teaching relationship that were stressed and ones that were manifested frequently (see Figure 6).

I was unable to carry out a similar exercise at the other universities, so there is no direct evidence on whether these aspects were stressed equally there. Inasmuch as the items measured were developed from close contact with the Sussex course, it seems reasonable to make the assumption that they are likely to represent overall a much closer fit to the underlying philosophy of the Sussex course. The aim was to produce a scale sensitive to the sort of attitude change that proved most likely to occur at Sussex.

I felt that perhaps the attitude scales in general use heretofore had been less sensitive to the differences in emphasis between the approaches in different institutions. If so, a failure to isolate different patterns in different universities would not demonstrate that none had existed, but only that none had existed in the broad, rather general areas in which it has been usual to measure attitudes.

Scores on the five attitude scales are presented in Figures 2 to 6. The five universities are designated as follows: Brunel–Br, Kings–K, Soton–St, Sussex–Sx, York–Yk.

Discussion

On each of the five attitude scales, Sussex students end the year with the highest mean score. This occurred despite the fact that in three cases out of the five, Brunel or York started the year with higher scores. This suggests that there is an institutional effect, over and above a social-climate effect. The evidence appears to support the hypothesis that the Sussex teaching scheme produces changes in the attitudes toward education of the student cohort which are consistently more radical than those produced by the other universities.

In this case, therefore, Stones and Morris are clearly wrong. My argument suggests that they are wrong because they adopted a simplistic view of socialization and an "oversocialized conception of man." The tensions between the "world of the school" and the "world of the university" produced among Sussex students an enhanced realization of themselves as apart from either world, a realization of their protected self. It was this "distance" that contributed to the radical perspectives at Sussex.[11]

CONCLUSION

This paper aimed to illustrate that a more complex view of man is required in empirical sociology. We have attempted to show how empirically derived concepts, intragroup competitive pressures, and the selection of social strategies raise new issues relating to the nature of man and his relationship to society.

REFERENCES

GLUCKMAN, M., *editor*
    1964   *Closed systems and open minds: the limits of naivety in social anthropology*. London: Oliver.
LACEY, COLIN
    1970   *Hightown Grammar: the school as a social system*. Manchester: Manchester University Press.
OLIVER, R. A. C., H. J. BUTCHER
    1962   Teachers' attitudes to education, the structure of educational attitudes. *British Journal of Social Clinical Psychology* 1:56–69.

[11]   We are unable in a paper of this length to go into a more detailed analysis of the way the tensions between the worlds of school and university contributed to increases in radicalism. We hope to do this in future publications.

PARSONS, TALCOTT
1951   *The social system.* Glencoe: Free Press.
SPINDLER, G.
1963   *Education and culture.* New York: Holt, Rinehart and Winston.
STONES, E., S. MORRIS
1972   *Teaching practice, problems and perspectives.* New York: Methuen.
WRONG, D.
1961   The oversocialized conception of man in modern sociology. *American Sociological Review* 26.

Students and Society: A Cross-National Comparison of Youth Attitudes and Values

MARISA ZAVALLONI

I shall present here some of the results of a cross-national study on the attitudes and aspirations of university students carried out in collaboration with Otto Klineberg and several colleagues in eleven countries: France, Spain, Italy, Great Britain, Austria, the United States, Yugoslavia, Japan, Australia, Nigeria, Tunisia.

Our aim was to make cross-cultural comparisons of the responses of university students to a wide range of issues and to determine from a comparative perspective different attitudinal clusters: political beliefs, personal aspirations, cultural orientations, and their interrelations.

During the last ten years we have witnessed an upsurge of interest in youth's attitudes, not unrelated to the various protest movements that have appeared in many parts of the world. Not only has protest disrupted the university, it has now filtered into high schools, and has brought about a critique of the commonly accepted values of everyday life. The social sciences have mainly responded in a speculative vein to this phenomenon. In a document prepared for UNESCO summarizing some of the conclusions found in current sociological studies, we note that the young around the world have created a kind of international culture, a specific youth culture in opposition to an adult culture still fixed on the traditional patterns. This interpretation of youth unrest poses certain problems; it may even raise more questions than we can answer. For instance:

1. Does this so-called new culture represent a modal orientation of youth in the countries where it appears, or is it a minority outlook? In other words, how widely accepted among university students are the different positions expressing this "new culture"?

In the questionnaire we made substantial use of statements found in the writings of Marcuse, Cohn-Bendit, and other representatives of political radicalism and counter-culture ideology in order to ascertain their acceptance among college students.

2.   What is the impact of this so-called new culture upon personal aspirations, the choice of a career, the basic sources of satisfaction in life, perspective on kind of family life, etc.? This question raises the problem of temporal trends in the value orientations of youth.

The questionnaire included some items from an earlier research study, the well-known Cornell survey of college students' attitudes, conducted in the fifties (Goldsen, et al. 1960). This previous study offered a baseline for determining eventual changes in career preference and ultimate goal values (career, family life, political activity, etc.). The temporal trend comparisons, however, must be limited to the United States sample, since no comparable information was available for the other countries.

3.   To what degree is there an interrelation between the different domains of attitudes studied? Is there any interdependence between a given political choice, broad cultural orientations, and personal aspirations? Do the various aspects of social, cultural, and personal ideologies represent an integrated pattern?

The theoretical question of the interdependence of attitudes has been the concern of social psychologists for a long time. However, these interrelations have usually been tested by comparing a limited number of attitude domains on a single sample. In this study we use a new method of statistical analysis (correspondence analysis — see Cordier 1968) in order to determine cross-nationally the degree of interdependence of attitudinal domains.

4.   How INTERNATIONALLY comparable is the new youth culture? Protest and the desire for innovation in one country could have a strictly political meaning; in another country it may express a need for change on the cultural level; in a third it may signify a personal concern with freedom and opportunity. A comparison of the structure of responses obtained in the different countries may help to clarify this issue.

5.   Are there social background factors (family origin, religion, etc.) that predetermine or facilitate the acceptance or rejection of radicalism and the new culture?

A number of studies (see, for example Keniston 1968) conducted in the United States consider this question. They show, for instance, that "radical" young people are emotionally close to their parents and basically have a similar political outlook. They just want to push their parents' original ideals further ahead. This relationship emerges from studies made on small samples of activists. Will a larger sample of students confirm these results? Will this relationship hold true in countries other than the United States?

THE SURVEY

The survey was conducted in 1970. The sample represents youth of college age (18-23), and its size varies with each country. Cooperation with colleagues in each of the countries studied was insured in the various phases of the research: questionnaire construction, pretest, and formal survey. In each of the countries studied we tried to obtain students from various disciplines (medicine, social sciences, pure sciences, etc.) in order to have certain units for comparison. In addition, our sample included students from all kinds of academic institutions. The respondents were confronted with a scale in which each occupational requirement was to be ranked from "very important" to "unimportant."

THE POLITICAL ORIENTATION OF THE STUDENTS

We determined the political orientation of the students by their answers to an open question: "How would you describe your political position?" The results were classified in a scale ranging from the conservative moderate to the far left. In no country studied did the conservative moderate represent a majority position. Austria ranks first in conservatism (46 percent), followed by Australia (37 percent), then Japan and the United States (both at 30 percent). The percentage of conservative students is smaller in the other countries. The opposite extreme, the far left, is also a minority position. This orientation is the greatest in Japan (26 percent), followed by France (22 percent) and Italy (18 percent). In the United States, the proportion of students representing such an extreme position is only 4 percent. The majority of the respondents in all the countries studied represents a leftist orientation, but in a moderate version (see Figure 1).

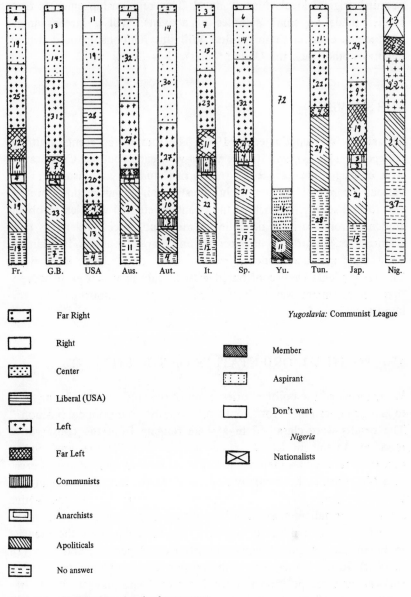

Fr.   G.B.   USA   Aus.   Aut.   It.   Sp.   Yu.   Tun.   Jap.   Nig.

Far Right

Right

Center

Liberal (USA)

Left

Far Left

Communists

Anarchists

Apoliticals

No answer

Yugoslavia: Communist League

Member

Aspirant

Don't want

Nigeria

Nationalists

Figure 1.   Political tendencies by country

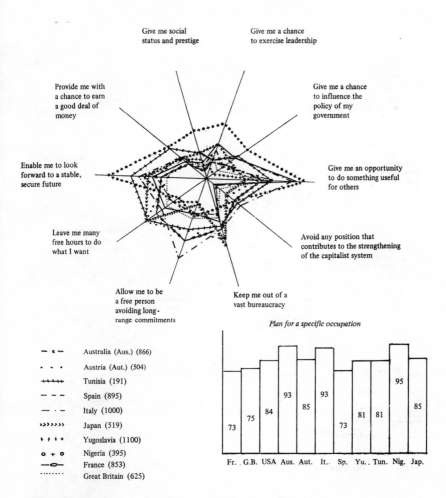

Figure 2. Importance of various occupational requirements — a cross-national comparison

CROSS-NATIONAL COMPARISONS OF OCCUPATIONAL RE-
QUIREMENTS (Figures 2, 3, 4)

During the fifties, research was conducted, among a large sample of college students, on the occupational requirements of youth (Goldsen 1960). Included in the present study are some of the same questions posed in the previous study, with the addition of a number of dimensions touching upon new and current concerns.

Figure 2 shows the principal results obtained from the eleven countries studied. In order to give a synthetic view of international differences in attitudes, we adopted a graphic representation of polar

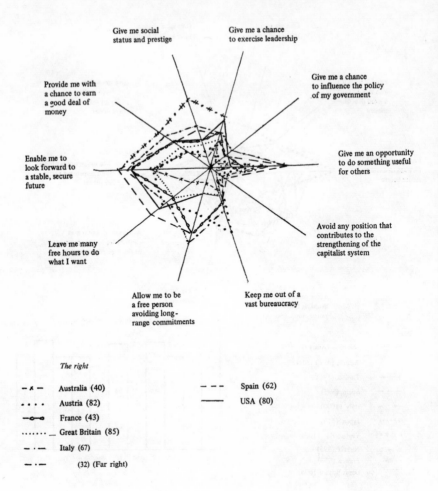

Give me social
status and prestige

Give me a chance
to exercise leadership

Provide me with
a chance to earn
a good deal of
money

Give me a chance
to influence the policy
of my government

Enable me to
look forward to
a stable, secure
future

Give me an opportunity
to do something useful
for others

Avoid any position that
contributes to the
strengthening of the
capitalist system

Leave me many
free hours to do
what I want

Allow me to be
a free person
avoiding long-
range commitments

Keep me out of a
vast bureaucracy

The right

— × —   Australia (40)   — — —   Spain (62)

• • • •   Austria (82)   ———————   USA (80)

—o—o   France (43)

⋯⋯⋯ _   Great Britain (85)

— · —   Italy (67)

— · —   (32) (Far right)

Figure 3.   Importance of various occupational requirements — a cross-national
comparison of students having a rightist political orientation

ordinates. Each axis represents 100 percent of the responses obtained
for a given question. For instance, examining Figure 2, we can read
that 90 percent of the Nigerian respondents consider "the opportunity
to do something useful for others" as an important occupational requirement. The great majority of Nigerian (86 percent), American
(84 percent), and Italian (83 percent) students consider the opportunity
for altruism an important occupational requirement. Among students
in the other countries in our study, it is less frequently considered an
important objective.

Practically all the Nigerian students (90 percent) express a desire
for a stable and secure future. The Tunisians rank second, followed

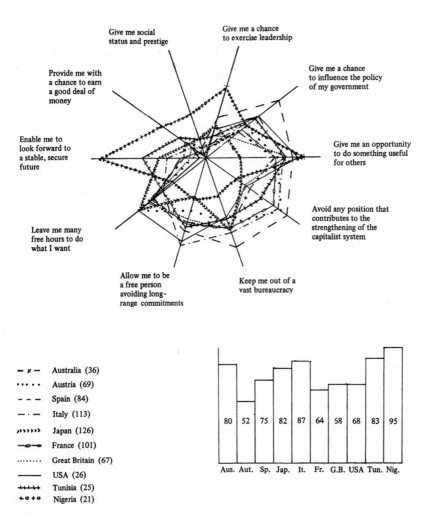

Figure 4. Importance of various occupational requirements — a cross-national comparison of students having far left political orientations

by the Italian and Yugoslav students. Students of the remaining countries appear to be less concerned with security.

A global overview of the responses indicates that the desire "to earn a good deal of money" and "desire for social status and prestige" is less frequently endorsed than altruism or the search for security. Nigeria and Tunisia rank first in this dimension (about 50 percent of the students consider it important); at the opposite extreme are the French, with only 20 percent attracted by the idea of wealth and social status.

Nigerians not only rank first in their expressed desire for wealth and prestige, but also in the desire to obtain a "position of leadership" and "to have a chance to influence the policy of their government." These two last occupational requirements are completely neglected by Yugoslav students (6 percent). They are considered important by one out of three Japanese and American students.

Another dimension included in the study in order to test an external political commitment ("avoid any position that contributes to the strengthening of the capitalist system" — this alternative was obviously omitted in the Yugoslav study) indicates interesting cross-cultural variations. In the United States, Australia, and Great Britain, students hardly favor this alternative (between 6 percent and 14 percent). For Italy, Tunisia, and France the percentage is approximately 40.

The rejection of bureaucracy is especially evident among Yugoslav students (64 percent) and Austrian and Japanese students (about 50 percent). The Nigerian students are least concerned with this question (30 percent), while the remaining countries fall somewhere in between.

Italian students (80 percent) — and to a lesser degree French students (60 percent) — are in favor of avoiding long-range commitments in their occupations. Japanese, Tunisian, and Nigerian students mention this occupational requirement even less frequently.

Occupational Requirements and Political Orientations: Right versus Far Left

Figures 3 and 4 permit us to compare the occupational requirements of students who indicate a rightist political outlook with those of students at the far left of the political spectrum.

In all the countries studied, students of the right favor more often than others the attainment of security, wealth, status, and prestige. In Italy students with a far right orientation differ from those of the conventional right only in so much as they strongly desire status and prestige. In other countries, we find no more than one or two students of this tendency; therefore they have been included in the "right."

In spite of the general similarities among students of the right, we notice that Austrian, British, and Australian students are comparatively less oriented towards money and security than students of the right in the other countries.

At the opposite end of the political spectrum, we note that in each country a radical political orientation implies a rejection of long-term engagements and a position bringing money, status, and prestige, and a refusal of any position that would contribute to the capitalist system. On the other hand, leftist students consider it important and desirable to have an occupation which leaves them many free hours and one which is not within the context of a bureaucracy.

Changes Over Time in the Importance of Occupational Requirements of United States Students

As mentioned above, we compared the occupational requirements of United States students in the seventies with those of students in the fifties. The results suggest some basic changes in values among college youth. Money and desire for status as an incentive has dropped and altruism has become a generalized orientation. Only 3 percent of the students studied in the fifties considered the possibility to earn a good deal of money as of NO importance in the choice of a career. In the present study this percentage has strikingly increased (35 percent). In the fifties, 43 percent of the students considered it very important to "have the opportunity to do something useful for others"; in the present study the percentage is as high as 87 percent. Similarly, in the fifties only 21 percent of the students considered it unimportant to obtain status and prestige through a career, as compared to 55 percent in the present study.

No change was observed in the proportion of students who seek power. Both in the fifties and in the seventies one-third of the total sample of American students considered it important that their future profession gives them "a chance to exercise leadership" and "an opportunity to influence the policy of [their] government."

CROSS-NATIONAL COMPARISONS OF THE IMPORTANCE OF UNIVERSITY GOALS (Figures 5, 6, 7)

We have just seen how in the United States some basic changes have taken place in the occupational requirements of college youth. A concern with altruism, for example, replaces the desire for success and wealth. If ultimate goals in life change, one might anticipate that young people's expectations with regard to the function and goals of the university change as well. These new expectations may have a bearing on both the content of the university's curriculum and the general goals of the institution.

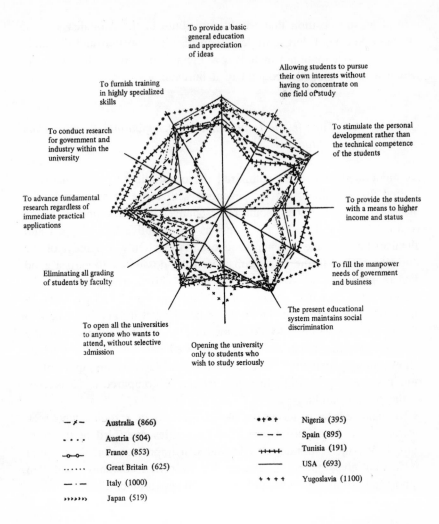

To provide a basic
general education
and appreciation
of ideas

Allowing students to pursue
their own interests without
having to concentrate on
one field of study

To furnish training
in highly specialized
skills

To conduct research
for government and
industry within the
university

To stimulate the personal
development rather than
the technical competence
of the students

To advance fundamental
research regardless of
immediate practical
applications

To provide the students
with a means to higher
income and status

To fill the manpower
needs of government
and business

Eliminating all grading
of students by faculty

The present educational
system maintains social
discrimination

To open all the universities
to anyone who wants to
attend, without selective
admission

Opening the university
only to students who
wish to study seriously

—✗—	Australia (866)	◆✦◦✦ Nigeria (395)
• • • •	Austria (504)	— — — Spain (895)
—○—○—	France (853)	++++ Tunisia (191)
. . . . . .	Great Britain (625)	——— USA (693)
— · —	Italy (1000)	+ + + + Yugoslavia (1100)
›››››	Japan (519)	

Figure 5.   Importance of various university goals — a cross-national comparison

Figure 5 indicates various alternatives, representing a number of universities' goals and the frequency with which the respondents of all the countries studied agree with them.

Some of these alternatives are accepted by the great majority of students in all countries studied: e.g. the university should "provide a basic general education and appreciation of ideas," it should "stimulate the personal development rather than the technical competence of the students" (with the exception of Nigerian students). It should "maintain social discrimination" (with the exception of Yugoslav students) and it should "advance fundamental research regardless of immediate

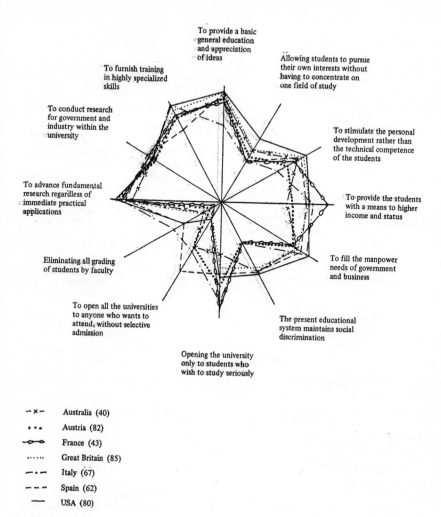

Australia (40)

Austria (82)

France (43)

Great Britain (85)

Italy (67)

Spain (62)

USA (80)

Figure 6. Importance of various university goals — a cross-national comparison of students having a rightist political orientation

practical applications" (with the exception of Japanese students). On other issues the cross-cultural differences are extreme. The majority of Nigerian students agree "to conduct research for government and industries within the university." The Japanese and Tunisians disapprove of the university's collaboration with government and industry. American and French students are evenly split on this issue; the remaining countries tend to approve such collaboration.

One finds a similar pattern of response with regard to the role the university should play in fulfilling "the manpower needs of the government." All the Nigerian students approve of this objective, followed

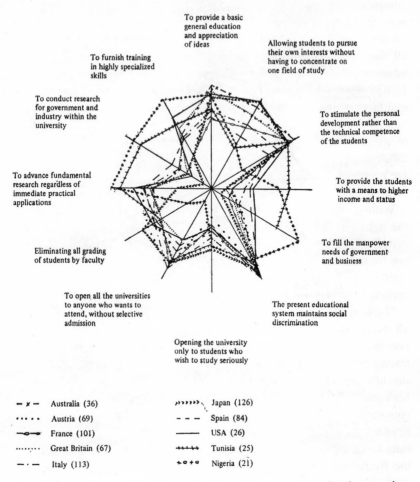

To provide a basic
general education
and appreciation
of ideas

To furnish training
in highly specialized
skills

Allowing students to pursue
their own interests without
having to concentrate on
one field of study

To conduct research
for government and
industry within the
university

To stimulate the personal
development rather than
the technical competence
of the students

To advance fundamental
research regardless of
immediate practical
applications

To provide the students
with a means to higher
income and status

Eliminating all grading
of students by faculty

To fill the manpower
needs of government
and business

To open all the universities
to anyone who wants to
attend, without selective
admission

The present educational
system maintains social
discrimination

Opening the university
only to students who
wish to study seriously

— x —   Australia (36)   ⟩⟩⟩⟩⟩⟩⟩ Japan (126)

• • • • •   Austria (69)   – – –   Spain (84)

—o—o   France (101)   ———   USA (26)

·········   Great Britain (67)   +++++ Tunisia (25)

— · —   Italy (113)   +o+o   Nigeria (21)

Figure 7.   Importance of various university goals — a cross-national comparison
of students having a far left political orientation

by a majority of students from the other countries approving with the
exception of the French (40 percent) and the Japanese (20 percent).
Yugoslav and Japanese students disapprove of the notion that the
university "should provide means to higher income and status." The
great majority of Nigerian and Tunisian students approve of it. The
remaining countries fall in between.

These results indicate a great discrepancy in the degree to which
students accept the university's collaboration with the government.

There are three additional domains where opinions diverge significantly: grading, selection, curriculum. Few Nigerian (20 percent) and
French (30 percent) students are in favor of eliminating all grading as

compared to a majority of Japanese (70 percent) and Yugoslav (70 percent) students who favor it. The remaining countries tend to be split on the issue. The Nigerian (90 percent) students are opposed "to open all the universities to anyone who wants to attend, without selective admission." Only one out of three students from Great Britain and the United States are in favor of it. A majority of students from the remaining countries are in favor of it. Freedom in the choice of curriculum (pursuing one's interest without having to concentrate on one field of study) is approved by almost all Japanese and Yugoslav students, followed by Americans (80 percent). Nigerian and Tunisian students are evenly split on this issue. In the remaining countries, the majority favor freedom in this domain.

Within each country, students who are politically oriented towards the right (see Figure 6) are inclined to opt for a traditional university system. They are in favor of highly specialized instruction, of advancing fundamental research, of a university as a means to obtain high status, and of opening it only to serious students. We find national variations concerning selective admission to the university.

Students of the new left (see Figure 7) show an opposite profile. In all the countries studied they favor complete revision of the university system. The university should be an autonomous institution concentrating on the individual's interests and his self-fulfillment. Students of the left are less likely to use the university as a means of obtaining high status and income and less likely to approve of government-sponsored research (especially in Japan, the United States, England, and France). In the context of these permissive attitudes, selective admission and grading have no meaning. There are, however, variations in the frequency with which students in the different countries endorse specialized training and fundamental research.

In all the countries studied, students of the far left (see Figure 6) appear hostile to the idea that the university should conduct research for the government or fill its manpower needs, or that the university should be seen as a means of obtaining an elite position in society. Although from a global perspective students of the far left agree on these views, the DEGREE to which they endorse them varies from country to country. (This would seem to imply that the nationality variable, i.e. the situation specific to each country, interacts with political orientation in determining the type of responses obtained.)

ADDITIONAL COMPARISONS

We have presented some detailed cross-national comparisons of the attitudes of college youth towards their career expectations and the ideal goals of a university. The following summarizes the principal results obtained on other issues.

The Position of Women in Society

Particularly within the last few years in the United States and subsequently in Western Europe, women of diverse political tendencies have formed groups in order to explore the various ways of fighting the psychological and material oppression imposed by their society, question their role in the social system, and finally, to investigate the very nature of that system.

A number of questions were included in the questionnaire dealing with normative aspects of sex roles and attitudes towards the women's movement.

The results indicate that the idea that women constitute an oppressed group is generally acknowledged in countries of such diverses political and social orientations as Yugoslavia, Japan, Austria, and Spain. On the other hand, the French and Italian students are less inclined to admit to this oppression. In Nigeria, the idea is popular only among a minority. In the case of the latter, it is perhaps interesting to note the important role women play in the economy of the country.

Students of all political tendencies, in all the countries studied, readily accept equality in the realms of employment and salary; in the realm of sexual equality there exists a greater divergence of opinion. Generally speaking, the Nigerian and Japanese students accept a double standard: they do not believe that the same principles must govern the sexual life of both men and women. The Tunisians, the French, and the Italians more readily accept the idea of sexual equality. In Spain, Austria, Yugoslavia, America, Australia, and Great Britain, students go even farther, generally accepting the idea without reserve.

Although many students favor social and sexual equality among men and women, few advocate an active struggle to achieve that equality. Less than one out of every two students in the study consider organized protest a viable means of improving the situation of women.

A greater number of women than men in our study recognize that women constitute an oppressed group within their respective societies;

however, more men than women favor organized protest to eliminate that oppression, and accept birth control and abortion. This fact, surprising as it is, becomes comprehensible if one considers the political tendency of students involved. It is not the sex of the individual that explains his attitude towards the oppression of women and the means for combating that oppression. Rather, his political orientation, although not necessarily the determinant, seems to explain his attitude. The farther the student is to the left of the political spectrum, the more he is in favor of birth control and abortion, and all the principles and actions which might better the situation of women. Women, in general to the right or center of the spectrum, maintain a conservative position towards their role in society and hence towards the question of abortion and contraception.

Examining specific countries, one finds a great discrepancy in male and female attitudes in Nigeria and Tunisia. In these two nations female students strongly favor the status quo. On the question of abortion and students adopt what seems a clear-cut feminist position, while male birth control, however, Tunisian and Nigerian students of both sexes hold conservative attitudes.

In Austria and America, men and women come much closer to sharing the same attitudes. Among the students, both the men and women of these countries accept the feminist views, even on questions of contraception. The American women, however, appear to be more feminist than the Austrian women. Although Spanish students of both sexes recognize the oppression of women, Spanish women seem to accept the status quo. Both Spanish men and women hold traditional attitudes on the subject of contraception and abortion. French and Italian men have conservative views about women, and French and Italian women, like the Spanish, also accept the status quo. Italian women hold conservative views on the question of contraception.

One should bear in mind, however, that the cultural and national context of students in the study, regardless of the students' political tendencies, tend to modify their feminist attitudes. A French student of the far left, for example, holding radical feminist views, is perhaps less radical on the question of women in society than an American student of the far left.

Perception of the Generation Gap

The majority of students (between 60 and 94 percent) in all the countries studied agree to the fact that "the difference between youth and the older generation in moral and social values is greater than in the past" and that the generation gap is more acutely felt than before (between 70 and 80 percent).

Proximity to Parents

The students were asked to indicate how close they felt to their parents in emotional terms, in moral values, and in political outlook. Few students, whatever their nationality, admit affective conflict. However, moral values and political outlook seem to oppose students to their parents to a greater extent. The students that consider themselves closest to their parents in moral values are Nigerian (90 percent), followed by Tunisian (74 percent), Italian, and American students, whereas the most distant are Austrian students (30 percent). The greatest distance between parents and students is found in political outlook. This opposition is especially evident in the case of Japanese students (30 percent). Those that felt closest politically to their parents are the English-speaking students (about 60 percent).

Within each country, the results indicate that the more a student is to the left, the more he tends to be alienated from his parents when it comes to moral values and political outlook. Affectivity does not seem to be a cause for conflict between students of the far left and their parents. With the exception of Austrian students (50 percent), the large majority (about 80 percent) of far left students are close to their parents in emotional terms. These results would seem to show that there is no antagonism between radical students and their parents and do not confirm the oedipal-conflict hypothesis which is so often offered as an explanation of youth protest.

Specific differences in values between students and their parents were assessed. The areas of investigation included sex, money, drugs, achievement, leisure, individualism, the present moment, art, and creativity.

The greatest difference in attitude between students and their parents is found in the area of sexual relations. Whatever the country, students feel that their views on sexual experiences are radically different from those of their parents. This sentiment is especially marked in Tunisia (86 percent) and Spain (80 percent). Drugs are rarely a source of conflict between parents and students (less than 40 percent in all the countries studied) except in English-speaking countries (e.g. United States 60 percent).

Comparing the countries, the greatest number of differences in value between parents and students are found in Tunisia (leisure, present moment, nature, art, creativity) and Spain (religion, money, achievement, individualism) followed by France and Italy. The least number of differences are mentioned in Austria, in Japan, and in the English-speaking countries. It is interesting to note that in the English-speaking countries, where one speaks the most often of a generation gap, relatively little difference in parent-student attitudes (except concerning drugs) is found compared to the other countries.

The notion that the family is a universally oppressive institution is endorsed to a lesser extent and differentiates the various countries. The rejection of the family unit especially characterizes Tunisian students (56 percent), followed by Spanish, Yugoslav, and Japanese students. American (14 percent), British (18 percent), and Australian (20 percent) students are less ready to reject the family as oppressive.

Within each country, one finds that the more to the left the student is, the more sensitive he is to the existence of a generation gap. Radical students are most likely to express a conflict with traditional values and ideas, to feel distant from their parents in political and moral views, and to consider the family as an oppressive institution. At the opposite extreme, students having a rightist orientation tend to value the family as an institution and to share the same attitudes as their parents.

From the beginning of the study we were concerned with the possibility of an organization of attitudes expressing a coherent view of the world, one which links political, cultural, and personal orientations.

We used factor analysis to determine the existence of an attitude structure. The method employed, "correspondance analysis" (Cordier 1968), permits the extraction of factors explaining the covariation of responses. By grouping the attitudinal variables as a function of their proximity, this method permits us to obtain the underlying ideology or attitudinal system which determines the responses obtained.

In the present study we hoped to discover the functional relation between the ways of "experiencing" society (through both its political and social aspects and its cultural and normative aspects) and the responses of the individual to his situation as a student, to his career aspirations, and to his family relationships.

The data obtained from three of the countries studied (France, Great Britain, and the United States) indicate that in these countries attitudes can be organized into two dimensions. First, there exists an ideological orientation which could be characterized by either a desire or a lack of desire for change (acceptance or rejection of the status quo). The second dimension, more psychological in nature, seems to express the "motivational structure of the ideology."

Combining these two dimensions, we get a typology in which we can distinguish four types:

The first type, to whom we have given the name CONSERVATIVE-ALTRUIST (C-A), has definite career plans and is optimistic about realizing them. Satisfied with the present organization of the university and with university curriculum, he tends to be a serious student with traditional notions of work and effort, and he seeks specialized training. He does not fear long-term engagements or bureaucratic institutions.

The C-A type is a conformist in his cultural opinions. He feels close to his parents and wants to maintain traditional values. Family and religion will be his greatest sources of satisfaction in life. In all three countries studied he is a believer: a Catholic in France and a Protestant in the United States and Great Britain.

The political tendencies associated with this type tend to be "center" (France) and "right" (Great Britain).

In France and Great Britain we find this type in particular represented by students in medicine, engineering, and business, whereas in the United States, by law students. French students of this category come from families where the parents have had a high level of education. American students with this orientation come from families with little education. In Great Britain we found no relationship between the level of the parents' education and the conservative outlook of the student.

The second type, the CONSERVATIVE-INDIVIDUALIST (C-I), differs from the first mainly in terms of his professional aspirations. He is ambitious and wants to succeed in life by obtaining wealth, prestige, and power. Leisure and freedom of action are also important to him. He sees the university as a means to obtain high social status. The university should be selective, produce an elite, and cooperate with government and business. In his cultural opinions, the C-I is less tradition-oriented than the C-A, but he is still a conformist accepting middle-class morality, marriage, and the traditional role of the woman in society. He feels emotionally, morally, and politically close to his parents: for him, there is no generation gap.

In the three countries studied, C-I students tend to have a right or center political position and, like the C-A type, are students in medicine, law, engineering, and business. British and French students in this category appear to come from a higher social background than American students.

The third type, the INNOVATIVE-INDIVIDUALIST (I-I), contrary to the conservative type, is ill at ease in a society that he judges negatively. He is hostile to technology, which he considers an alienating force, has no precise professional goal, and is pessimistic about the possibility of finding the kind of job he would like. He rejects traditional occupational goals and puts the emphasis on leisure activities: work and play should be one. Critical of the university system, he objects to course requirements and would like to be free to pursue his own intellectual interests. One finds the same search for new values and alternative lifestyles in his cultural opinions. The I-I rejects middle-class morality and the family, which he finds oppressive, and would prefer a communal lifestyle and the legalization of drugs. Students of this category consider themselves distant from their parents in political, affective, and moral terms. This distance is particularly marked in France.

In France and in Great Britain, the I-I type tends to be anarchist, and in the United States he is generally to the left. In all three countries, this group is characterized by students in the social sciences, and also in law in Great Britain. In France and Great Britain, these students come from families where parents have little education, whereas in the United States, students of this type come from highly educated families.

Type four, whom we call the INNOVATIVE-ALTRUIST (I-A), like type II has a critical attitude towards the society in which he lives, but contrary to I-I he is highly involved in politics and he adopts a position of active struggle against the system. He desires a career in which he will be helpful to others, able to influence the politics of his government, and wants most of all to avoid any professional position that would reinforce the capitalistic system. His criticism of the university is on a political level.

Type I-A refuses conventional success goals, rejects a university that preserves privileges and that collaborates with government and business. The university should be a tool to transform society.

In his cultural opinions he appears less radical than the I-I type. While rejecting middle-class morality and traditional marriage he is not ready to adopt a communal lifestyle. The I-I is in favor of contraception and sexual equality.

The students of I-A type feel less distant from their parents as compared to those of the I-I type. This type is represented in all three countries studied by a far left political position. In addition, in France and Great Britain it is represented by the Communist position (this category was not found in the United States sample). In terms of university attendance, the type I-A (as the type I-I) is found mostly in the social sciences. In relation to their family origin, they share the same characteristics as the I-I type (low educational level in France, from all educational levels in Great Britain, and from highly educated families in the United States).

The discovery of these four typical orientations illustrates the existence of coherent and conflicting ideology covering widely different aspects of life.

If you know the political choice of an individual you can almost predict his attitudes in domains quite distant from the political one, e.g. his source of satisfaction in life and the content of his occupational aspirations. These results suggest that a much closer look at the interdependence between social ideology and personal desires will be fruitful for the understanding of the social actor.

Also, we may speculate that the function of ideology is to create on the cognitive level an ideal environment where one's desires can be maximally realized.

These results also do not lend support to the common notion in social science that there is a value-consensus relative to cultural and normative matters in society. The picture we obtain suggests that real conflict exists between people with differing notions of what a meaningful life should be and what ends are worth fighting for.

REFERENCES

CORDIER, BRIGITTE
  1968   *Analyse factorielle des Correspondances.* Thèse de Droit, 3ème Cycle. Rennes.
GOLDSEN, R. K., M. ROSENBERG, R. M. WILLIAMS, E. A. SUCHMAN
  1960   *What college students think.* Princeton, N.J.: D. Van Nostrand.
KENISTON, KENNETH
  1965   *The uncommitted alienated youth in American society.* New York: Harcourt Brace and World.
  1968   *Young radicals: notes on committed youth.* New York: Harcourt Brace and World.
  1971   *Youth and dissent: the rise of a new opposition.* New York: Harcourt Brace Javonovitch.
KLINEBERG, OTTO, MARISSA ZAVALLONI
  1969   *Nationalism and tribalism among African students.* New publications of the International Social Science Council. The Hague: Mouton. Paris: Ecole Pratique des Hautes Etudes.

Biographical Notes

Tsuneo Ayabe, a Japanese anthropologist, has done extensive fieldwork in Japan, Thailand, Laos, and Cambodia. He has been a visiting Professor of Anthropology at the University of Pennsylvania and at Stanford University. Currently he is Associate Professor of Anthropology, The Research Institute of Comparative Education and Culture, Kyushu University, Fukuoka, Japan.

Gail H. Davila was born in Seattle, Washington, and has a B.A. degree from Antioch College in Economics and International Relations. She also attended the Universidad de Concepción, Chile. She is currently a Research Associate at the Fels Research Institute where she has participated in numerous studies of child growth and development.

Edward J. Eckenfels is an Assistant Professor in the Department of Preventive Medicine and Special Assistant to the Office of the Dean at Rush Medical College. He also serves as Coordinating Consultant for the Holmes County Health Research Project.

Dzigbodi K. Fiawoo was born in Ghana. He received his undergraduate degree from Cornell University, his M.A. from Columbia University, and his Ph.D. from Edinburgh University. He was a postgraduate Research Associate at the Laboratory of Human Development at Harvard University (1961–1962) and a Senior Commonwealth Fellow at Cambridge University's Centre of African Studies (1970–1971). He was also a visiting lecturer at the Centre for West African Studies,

Birmingham University, Birmingham, England. He is Senior Lecturar (Acting Head) of the Department of Sociology, University of Ghane, Legon, Ghana. He has done research on child development in Ghana, as well as on traditional religion and social change, with special reference to the Ewe-speaking people, and is currently National Director of a Ghana Government Project on the Young Child, sponsored by UNICEF.

ESTELLE FUCHS received her Ph.D. from Columbia University and is now Professor of Anthropology, Division of Education, Hunter College, City University of New York. She has had considerable experience studying youth in metropolitan centers of the United States, in Denmark, and among American Indians. She is the author of numerous works, including *To live on this earth: American Indian education* (with Robert J. Havighurst).

K. S. GOKULANATHAN, M.D., has been Director of the Adolescents Program, Howard University College of Medicine, Washington, D.C., and Director of the Ernakulan Polyclinic, Kerala, India. He has done considerable research on problems of adolescent growth and development from both physical and cultural perspectives. He is himself a member of the Nayar ethnic group of Kerala, South India.

JORGE G. GONZÁLEZ, M.D., is a Colombian psychiatrist and psychoanalyst who is currently at work in the adolescent clinic in Manizales, Colombia, South America. Dr. Gonzalez has also been associated with the Metropolitan Hospital in New York.

ROBERT J. HAVIGHURST is world renowned for his major contributions to the research literature on education and society. His long and distinguished career places him as one of the leading authorities on youth. He is currently Professor of Education and Human Development at the University of Chicago.

WILHEMINA KALU is a young Ghanaian who was educated in the field of child study in Ghana and England. She is currently working with emotionally disturbed youths in Princeton, New Jersey.

MÁRIA KRESZ is an ethnologist working at the Néprajzi Museum, Budapest, Hungary. She has conducted ethnographic research in Transylvania over a period of many years.

GEORGE KURIAN received his degree in Literature and Philosophy in Sociology from the State University of Utrecht, The Netherlands. He has conducted considerable research in the area of family and social change in Asian countries. Among his extensive works in this area are *The Indian family in transition* and *The family in India*. Currently, Dr. Kurian is teaching at the University of Calgary, Canada, and is editor of the Journal of Comparative Family Studies.

COLIN LACEY is a social anthropologist working in the field of adolescent education. A research fellow lecturing in Sociology of Education at the Centre for Study of Social Organisation of Schools, Sussex University, England, he has been actively engaged in studies of schools for the last decade.

BELA C. MADAY is an anthropologist with the National Institute of Mental Health in Rockville, Maryland, and Adjunct Professor of Anthropology at The American University in Washington, D.C. Born in 1912, he was educated at the University of Budapest and received his Ph.D. in 1937. He has had a long and distinguished teaching career. His research interests are East European peasant cultures, especially Hungarian folk culture, culture change, acculturation, and the interface between anthropology and psychiatry. He has edited or co-authored 4 books and 58 articles in Hungarian, and 22 books and 14 articles in English. He is Editor of the Hungarian Studies Newsletter and was President of the Anthropological Society of Washington from 1973 to 1974.

LAWRENCE A. MALCOLM, M.D., is internationally renowned for the extensive research he has conducted on growth and development among the peoples of New Guinea. For the past several years he has been working with the Health Planning Unit of the Department of Public Health in Papua, New Guinea.

DAVID MELLITS is Associate Professor, Department of Pediatrics, School of Medicine, and Associate Professor, Department of Biostatistics, School of Hygiene and Public Health, Johns Hopkins University, Baltimore, Maryland.

JOHN PETERSON is an anthropologist with the Social Science Research Center, Mississippi State University. Dr. Peterson has taught Anthropology and Education at the University of British Columbia and has been working as Consultant with the Choctaw Tribe of Mississippi.

MARIO RENDON, M.D., is a Colombian psychiatrist who is currently Clinical Instructor in Adolescent Psychiatry at New York University, Bellevue Hospital. He is also a teaching analyst at the American Institute for Psychoanalysis.

ALEX F. ROCHE, M.D., is currently Senior Scientist, Head, Section of Physical Growth and Genetics and Joint Head, Fels Longitudian Study of Families, Fels Research Institute, Ohio. Dr. Roche comes from Australia. His many contributions to the research literature on physical growth include, among others, works on skeletal maturation and elongation, sexual and dental maturation, cranial growth in normal and abnormal children, and nutrition and body composition.

I. R. SHENKER, M.D., is Physician in Charge, Adolescent Medicine, Long Island Jewish–Hillside Medical Center, New Hyde Park, New York.

LORAND B. SZALAY is a social psychologist working with the American Institutes for Research in Kensington, Maryland, and teaching at the University of Maryland. Born in 1921, he received his M.A. in Modern Languages at the Academy of Foreign Trade and Languages in Budapest (1950) and his Ph.D. in Psychology at the University of Vienna (1961). In postdoctoral studies he spent a year at the University of Illinois (1961–1962). While Associate Professor in Research with The American University in Washington, D.C., he developed the Associative Group Analysis method and has validated it in several cross-cultural overseas applications. As Senior Research Scientist at The American Institutes for Research since 1970, he directed several research projects and developed three volumes of Korean-U.S. communication lexica, representing a new approach to area and language training.

MEI-CHUN TANG is Chairman and Professor, Department of Archaeology and Anthropology, National Taiwan University. He has been particularly concerned with research on the Chinese family. Dr. Tang received his Ph.D. from Columbia University in New York.

BENJAMIN WHITE is an anthropologist who has been conducting field research in Java since August 1972.

MARISA ZAVALLONI has conducted research and published widely on youth and social attitudes. Among her many works are *Adolescent values in a changing society* and *Nationalism and tribalism among African students:*

a study of social identity (with O. Klineberg). Dr. Zavalloni is currently Professor of Social Psychology at the University of Geneva and Associate Director of the International Center for Intergroup Relations, Paris.

Index of Names

Index of Subjects

Accra, Ghana, 81, 139–140, 142
Accra International School at the Cantonments, Ghana, 80
Achimota School, Ghana, 79–81, 86–87, 89–90
Akwapin people, 144
American Anthropologist (journal), 287
Anthropology today (Kroeber), 287
Asae people, 67, 68, 73
Associative Group Analysis, 274
Australia, 315–334
Austria, 315–334

Baganda people, 91
Boston Children's Hospital, 93
Brunel New Southern University, England, 303, 305, 308–313
Bundi people, 68–71
Butibum, Papua New Guinea, 73–74

Calgary, Alberta, 262
Canada, immigrants from India in, 262–272
Chicago, 8, 126, 129–133, 135
Children in crisis (Coles), 126
Child Research Council, Denver, Colorado, 29
China, 239–248. *See also* Taiwan
Choctaw Indians, 5, 161–165
Christ the King School, Ghana, 80–81
Columbia University, 187

Dawhenya Canal Construction Project, Ghana, 152–153

"Economic cost and value of children in four agricultural societies" (project), 187

Fels Longitudal Sample, 26, 27, 29–30, 31, 34–36, 56, 59, 61–62
Fels Research Institute, Yellow Springs, Ohio, 31
First Row Little Rock, Taiwan, 244–248
France, 315–334
Fusion of capitellum of humerus (FCH), 47
Gadjah Mada University, Jogjakarta, 187
Ga people, 9, 137–157
Ghana, 9, 79–91, 138–157; Educational Tryst, 140–142; English language in, 149; National Youth Service, 144–145, 152–153
Great Britain, 287–313, 315

Hightown Grammar School, Manchester, England, 288–302
Holmes County, Mississippi, blacks in, 8, 125–135, 164
Holmes County Freedom Democratic Party, 125–126
Holmes County Health Research Project, 125–135

Ibo people, 4
Inanwantan people, 66
India, Indians, 253–257, 259–262; in